Crime Fighting Heroes of Television

Crime Fighting Heroes of Television

Over 10,000 Facts from 151 Shows, 1949–2001

VINCENT TERRACE

McFarland & Company, Inc., Publishers
Jefferson, North Carolina, and London

Library of Congress Cataloguing-in-Publication Data

Terrace, Vincent, 1948–
    Crime fighting heroes of television : over 10,000 facts from
151 shows, 1949–2001 / Vincent Terrace.
        p.   cm.
    Includes bibliographical references and index.

    ISBN 0-7864-1395-6 (softcover : 50# alkaline paper)

    1. Adventure television programs— United States— Catalogs.
2. Crime on television.   I. Title.
⌐ PN1992.8.A317 T47   2002
791.43'655 — dc21   2002013181

British Library cataloguing data are available

Cover image: ©2002 PhotoSpin

Manufactured in the United States of America

McFarland & Company, Inc., Publishers
  Box 611, Jefferson, North Carolina 28640
    www.mcfarlandpub.com

Contents

Preface

As a young girl, Buffy (*Buffy, the Vampire Slayer*) would dream about battling crime as Power Woman, not knowing that one day she would become the Slayer. When an ordinary citizen named Wayne (*Honey, I Shrunk the Kids*) felt the need to fight crime, he became Captain Astounding; however, because of the costume he chose, he became known as "Buckethead." When Peter Brady (*The Invisible Man*) saved the life of a ventriloquist, she made a marionette of him called "Dr. Brady, the Invisible Puppet." This is a very small sampling of the more than 10,000 facts that can be found in *Crime Fighting Heroes of Television*.

It appears that no matter where crime is, television has given us someone or something to battle it. If evil reared its ugly head in a past century, there was the Queen of Swords and Zorro to battle it. When crime strikes the modern-day world, television has given us such heroes as Batman, Black Scorpion and the Tick to suppress it. When crime becomes extraordinary, a means just as extraordinary is created to battle it—from the awesome attack helicopter *Airwolf* to Erica West's (*Team Knight Rider*) "sexy" motorcycle, Kat. Could the crime fighter of the future be part human, part robot or all robot? Series such as *The Bionic Woman*, *Mann and Machine* and *RoboCop* have sought to explore that possibility. And what about outer space? Could an alien life form pose a threat? To safeguard the Earth, television has given us such heroes as Captain Video, Flash Gordon and Buzz Corry (*Space Patrol*).

Television's extraordinary crime fighters are not limited to just regular series. In addition to the 125 series detailed here, there is information regarding the almost heroes—the characters who surfaced only to star in a project that never made it past the pilot stage (for example, *Chameleon in Blue*, *Infiltrator* and *The Phantom*). Each of these 26 titles (both aired and unaired) are clearly marked "Pilot" to distinguish them from an actual series. Additional pilot film information is contained within specific entries (for example, "Wonder Woman" in *Wonder Woman*).

1

Entries, listed alphabetically, relate factual information (trivia) regarding character development (for example, how Sara acquires the powers of the "Witchblade"; how Darcy becomes "Black Scorpion"), personal information, addresses, phone numbers, pets, costume colors, hometowns, catchphrases, favorite foods, clothing sizes—anything and everything that adds interest to a program and its characters. This book features live action programs broadcast on network (ABC, CBS, Dumont, Fox, NBC, UPN, WB), cable (Family Channel, NIK, SciFi, TBS, TNN) and in syndication from 1949 through 2001. Animated series, for the most part, have been excluded. The book also contains program openings, a performer's index and an appendix of the super heroes listed (by costumed name, by alias) and an appendix of crime fighting machines.

The author would like to thank Jennifer Mormile, Thomas Gallucci, James Robert Parish and Robert (Bob) Reed for their help in making this book possible.

The Shows

1. *The A-Team* (NBC, 1983–1987)

Hannibal Smith, B.A. Baracus, Templeton Peck and H.M. Murdock are soldiers of fortune who comprise the A-Team, military fugitives who help people unable to help themselves. The four were members of the U.S. armed services A-Team during the Vietnam War. On Sunday morning, January 27, 1971, they received orders from Colonel Morrison to rob the Bank of Hanoi. Believing they are performing a mission to end the war, they successfully withdraw 100 million yen (ten million pesetas in another episode). Morrison, a Vietnamese supporter, informs military officials of the robbery then escapes with the money by staging his own death. The A-Team is captured by Colonel Roderick Decker and imprisoned. Before they can be tried, they escape from Fort Bragg and retreat to the Los Angeles underground. They are branded fugitives and $20,000 is offered for their capture (1-HG-4227 is their military file number). Military brass believe only Hannibal, B.A. and Peck comprise the A-Team. Murdock, a pilot, was on another mission at the time and now secretly helps them.

Colonel Lynch (William Lucking) first pursued the team. He was replaced by Colonel Decker (Lance LeGault). The army wants the file on the A-Team closed. They were convicted at a time of great political pressure. They were virtually forgotten until Lynch started his fruitless pursuit "and now the whole thing has mushroomed into a highly embarrassing series of situations." Decker is ruthless, a man who will get the job done at any cost and not lose any sleep over it (in Vietnam, Hannibal says "he blew up Cong hospitals like it was his favorite sport"). "Next time Hannibal Smith, next time" became his catchphrase when the A-Team always managed to escape his clever military traps. Colonel Briggs (Charles Napier) replaced Decker and Colonel Harlan "Bull" Fulbright (Jack Ging) replaced Briggs; each failed to capture the A-Team.

In last season episodes the team is captured by Colonel Hunt Stockwell (Robert Vaughn). They are tried, convicted of murder and robbery, and sentenced to death by firing squad. They are given a chance to redeem themselves by performing assignments for Stockwell. The team is given a permanent base in Langley, Virginia, and operate under the code name Empress 6 (Stockwell's code is Empress 1). Stockwell is assisted by Carla (Judy Ledford); 555-6162 is the A-Team's mobile phone number; NRB 729 is Stockwell's car license plate.

John "Hannibal" Smith (George Peppard) was a colonel in command of the 5th Special Forces Group. His Social Security number is 844-31-3142; 61-5683-1 is his FBI file number (wanted as a fugitive). Hannibal is also a part-time actor and takes roles in horror movies as the Slime Monster or the Aquamaniac. He is famous for his expression "I love it when a plan comes together" and has an M-60 gun he calls "Baby." He also gets "on the jazz" (a feeling of excitement during each assignment) and plays Mr. Lee, the Chinese owner of Mr. Lee's Laundry Shop in Los Angeles (each client must meet with

Mr. Lee before the team will take on a case. Hannibal believes this deception is necessary to avoid a military trap).

Bosco "B.A." Baracus (Mr. T), a sergeant, is the toughest and meanest member of the team (he says the "B.A." stands for bad attitude). His Social Security number is 554-04-3106 and 61-5683-3 is his FBI file number. B.A. grew up at 700 Foster Avenue in Chicago and was called "Scooter" by his mother (his real first name is Elliott). B.A. loves children (he runs a day care center in his spare time) and gold jewelry. "Pity the fool" is his catchphrase and he has a fear of flying. To rid B.A. of this fear, Hannibal does one of three things: injects him with a tranquilizer; spikes his favorite drink (milk); or gives him his "beddy-bye drink" (a conk on the head with a two-by-four). B.A. lives at the Hotel Regina and drives a black with red trim GMC van (plates seen as 218 3000, S96 7238, 2A22029 and 2E14859).

Templeton Peck (Dirk Benedict), known as "Face" and "The Faceman," is a lieutenant and a master con artist (he schemes to get the team what it needs without paying for it). His Social Security number is 522-70-5044 and 61-5683-2 is his FBI file number. Peck, orphaned at the age of five, was raised by the Guardian Angels Orphanage in Los Angeles. He learned most of his cons from his favorite TV show (*Dragnet*) and is an expert at bending the rules. He is also an expert liar and "has such a face that everybody believes what he is saying." His favorite scam is to find investors for his mythical movie company, Miracle Films ("If It's a Good Picture, It's a Miracle"). He has a script called *The Beast of the Yellow Night* ready for production (in the pilot episode his scam was a film called *Boots and Bikinis* for 20th Century–Fox; it was set to star Loni Anderson, Bo Derek and Farrah Fawcett). Peck lives in a beach house (that he scams) at 1347 Old Balboa Road and drives a car with the plate IHG 581. Tim Dunigan played Face in the pilot (replaced when producers felt he was too young to have served in Vietnam).

Before the war H.M. ("Howling Mad") Murdock (Dwight Schultz) was a pilot with the Thunderbirds. He performed heroic missions in Vietnam and pretends to have gone insane as a result. He lives in Building 16 (the psychiatric ward) of the V.A. Hospital in Los Angeles and is suspected by the military of being a member of the A-Team (but they can't prove it). Murdock has been diagnosed with paranoid delusions and ammonia is the key word that triggers his aggression. In last season episodes Murdock is found to be sane, released from the hospital and then resides with the team in Virginia.

Murdock has an invisible dog (Billy), an alligator (Wally Gator) and a house plant (The Little Guy). His heroes are "The Range Rider" (from the 1950s TV western series) and Captain Bellybuster (mascot of the Burger Heaven Food Chain). Murdock (and B.A.) have AB negative blood and although Murdock is pretending to be crazy B.A. believes "he ain't pretending, he is crazy."

Amy Amanda Allen (Melinda Culea), called "Triple A" by Hannibal, assists the team when a beautiful girl is needed to help in a scam. She is a reporter for the Los Angeles *Courier-Express* and became part of the team when she hired them to find a missing reporter (and became actively involved in the case). Her car license plate numbers read ILBJ 1247, IFH 480, IFHJ 484. Amy was replaced by her friend, Tawnia Baker (Marla Heasley), a reporter for the *Courier-Express*, when Amy was transferred overseas. Like Amy, Tawnia helps the team when needed. Her license plates are seen as IJFY 515 and 854 022. Tawnia left the team to marry archaeologist Brian Lefcourt (Barry Van Dyke) in the episode "Bend in the River" (before her role as Tawnia, Marla played Cahrise, a bikini clad coed in "Bad Time on the Border." Mike Post and Pete Carpenter composed *The A-Team* theme.

The program opened with these words: "In 1972, a crack commando unit was sent to prison by a military court for a crime they didn't commit. These men promptly escaped from a maximum security stockade to the Los Angeles underground. Today, still wanted by the government, they survive as soldiers of fortune. If you have a problem, if no one else can help, and, if you can find them, maybe you can hire the A-Team."

2. *Acapulco H.E.A.T.* (Syndicated, 1993)

The Hemisphere Emergency Action Team, H.E.A.T. for short, is a secret organization designed to fight international terrorism and crime. It is based in the ruins of a Mayan temple in Puerto Vallarta in Acapulco, Mexico, and its operatives live in the nearby Regina Hotel. Officially, H.E.A.T. does not exist. This enables them to help governments or companies without the impediments of red tape (or ever being traced). The main operatives are Ashley Hunter Coddington (Catherine Oxenberg), Catherine Avery Pascal (Alison Armitage), Mike Savage (Brendan Kelly) and Krissie Valentine (Holly Floria).

Ashley, the leader of the group, has the code name Sarong. She is beautiful and intelligent and was formerly with MI-6. She was born in England and although she constantly displays her legs in swimwear, shorts and miniskirts, she hates to be called "Legs." Ashley is an expert on weapons, explosives and the martial arts. Catherine, who prefers to be called Cat, has the code name High Dive. She is a cunning thief who was recruited from prison (promised a pardon to work for H.E.A.T.). She is an expert pickpocket and can open virtually any safe (and pick any lock). When a safe proves too difficult to open, she uses plastic explosives to crack it.

Mike, codename Platform, hates to be called Michael. He was born in Brooklyn, New York, worked as a bartender and was formerly with the CIA. He eats Sugar Crispies cereal for breakfast and likes to incorporate the technical "gizmos" they have available to them (like the thermal scanner — which can monitor buildings for activity). Krissie is the team's computer operator.

She has the codename Springboard and is basically a non–field operative (she is based at headquarters).

Marcos (Randy Vasquez) is an undercover agent for the Mexican government who poses as a cab driver (cab number 2661) but works with the H.E.A.T. team. Claudio DiVanti (played by male model Fabio) is the owner of the Regina Hotel; Mr. Smith (John Vernon) is the mysterious head of a government organization called C-5 that hires the H.E.A.T. team.

A casting change dropped Ashley and Krissie and added Nicole (Lydie Denier) and Joanna (Christa Sauls). H.E.A.T. was still located in Acapulco but the team was now headed by Nicole DeNaurd. She was born in France and was a former CIA agent. Nicole keeps a poison capsule in her bra (for use on her enemies) and uses her beauty and charm to get men to do what she wants. She can read lips, is an expert on weapons and explosives and skilled in the marital arts. Joanna, born in the Midwest, replaced Krissie as the team's computer operations specialist. She calls headquarters "The Heat Room."

See also *The Dream Team.*

3. *The Adventures of Sinbad* (Syndicated, 1998–2000)

The *Nomad* is a ship captained by Sinbad (Zen Gesner) that sails the Seven Seas to fight evil wherever it is found. Sinbad is assisted by his older brother, Doubar (George Buza), his best friend, Rongar (Oris Erhuero), Firouz (Tim Progosh), the inventor, and Maeve (Jacqueline Collen), a beautiful sorcerer's apprentice.

The series is set in a time of ancient myths and legends. Sinbad and Doubar were born in Baghdad and cared for by a sorcerer named Dim Dim after their parents were lost in a storm at sea (Sinbad, a toddler at the time, was saved by Doubar). When Sinbad was eight years old he had a crush on a girl named Lea. A short time later, when Lea fell into the sea and drowned, Sinbad decided to become a sailor and master the sea. He took whatever sea-related jobs he could find and by the age of 15 was his own captain. At an unspecified time after, his ship sank but Sinbad managed to stay afloat on some driftwood. He passed out and awoke on an island where he not only found food and water, but a mysterious rainbow bracelet on his left wrist. It is not said how, but Sinbad managed to get back to Baghdad and learned that two years had passed. Unable to explain what happened, Sinbad accepted the notion that the fates saved him. Later, when the Caliph's daughter is kidnapped by the evil sorcerer Turok, the Caliph asks Sinbad to rescue her. He gives Sinbad the *Nomad* and Sinbad rounds up his crew: Doubar, Rongar and Firouz. En route they dock at Dim Dim's island and meet Maeve, who becomes part of the crew (assigned by Dim Dim to assist Sinbad). Dim Dim, however, is swept away by an evil demon and this sets up one aspect of the storyline: Sinbad's oath to someday find him. As the *Nomad* continues with its rescue mission, Sinbad encounters the evil Turok and kills him. He rescues the princess but enrages Turok's daughter, Rumina (Julianne Morris), an evil and powerful sorceress who has sworn to kill Sinbad and his crew (a recurring aspect of first season episodes). With his first successful venture behind him, Sinbad is permitted to keep the *Nomad* and use it for the good of others.

Doubar calls Sinbad "Little Brother" and is looked upon by Sinbad as a father figure, protector and best of friends. He has incredible strength and often plunges head first into dangerous situations without thinking. Rongar the Moor is an expert knife thrower (his only weapons; Sinbad and Doubar use swords) and had his tongue cut out for not betraying his brothers when they were sought by the Caliph. Rongar does not speak but his gestures are easily understood. Firouz, "a master scientist" as he calls himself, is an old friend of Sinbad's (how they met is not related). He is a bit absent-minded and has invented a number of items, from a telescope to explosives, to save the day (Sinbad calls his dynamite invention "exploding sticks").

Maeve is Dim Dim's Celtic sorcerer's apprentice. She is traveling with Sinbad not only to help him find Dim Dim but to kill Rumina, who has turned her younger brother into a hawk named Dermott (it is mentioned that Maeve and her brother had a past encounter with Rumina; when he refused her love she turned him into a hawk). Dermott travels with Maeve (acts like a scout) and can telepathically communicate with her; Rumina's death will lift the curse.

The first episode of the second season, "The Sacrifice," finds Maeve being replaced by Bryn (Mariah Shirley), a beautiful warrior who possesses the same mysterious rainbow bracelet as Sinbad. During a storm at sea, Maeve is swept overboard. In an attempt to save her, Sinbad jumps into the water but is overpowered by the waves and washed upon the shore of an island that is ruled by the Kamin, a large reptile-like creature that has the inhabitants living in fear. Back at the ship, it not only appears that Maeve has drowned, but Dermott has also disappeared.

As Sinbad regains consciousness, he first sees Bryn, then the Kamin, who is seeking her (a sacrifice by the villagers to appease the Kamin and save their homes). After escaping to safety, Sinbad notices Bryn's bracelet and learns that she was lost in a storm at sea and awoke to find herself on this island and in possession of the bracelet. She has no memory of how she got the bracelet, who she is (other than her name) or where she came from. She also possesses a power to discharge energy bolts from her eyes by concentrating ("But it comes and goes" she says). With the help of Doubar, Rongar and Firouz, who have come to the island to find Sinbad, they defeat the Kamin (in a story that borrows heavily from the 1933 movie *King Kong*) and return to the ship. There, as Doubar shows Sinbad the only item found of Maeve's—the leather wrist band she used for Dermott—a glowing blue light, representing the spirit of Dim Dim, appears and speaks: "Maeve is safe, Sinbad, alive and well. The curse I am under prevents me from being here in all but spirit. The forces of darkness are growing too strong, Sinbad. Rumina would have killed Maeve before her time. She is safe under my protection until she has mastered the art of white magic. Fight the dark powers, Sinbad. You will find Bryn a powerful assist in your travels." As the blue light fades Dermott returns and lands on Bryn's arm (like he did with Maeve). "Until we meet again, Maeve, until we meet again" closes the episode as Sinbad speaks these words into the sky. Matthew McCauley composed the theme.

4. *The Adventures of Superboy* (Unaired, 1961)

Pilot. Clark Kent (John Rockwell) is actually Kal-El, the only known survivor of the doomed planet Krypton. (Before the planet exploded, Kal-El's father placed him in an experimental rocket and programmed it to land on Earth. The ship landed in Smallville, Kansas, and its infant passenger was found by Jonathan and Martha Kent, a childless farm couple who raised him as their son, Clark. As Clark grew and showed evidence of incredible abilities, Martha fashioned him a costume made from the red and blue blankets that were originally wrapped around him.)

Clark, now a teenager, attends Smallville High School and assists the police as the mysterious Superboy. Clark's base of operations is a secret room behind the bookcase. Here, Clark has a communications center and a trap door that leads to a cave-like area that he uses as Superboy to exit the house. Lana Lang (Bunny Henning) is Clark's girlfriend; only Clark's mother, Martha (Monty Margetts), appears. Screen credits for Clark and Lana read John Rockwell and Bunny Henning; in printed sources, they are Johnny Rockwell and Bonny Henning.

See also *The Adventures of Superman*; *Lois and Clark: The New Adventures of Superman*, *Smallville* and *Superboy*.

The Adventures of Superboy (1988) see **Superboy**

5. *The Adventures of Superman* (Syndicated, 1952–1957)

As the theme music (written by Leon Klatzkin) plays, an announcer begins the program: "Faster than a speeding bullet. More powerful than a locomotive. Able to leap tall buildings in a single bound." Voices are then heard: "Look, up in the sky, it's a bird, it's a plane, it's Superman." The announcer returns: "Yes, it's Superman, strange visitor from another planet who came to Earth with powers and abilities far beyond those of mortal men. Superman, who can change the course of mighty rivers, bend steel in his bare hands. And who, disguised as Clark Kent, mild-mannered reporter for a great metropolitan newspaper, fights a never-ending battle for truth, justice and the American Way."

But who is Superman — and where did he come from? The story begins many years ago on a distant planet called Krypton, which is inhabited by a race of super intelligent beings. Jor-El (Robert Rockwell) is a leading scientist who believes the planet is being drawn closer to its sun and destruction. When he is unable to convince the Council of Scientists of his beliefs, he begins developing a rocket ship to save his wife, Lara (Aline Towne) and their infant son, Kal-El, from the impending disaster. Jor-El, however, has only time to complete a small, experimental rocket before the planet is struck by earthquakes. He and Lara decide to save Kal-El. The baby is placed in the rocket and Jor-El programs it to land on Earth, a planet he knows is inhabited. Shortly after the rocket is launched, Krypton explodes and scatters billions of particles of Kryptonite, the only substance that will be able to harm Kal-El, into the universe.

The rocket enters the Earth's atmosphere on April 10, 1926, and crash lands near the Jones farm in Smallville, Kansas. Eben and Sarah Kent (Tom Fadden, Dina Nolan), a childless farm couple, witness the landing. Eben risks his life to save the baby from the burning rocket. The baby, wrapped in red and blue blankets, is miraculously unharmed. The rocket explodes seconds later, destroying all evidence of its ever having been there. Realizing that no one would ever believe their fantastic story, Eben and Sarah decide to raise the baby as their own and name him Clark Kent. As young Clark (Stuart Randall) begins to grow, he develops amazing powers (X-ray vision, incredible strength, the ability to fly). In 1951, following Eben's death from a heart attack, Sarah urges Clark to use his great abilities to help mankind. Before Sarah moves in with her cousin, Louise, she makes Clark a costume from the blankets that were originally wrapped around him (how she managed to cut and sew the indestructible material was not explained). To keep his true identity a secret, he maintains the alias of mild-mannered Clark Kent and moves to Metropolis, where he becomes a reporter for the *Daily Planet*, a crusading newspaper.

Clark (George Reeves) lives in Apartment 5H of the Standish Arms Hotel; West 3-0963 is his phone number. While it appeared that Sarah had made only one costume for Clark in the pilot ("Superman on Earth"), later episodes show that Clark has three Superman costumes in his secret closet (located behind a false wall in his regular closet). Although Clark has X-ray vision, he cannot see through lead — a fact many criminals try to use as a means to outwit Superman (lead also neutralizes the effects of Kryptonite on Clark). While Superman expects no rewards for his battle against crime, he was voted "First Citizen of Metropolis" for his tireless efforts.

Lois Lane (Phyllis Coates, Noel Neill) is the *Daily Planet* reporter always in distress. She was born in the small town of Clifton-by-the-Sea and now lives in Apartment 6A of an unidentified building. She drives a car with the plate

ZN 18683 and suspects that Clark is Superman but can't prove it (she believes that every time Clark disappears in an emergency to become Superman, he is a coward—"Looking for a hole to hide in, Clark?").

Jimmy Olsen (Jack Larson) was originally depicted as the paper's photographer, then a cub reporter. He has the middle name of Bartholomew and lives with his mother in an undisclosed location. Like Lois, he too faces perilous situations and must be rescued by Superman. Perry White (John Hamilton) is the editor of the *Daily Planet*. He was a top notch reporter, then the mayor of Metropolis before becoming editor. He is a member of the Amateur Magician's Society and MX 31962 is his mobile car phone number. "Great Caesar's Ghost" is the expression Perry uses when he becomes upset or angry; and "Don't Call Me Chief!" is what he yells at Jimmy for constantly calling him "Chief."

William "Bill" Henderson (Robert Shayne) is the police inspector who is most helped by Superman. Professor Twiddle (Sterling Holloway) and Professor J.J. Pepperwinkle (Phillips Tead) are slightly off-center scientists who complicate Clark's life with their wacky inventions. Professor Twiddle, originally called Uncle Oscar, devised a machine that could plot crimes and one that could send people back in time. Professor Pepperwinkle invented the Topsy Turvy Machine (makes people think they are upside down), a device that could send people anywhere in the world via telephone lines, an aerosol spray to erase one's immediate memory, a robot called Mr. McTavish, and a machine that could turn cheap base metals, unshelled peanuts and apple cider into gold (the secret ingredient was platinum, which cost more than the gold was worth).

Professor Pepperwinkle lived at 64 Hope Street and Green Leaf 8975 is his phone number. He also believes there are two kinds of Kryptonite—Kryptonite Negative, which can take away Superman's powers, and Kryptonite Positive, which gives him his powers. Prior to this role, Phillips Tead played Mr. J. Willy, the owner of the Superman Souvenir Shop (in the episode "The Seven Souvenirs").

The Daily Planet Building (seen with the street number 5045) is located next to the Thomas Drug Store (in close-up scenes, in establishing shots, the building is actually Los Angeles City Hall). The building is characterized by a metal model of the planet that can be seen through the front doorway in the lobby. Metropolis 6-0500 is the paper's phone number and copies sell for five cents each. Black and white episodes feature a steam locomotive in the opening sequence; color episodes use stock footage of a diesel engine owned by the Southern Pacific Railroad (it's orange and red color scheme indicates that it is the Southern Pacific Daylight passenger train). The series is based on the comic strip by Jerry Siegel and Joe Schuster.

See also *The Adventures of Superboy*; *Lois and Clark: The New Adventures of Superman*; *Smallville* and *Superboy*.

6. *The Adventures of Superpup* (Unaired, 1958)

Pilot. "Your product, the best of its kind in the world, presents *The Adventures of Superpup*. Faster than the speediest jet. More powerful than the mightiest rocket. Able to fly around the world faster than you can say Superpup." This opening introduced viewers to a takeoff on the Superman saga with actors dressed in dog costumes. Bark Bent (Billy Curtis) is a reporter for the Metropolis *Daily Bugle*. He is, in reality, Superpup, a daring crime fighter. The origins of Superpup are not given. He does, however, wear a costume that is identical to Superman's and uses glasses to hide his true identity as Superpup. Pamela Poodle (Ruth Delfino) is the paper's star reporter (and Bark's forever in distress girlfriend). Perry Bite (Angelo Rossetto), a bulldog, is the paper's easily aggravated editor (when he gets upset, he walks across the top of his desk and says "Trouble, trouble, trouble"). Sergeant Beagle (Frank Delfino) is the police officer Superpup helps. The pilot finds Superpup attempting to save Pamela from the evil Professor Sheepdip (Harry Monty), who has her tied to a rocket and plans to send her to the moon. The series was made to be sponsored by a particular product (hence the first line in the opening). "Be with us again next week when your product, the best of its kind in the world, presents *The Adventures of Superpup*."

7. *Airwolf* (CBS, 1984–1986; USA, 1987–1988)

Under the guidance of a scientist named Dr. Moffet (David Hemmings), an awesome attack helicopter called *Airwolf* is built for the Firm, a U.S. government agency that handles sensitive issues. Moffet, however, betrays his country by stealing *Airwolf* to sell it to a foreign power. Michael Archangel (Alex Cord), head of the Firm, recruits a former employee, Stringfellow Hawke (Jan-Michael Vincent), to retrieve the helicopter. In return Michael promises him the government will look for his brother, Saint John (pronounced Sin-Jin), who is listed as missing in Vietnam. With the help of his friend, Dominic Santini (Ernest Borgnine), Hawke retrieves *Airwolf* but elects to hold it as hostage to force the government to keep its promise. In the meantime, Hawke uses *Airwolf* to help Michael when the need arises.

Hawke, called "String," was orphaned at the age of 12 and raised by Saint John (Christopher Connelly) and Dominic Santini (for whom he now works). String, 34, served with the 328 AHC unit in Vietnam and previously worked as a pilot for the Firm. String has a dog named Tet and is somewhat of a recluse (he lives in a remote, forest-like area of California). He has hidden *Airwolf* deep in "The Valley of the Gods" (a secret mountain location in the California desert).

Dominic, called Dom, runs the Santini Air Charter Service from the Van Nuys Airport (also given as the Municipal Airport) in California. Dom's helicopters are red, white and blue and equipped for motion picture stuntwork. Dom was born on the island of San Remo and calls *Airwolf* "The Lady." Dom has a jeep (plate 1-BOX-070), a station wagon (plate IDT 0406) and the Santini Air gas truck (plate 26 15622).

Caitlin O'Shaughnessy (Jean Bruce Scott) is a former deputy with the Texas Highway Patrol, Aerial Division, who now works as a pilot for Dom. She was a member of the Kappa Lambda Chi Sorority at Texas University and lives in an apartment at 703 LaSorda Place in Van Nuys.

Michael Coldsmith Briggs III, code name Michael Archangel, heads the Firm. Angel One is Michael's code to *Airwolf*; FIRM 1 is his limo plate number and he is assisted by several beautiful women on the CBS version: Belinda Bauer (Gabrielle, pilot), Deborah Pratt (Gabrielle, series), Sandra Kronemeyer (Lydia), Kandace Kuehl (Amanda) and Leigh Walsh (Rhonda).

Airwolf, government file A56-7W, is a black with white underbelly Bell 222 helicopter with a cruising speed of 300 knots and a maximum speed of 662-plus miles with the main rudder disengaged (in some episodes the top speed is mentioned as Mach 2). *Airwolf* can travel up to a height of 82,000 feet and has the Coast Guard code Ranger 276. It has a sophisticated computer control system, radar scanners, turbos for fast flight and movie and infrared cameras. When an unauthorized person attempts to touch *Airwolf*, he or she receives an electric shock.

Airwolf armaments include four 30mm chain guns (in the wings) and two 40mm wing cannons. It also carries a series of missiles. Air-to-Air missiles include Redeye (short range), Sidewinder and Sparrow (radar homing) and Phoenix (programmable, radar homing). Air-to-Surface missiles include Hellfire (short range), Copperhead (long range), Maverick (infrared radio imaging) and Shrike (electromagnetic homing). *Airwolf* also carries two warheads: Bullpup (radio command) and Harpoon (radio homing, anti-sky). The USA version, called *Airwolf '87* (but syndicated as *Airwolf* with the CBS episodes) drastically changes the storyline. Michael Archangel has been transferred to the Far East and has been replaced by Jason Locke (Anthony Sherwood) as the head of the Company (not the Firm as in the CBS episodes). Caitlin has returned to the Texas Highway Patrol and has been replaced by Dominic's niece, JoAnn "Jo" Santini (Michele Scarabelli), who works as a helicopter pilot for Santini Air (like Caitlin, she knows about *Airwolf*). The new version begins when String acquires positive proof that Saint John is alive. However, before he can use *Airwolf* to affect a rescue mission, he is seriously injured in a helicopter explosion at the airport that kills Dom. Jo decides to continue with the mission but is stopped by Jason who, with U.S. Air Force pilot Mike Rivers (Geraint Wyn Davies) tracked *Airwolf* through high-resolution photography. Although Jason has been ordered to return *Airwolf* to the government, he allows Jo to complete her mission (which she does with their help). Fearing that the copter may fall into enemy hands if it is returned, Jason decides to keep *Airwolf* a secret and forms the new *Airwolf* team: himself, Mike, Jo and Saint John (Barry Van Dyke). Jo and Saint John continue to run Santini Air and use *Airwolf* to help Jason and Mike when the need arises (String is only seen in the first episode. He is flown by Saint John to a secret location to recover from his injuries).

Jo is called "Little Lady" by Company officials. The team's code for Airwolf's hideout is Wolf (also called "The Company Store"); their code for Santini Air is "Cubs" (for example, "Wolf to Cubs"). During assignments, Saint John uses "Plan B" (make it up as you go along).

Sylvester Levay composed the CBS theme version; Dan Milner composed the adaptation for the USA version.

8. *Alias* (ABC, 2001)

Sydney Bristow (Jennifer Garner) appears to be an ordinary girl. She is young and attractive and attends the University graduate school. She is also a double agent—working as a spy for the real CIA in an effort to destroy SD-6, a branch of the CIA that is actually a secret enemy of the U.S. government.

For Sydney, it began one fall afternoon during her freshman year at the University (as the school is called). She was seated on a bench when approached by a man representing the U.S. government. "He said he might be interested in talking to me about a job. When I asked why me, all he told me was that I fit a profile. I felt like I didn't belong anywhere, even college and I needed the money... I met with him and he offered me a job."

That job, Sydney was told, was as an agent for SD-6, a covert branch of the CIA. In reality, SD-6 "is part of the enemy." It was formed a number of years ago by a dozen rogue agents who went freelance to form "The Alliance of Twelve," an enemy of the government who uses the facilities of the CIA to acquire what they need for themselves.

Sydney is trained and advances quickly—"They said I was a natural." Sydney has a photographic memory, is an expert shot and skilled in the martial arts. She carries lockpicks in the heels of her shoes, is proficient with explosives and a master of disguise. Her actual status as a student provides her with the perfect cover. Sydney, however, makes one fatal mistake: she tells her fiancé that she is a spy. This results in his murder by the agency and Sydney discovering that her superior, Arvin Sloane (Ron Rifkin) is an SD-6 leader and only using the CIA as a cover. She also learns that her father, Jack Bristow (Victor Garber) is not who he appears to be. Sydney believed her father "sold airplane parts" for Jennings Aerospace. He is, however, a double agent—working for the CIA as an undercover agent in SD-6 to help bring it down. To get even for the wrong that was done to her, Sydney sides with her father and offers her services to Jack's superior, Michael Vaughn (Michael Vartan), a real CIA agent who is also seeking to destroy SD-6. (All that is revealed about Sydney's mother is that she was aware that Jack was a CIA agent and that "she died in an accident").

When Sydney first meets with Vaughn, the operations director, she believes she can complete her mission "in a matter of months and then I quit." But when Vaughn shows her a map of how "The Alliance of Twelve" has grown to all areas of the country, Sydney agrees to stay until she can expose the leaders of SD-6. SD-6 is so secretive and elite that agents of the CIA headed by Sloane are unaware that they are actually working for the enemy. One such agent is Dixon (Carl Lumbly), Sydney's partner on assignments. Dixon's cover is that of an investment analyst "who loves his job" (even his wife, Diane [Yvonne Farrow] is unaware of his true occupation). Sydney becomes a double agent when she performs missions for SD-6 but passes the results of those missions on to the CIA.

A bank called Credit Dauphine houses the secretive SD-6. Marshall (Kevin Weisman) is another in-the-dark CIA agent who is actually helping SD-6 with the ingenious weapons he creates for Sydney's extremely dangerous assignments.

Sydney is an A student and has received only one D in her entire school career — in high school home economics. She lives in an apartment at 425 Kochran Place in Los Angeles. She is extremely careful during assignments — "I have to be. If I get careless, it's over for me." When Sloane needs Sydney, he beeps her; the message on her screen reads "Sloane 911." In the episode of 11/18/01, Jack's cover for Jennings Aerospace is closed and he is given a new cover — that of Portfolio Manager for Credit Dauphine (in reality, he oversees operations established by Sloane). J.J. Abrams composed the theme.

9. *The Amazing Spider-Man* (CBS, 1978–1979)

Peter Parker (Nicholas Hammond) is a graduate student at Empire State University in New York City. While hoping to become a physicist, he works part time as a freelance photographer for the *Daily Bugle*, a crusading newspaper (founded in 1890 and housed in the Bugle Building in Manhattan). While on an assignment to cover an experiment on radioactivity at the university, Peter is bitten by a spider that had been exposed to the deadly effects of the demonstration. Later, he realizes the spider's venom has become a part of his bloodstream and he has absorbed the powers and abilities of a living spider. He creates a special red and blue costume to conceal his true identity while he battles crime as the mysterious Spider-Man (he can scale buildings and spin a web with a special web dispenser he builds into the cuff of the costume).

Peter lives at 1231 Maple Drive with his aunt, May Parker (Irene Tedrow); 555-1834 is their phone number. J. Jonah Johnson (Robert F. Simon) is the editor of the *Bugle* (49NEJJ is his Rolls-Royce license plate number). Julie Masters (Ellen Bry), a reporter for the rival newspaper, the *Register*, drives a car with the plate 376 KNP. Rita Conway (Chip Fields) is Jonah's administrative assistant; Police Captain Barbera (Michael Pataki) is headquartered at One Police Plaza in Manhattan. Fred Waugh plays Spider-Man in stunt sequences; Jeff Donnell played May Parker in the pilot and David White was Jameson in the pilot. Stu Phillips composed the theme.

The Marvel comic book character first appeared on TV in 1969 when ABC aired the animated series *Spider-Man*. Here Peter Parker (voice of Peter Soles) is a student at Central High School and completing notes on a radiation experiment when he is bitten by a spider. He creates his own costume and acquires a position on the New York *Daily Bugle* to learn of trouble and act as Spider-Man. Betty Brandt (Peg Dixon) was a fellow reporter and J. Jonah Jameson (Paul Kligman) was the editor of the *Bugle*.

Ten years later ABC presented Peter Parker's female counterpart, Jessica Drew, in an animated series called *Spider-Woman*. Jessica Drew (voice of Joan Van Ark) is the daughter of a famous scientist who is experimenting with spider venom. One day, while in her father's lab, Jessica is bitten by a poisonous spider. To save Jessica, Dr. Drew injects her with an experimental spider serum. The serum saves Jessica's life but also endows her with amazing spider-like powers. Jessica, the publisher of *Justice Magazine*, creates a red and blue costume and battles crime as the mysterious Spider-Woman.

10. *Angel* (WB, 1999)

Angel Investigations is an unusual company that operates out of Los Angeles. It helps people lost in the night and battles evil that preys on them. It is run by a man known only as Angel (David Boreanaz), a former evil vampire who uses his skills of the undead to help humans. He is assisted by mortals Cordelia Chase (Charisma Carpenter) and Wesley Windom Price (Alexis Denisof); 555-0162 is the agency's phone number; NKO 714 is Angel's license plate number.

Angel, born in Ireland in 1746, was transformed into the living dead by Darla (Julie Benz), a beautiful vampire who seduced him. He terrorized Europe as Angelus, "The vampire with the angelic face" (after killing his victims, Angel would carve a cross on their left cheek to let people know he was there). In the late 1850s, Angelus killed a young Gypsy girl. Her clan cursed him by restoring his soul and with it, his conscience. Overcome with guilt for the misery he caused, Angel fled to America and vowed never to feed on humans again. Rejecting the lifestyle of a vampire, Angel chose to remain above ground and do whatever he could to atone for the sins of his past. He is first introduced on the series *Buffy, the Vampire Slayer* (see *Buffy, the Vampire Slayer* for information) and forms an uneasy alliance with Buffy (Sarah Michelle Gellar) to help her destroy the vampires who invade Sunnydale. Being a Slayer, Buffy should kill Angel, but she is attracted by his mysterious aura. At the end of Buffy's second season, *Angel* was spun off into a series of its own.

Although he has a soul, Angel still possesses vampire traits. He cannot function in sunlight (Cordelia says, "He uses the rat-infested sewers to get around in the daytime") and survives on pig's blood. He wears a long black trench coat and can be killed by a stake through the heart.

Cordelia, called "Cordy," was originally a friend of Buffy's and a student at Sunnydale High School. Rather than attend college after graduating, she chose to pursue a career in acting and took a job as Angel's secretary to make ends meet (in high school Cordelia was a member of the Cordetts, a clique of rich girls. During her senior year, Cordelia's parents lost their wealth. The once spoiled and rich Cordelia now had to make it on her own. Cordelia actually became a part of Angel's team when she helped Angel defeat a vampire preying on young actresses. She suggested to Angel that he should charge people for his services and thus the agency was born). Cordelia appeared in a commercial for Tan 'n' Screen lotion and hands out Angel's business cards at every opportunity. Cordelia first lived above Angel's loft, then in a small, dingy apartment and finally in Apartment 212 at 118 Silver Lake Road with a ghost named Dennis. As long as Dennis does his haunting quietly and doesn't invade her privacy, Cordelia puts up with him (Dennis was bricked up behind a wall by his mother, who didn't want him to marry a prostitute; she felt the girl would ruin her son's life).

Cordelia's minor role as a secretary was dramatically increased when Angel's original assistant, Alan Francis Doyle (Glenn Quinn) was killed off. Doyle, as he was called, was sent by "The Powers That Be" to help Angel (Doyle's father was a demon, his mother was a human). Doyle considers himself a messenger (he receives telepathic images of people in need and relates the information to Angel). In a fierce battle against demons, Doyle is mortally wounded. Before he dies, he kisses Cordelia and passes his "gift" to her, making her Angel's contact to the other world (Cordelia doesn't consider it a gift as "it gives me mind-bending, bone-crushing vision headaches"). Cordelia calls herself "Vision Girl" and designed the agency's business cards (a drawing of an angel). She says "We specialize in strange."

Wesley is a rogue demon hunter who worked previously as a Watcher (one who looks after Slayers, like Buffy). He joins with Angel when they cross paths on several cases. He was originally a third grade school teacher and does volunteer work at the Food Bank. Wesley uses an array of demon fighting weapons but relies most on ancient prophecies to battle the unknown.

Also assisting Angel is Charles Gunn, called "G" (J. August Richards), a young man who heads a team of demon fighters (he is aware of the problem Los Angeles has with vampires and began his own vigilante group); and the Host (Andy Hallett), a green demon with horns who owns the Karaoke Spot (also called Caritos), a nightclub for demons. The Host, real name Lorne, is actually Kerlansworth of the Deathwolk Clan from a dimension called Pylea (he accidentally found a dimensional portal, crossed over into this world, found it better and stayed). He now assists Angel as a snitch. While Angel is not on a friendly basis with authorities, he does assist Kate Lockley (Elisabeth Rohm), a detective with the L.A.P.D. Wolfram and Hart is the prestigious law firm that secretly helps demons.

Winifred Berkel (Amy Acker), called "Fred," is a young woman who fell through a time portal and was trapped in Pylea for five years. Here, she was a fugitive, having escaped her captors (humans are used as slaves). She lived in a cave and stole food to survive. Fred's experiences in Pylea have given her a power to see demons; she now helps Angel in his battle against evil (she was rescued by Angel when he, Cordelia, Wes, Gunn and Lorne were transported to Pylea. Fred now lives with Angel in his hotel).

Angel Investigations was originally housed in a small office in downtown Los Angeles. When a fire destroyed the building, Angel set up operations in the Hyperion Hotel. Angel's exact age is unknown. It is first said that he was 241 years old (in 1997, making his birth year 1756). He is next said to have been 18 years old in 1775 — right before he was bitten by Darla (making his birth year 1757). Next he is said to have been bitten by Darla in 1753; in a later episode, Angel says he was born in 1723. The exact date of Angel's restoration is also a mystery. It is first mentioned that Angel's soul was restored in the 1850s, then the 1920s and finally (as of 2001) it is mentioned as taking place in 1898.

See also *Forever Knight*.

11. *Automan* (ABC, 1983-1984)

Walter Nebecher (Desi Arnaz, Jr.) is head of the computer department of the Parker Division of the Los Angeles Municipal Police Department. He lives in Apartment 2 at 3611 Alameda and yearns to fight crime on the streets— not from an office (called "The Cage" by his superior). Walter has an advanced knowledge of electronics and begins experimenting with holographic images on his computer. He creates an image called Automan and programs it with all the knowledge of sleuthing from Sherlock Holmes to James Bond. Hoping to use Automan as part of his computer crime solving, Walter increases the program's power to a point where Automan materializes before him. The force for good created by Walter is accompanied by Cursor, a glowing hexagon that can create anything Automan requires. Walter calls Automan (Chuck Wagner) "the world's first truly automatic man." He has programmed him to be honest and to sound and feel human. A glitch, however, had gotten into the program and made Automan afraid of the dark. Automan can learn by observing people ("I do what they do— only better. On a scale of one to ten think of me as an eleven").

Automan lives with Walter and needs to be recharged often ("If I'm away from a computer for too long I have a power failure and can't function"). When Automan needs to become human he asks Cursor to make him acceptable based on the situations he encounters. Since Automan is an electronic display, he is prone to interference from above-the-ground power lines. When Walter needs Automan he uses the access word "Crime Fighter" to bring Automan from the computer world to the real world. Since Automan physically assists Walter on cases, he first introduced him as "This is my assistant, Auto." When Automan's presence became known to Walter's superiors, Lt. Jack Curtis (Robert Lansing) and Captain E.G. Boyd (Gerald S. O'Laughlin), Automan adopted the alias of Agent Man, a federal (FBI) agent assigned to assist the department (when Auto introduces himself to people he calls himself Auto J. Man). Auto's favorite TV show is the serial *Albeline* and Veronica Everly (Michelle Phillips) is his favorite movie actress (he has seen her film, *Queen of the Nile*, 100 times). Auto also went undercover as an actor (to bust a drug ring) and starred in the movie, *The Silver Dawn* (he believes "there's a bit of Robert Redford in me"). When asked a question (for example, "Are you game?") Auto always responds literally ("I started out as one"). Auto's most unique weapon is his car — the holographic AutoCar (capable of high speeds and 90 degree right-angle turns). While it is possible for Auto to ride in the car, it is not explained how Walter can ride in something that does not exist — and feel the impact of those turns. Cursor, who creates the car, can also turn it into the AutoCopter. Cursor, however, is not always as helpful as Auto and Walter would like. Cursor is constantly preoccupied with beautiful women and is easily distracted (Cursor is often seen chasing women and looking at cleavage; in the opening theme, Cursor sketches a heart around a poster of then sex star Heather Thomas).

While others can see Auto, only Officer Roxanne Caldwell (Heather McNair) is aware of Auto's true identity (she accidentally stumbled upon Walter's secret when she witnessed Auto's jump from the computer to the real world). Roxanne has a crush on Walter and calls him "Wally." Walter wears badge number 412. Gloria LeRoy is Walter's landlady, called Miss Moneypenny by Auto (after the secretary in James Bond films who has an eye for 007; Auto feels the landlady has an eye for him). William Conrad does the narrating; Billy Hinsche composed the theme.

12. *The Avengers* (ABC, 1966–1969)

"Extraordinary crimes against the people and the state had to be avenged by agents extraordinary. Two such people are John Steed, top professional, and his partner, Emma Peel, talented amateur, otherwise known as the Avengers."

These words, spoken by an announcer over the opening theme music, introduced American viewers to John Steed (Patrick Macnee), a suave and sophisticated British government Ministry agent who exudes Old World charm and courtesy, and Emma Peel (Diana Rigg), a woman skilled in the martial arts, who joins him on assignments for the sheer love of adventure. Steed's battle against crime, however, began on British TV in 1961 when he was partners with David Keel (Ian Hendry), a private practice doctor. At this time Steed is a man of mystery (it is not clear whether he is a lone avenger or working for some secret agency of the British government). Dr. Keel is seeking the thugs who killed his fiancée, Peggy (Catherine Woodville), when he meets Steed, a mysterious figure who enlists his help to find the same people (drug dealers). They soon become a team and Steed enlists Keel's help whenever the need arises. Although they became actively involved in fighting crime, they work independently of the police (David is bitter because the police did nothing to find Peggy's killers and once on a case David has only one objective — to get the criminals behind bars).

The first change occurs in 1962 when Dr. Keel accepts a fellowship overseas and Steed becomes partners with Catherine Gale (Honor Blackman), a beautiful blonde with a Ph.D. in anthropology. She is a widow and works for the British Museum (she previously worked with her husband on a remote farm in Kenya. When he was killed in a Mau Mau raid, Catherine returned to England). While Steed is revealed to be a Ministry agent, Catherine is not a professional undercover agent until 1963. Catherine, called "Cathy," is first depicted as an amateur with unique skills that Steed's superiors recognize and accept. Catherine is a skilled mechanic, expert photographer and highly knowledgeable in the use of firearms. She possesses scientific knowledge, martial arts abilities (judo) and, unlike Steed, finds it necessary to carry a gun. Cathy lives at 14 Primrose Hall and rides a Triumph motorcycle with the license plate 987 CAA.

In 1965 the second change occurs when a minor car accident unites Steed with the totally emancipated Emma Peel, the beautiful, wealthy widow of test pilot Peter Peel (no mention is made regarding Cathy's disappearance). Emma was originally said to be the daughter of a rich ship owner; later she is the daughter of Sir John Knight, the owner of Knight Industries (located in the Knight Building in London). Emma became head of the company when she was 21 (at which time her father died; no mention is made of her mother or if Emma still has a vested interest in the company). Emma is a skilled karate expert, interested in science and anthropology (she has a mini lab in her rooftop penthouse in Hampstead) and loves to play bridge (the June issue of *The Bridge Players International Guide* published her article "Better Bridge with Applied Mathematics"). She also enjoys painting and rock sculpting (which she does in her living room). Emma drives a 1966 Lotus Elan that was seen with the following license plates: SJH 4990, HNK 9996 and HN 9996. Emma's "fighting clothes" are called the "Emmapeelers" (two piece outfits that came in a variety of colors; for example, blue and gray, blue and pink, black, purple, and maroon and tan). For protection, Emma carries a small handgun. Her least favorite assignment was posing as the sexy but dense harem dancer, Emma, Star of the East in the episode "Honey for the Prince."

The final change occurs in 1968 when Emma returns to her husband (believed to have been killed but found alive in the Amazonian jungle) and Steed is teamed with Tara King (Linda Thorson), a gorgeous and shapely Ministry agent. Tara, recruit 69, first met Steed when she accidentally tackled him during a training exercise (thinking he was part of the exercise). Tara is the daughter of a prosperous farmer. She attended a prestigious finishing school where she acquired the sophistication of the young international set. She has skills associated with the outdoor life, can ski and fly an airplane. Tara is single and is the only one of Steed's partners who screams for help when she is in extreme danger. Tara does not have any particular fighting skills. She will use whatever is handy as a weapon to protect herself. She lives at 9 Primrose Crescent and drives a red Lotus Europa MKI (plate PPW 999F). She loves music, auto racing and her wardrobe consists mainly of miniskirts and tight fitting sweaters (in an interview regarding the sweaters, Linda said "They had to pour my 39-inch bosom into 36-inch sweaters so that Patrick Macnee could get near me").

The relationship between Steed and his female partners was also different. With Cathy and Emma affection was rarely shown; they respected each other and had a bond of friendship. With Tara, a warmer relationship developed as there was a hug and an occasional kiss. Emma and Tara were the only partners of Steed that actually met each other (in the transition episode "Forget-Me-Knot"). Steed mentioned Cathy to Emma in several episodes.

John Steed, rarely called by a first name (for example, it was "Steed and Mrs. Peel") lived first at 5 West Minster Mews then 3 Stable Mews in London. He is television's answer to filmland's James Bond. He is trained to withstand brainwashing and torture and is an expert on explosives, poisons and codes. When it comes to fighting he uses every dirty trick in the book to get the best of his enemies. He carries no gun, but, as part of the Edwardian-style suits he wears, he carries an umbrella with him at all times (the handle conceals a sword). Steed is a connoisseur of fine wine, plays polo and croquet and reads the Royal Edition of the *London Times*.

Steed is the scion of a noble family. He attended school at Eton but spent much of his time in amateur stage productions. He left Eton in 1939 and joined the Royal Navy (where he was a lieutenant and in command of a torpedo boat). After the war he captained an ex-naval launch in the Mediterranean that dealt with illegal cigarette trafficking. He gave this up to become a civil servant in London. This led to his becoming an economic advisor to a sheik in the Middle East. When Steed settled a dispute between two neighboring states that made the sheik rich through oil deals, he was given life royalties from two of the oil wells by the sheik.

Steed's first car was a yellow 1926 vintage Rolls-Royce Silver Ghost, then a dark green 1929 vintage 4.5 liter Bentley (license plate YT 3942; later RX6180 and VT 3942). He also has a white Rolls-Royce "that I usually keep in mothballs" as it doesn't always start and is used only for special occasions (like treating Emma to lunch). Steed takes three sugars in his coffee and has a weakness for the opposite sex. He originally had a dog named Juno (Great Dane) then a Dalmatian he called Freckles.

Steed's first superior (with Cathy) was One-Ten (Douglas Muir), then the wheelchair-bound Mother (Patrick Newell). Mother, only seen in the Tara King episodes, was a top notch secret agent who was crippled in an explosion. He is in constant pain and is not the kindest man to work for. He can walk with the aid of special straps and ladders suspended from the ceiling and like Steed, has an eye for the ladies and a taste for fine wine. He is assisted by Rhonda (Rhonda Parker), a 6-foot-tall blonde who never speaks but carries out his every command. Mother's counterpart is Father (Iris Russell), a blind woman who was much more gentle, but just as sharp witted and perceptive as Mother. See also *The New Avengers*. Johnny Dankworth composed the original theme (1961–65), Laurie Johnson the revised theme (1965–69).

13. *Batgirl* (Unaired, 1968)

Pilot. Before Batgirl became a part of the *Batman* series (see entry), an eight minute test film was produced about "a dazzling dare doll" called Batgirl. Here Barbara Gordon (Yvonne Craig), the daughter of Police Commissioner Gordon (Neil Hamilton) works at the Gotham City Library. She also has a secret — she is the mysterious Batgirl, a daring avenger who helps the police solve baffling crimes. Barbara has a secret room in the library that contains her Batgirl costume (which she patterned after her hero, Batman). In addition to the Batgirl Cycle, Barbara has an electronic makeup compact equipped with a deadly laser beam. In the pilot story, Batgirl helps Batman and Robin (Adam West, Burt Ward) foil a plot by the evil Killer Moth to kidnap the wealthy Roger Montross (there are no screen credits; the regulars from *Batman* appeared to help Yvonne launch her series). William Dozier does the narrating.

14. *Batman* (ABC, 1966–1968)

Gotham City is a metropolis like no other. While populated by hard working people, it is also home to diabolical villains who seek to conquer it. One person, however, stands in their way — Batman, a mysterious caped crusader who risks his life to save Gotham City from evil. But who is Batman? And where did he come from? The legend begins many years ago with a ten-year-old boy named Bruce Wayne. Bruce and his parents, millionaire Thomas

Wayne and his wife, Martha, are walking home from a dinner party when they are approached by a thug. When Thomas refuses to give the thief Martha's jewels, a scuffle ensues. Martha and Thomas are shot. The thief is about to shoot Bruce when approaching police officers scare him off. Bruce, suddenly orphaned, is determined to get even — "I swear by the spirits of my parents to avenge their deaths by spending the rest of my life fighting criminals. I will make war on crime!"

Bruce lives at stately Wayne Manor in Gotham City. He is now cared for by Alfred Pennyworth, the faithful family butler. Backed by his family's vast wealth, Bruce works in almost total isolation to become a master scientist and to perfect his mental and physical skills. In time Bruce creates the world's greatest crime lab (later to be called the Batcave) beneath Wayne Manor.

Ten years later, on the anniversary of that tragic night, Bruce feels it is now time for him to fulfill the promise he made. "I must have a disguise," he tells Alfred. "Criminals are a superstitious, cowardly lot. So my disguise must be able to strike terror in their hearts. I must be a creature of the night, black, mysterious." Just then, Bruce and Alfred hear a noise at the window — a bat that has been attracted by the light. "That's it," Bruce says, "it's an omen; the perfect disguise. I shall become a bat!" Bruce develops his bat-like costume, utility belt and car (the Batmobile). Batman soon becomes the legendary "Caped Crusader" for justice.

Shortly after, Bruce establishes the Wayne Foundation, a charity that sponsors worthwhile causes. One day Bruce involves himself with one of those causes — taking a group of orphans to the circus.

A high wire act called the Flying Graysons is performing without a net when the rope snaps. The ensuing fall kills the parents of young Dick Grayson. Bruce, as Batman, investigates and discovers that racketeers sabotaged the act to force the circus owner to pay protection money. Batman approaches Dick and tells him what he has learned. He also tells him about the circumstances that led to his becoming Batman. "If only I could do something like that," Dick says, "it will help avenge their deaths. Let me join you, please." "With your acrobatic skills, plus with what I could teach you, maybe you can make the grade," says Bruce.

Bruce (Adam West) takes on the responsibility of raising Dick (Burt Ward) and eventually becomes his legal guardian. As Dick perfects his mental and physical skills, he becomes Batman's aide, adopting the alias of Robin, the Boy Wonder (and forming the Dynamic Duo when working as a team). As a normal teenager, Dick attends Woodrow Roosevelt High School.

Batman, hiding behind the guise of millionaire Bruce Wayne, and Robin, as his youthful ward, Dick Grayson, are fully deputized agents of the law. At Wayne Manor, the button used to gain access to the Batcave is located in the bust of Shakespeare in Bruce's den. When the button is pressed, a wall moves to reveal the Batpoles. When Bruce and Dick descend their respective Batpoles (like those in a firehouse) Bruce hits the Instant Change Costume lever. Their street clothes change to their costumes. In the Batcave, located 14 miles from Gotham City, are various Bat Computers and the black with red trim Batmobile (license plate 2F 3567; later B-1), Batman and Robin's main mode of transportation. The Batmobile is powered by atomic batteries, uses turbines for speed and has controls such as the Bat Ray Projector, a Bat Homing/Receiving Scope, the Bat Ram, the Bat Parachute (to stop the car at high speeds) and the start decoy button (which fires a rocket if an unauthorized person tries to start the car). Batman also has the Batcopter (I.D. number N3079; later N703) and the Batman Dummy Double (which Bruce stores in the Bat Dummy Closet). After an assignment, Alfred (Alan Napier) serves Bruce and Dick milk and sandwiches in the study. According to the villain King Tut (a.k.a. William Omaha McElroy), there is a supply of Nilanium, the world's hardest metal (once refined) under the Batcave.

In last season episodes, Batman and Robin find help in fighting crime when Batgirl suddenly appears and forms the Terrific Trio when working with them. Batgirl is in reality Barbara Gordon (Yvonne Craig), the beautiful daughter of Police Commissioner Gordon (Neil Hamilton). After graduating from college, Barbara returns home to take a job at the Gotham City Library. To help her father fight crime, she dons a bat-like costume and becomes Batgirl. Barbara lives in midtown Gotham City in Apartment 8A with her pet bird, Charlie. She conceals her Batgirl costume in a secret closet behind her bedroom wall (she opens the wall with a hidden button on her vanity table). Her mode of transportation, the Batgirl Cycle, is hidden in a secret freight elevator in the back of her building.

Barbara is also the chairperson of the Gotham City Anti-Littering Committee and, as Batgirl, received the first Gotham City Female Crime Fighting and Fashion Award, the Battie, for her crusade against crime and her sexy costume. Barbara's favorite opera is *The Marriage of Figaro* and she rode Bruce's horse, Waynebow, in the Bruce Wayne Foundation Handicap.

Bruce, chairman of the Gotham City Boxing Commission, has an office in the Wayne Foundation Building in downtown Gotham City. As Batman, he works closely with Commissioner Gordon and his assistant, Police Chief O'Hara (Stafford Repp). Gordon has two ways of contacting Batman: the red Batphone in his office, and the Bat Signal (flashes from the roof of City Hall). O'Hara's catchphrase is "Saints preserve us" (which he says when a criminal is on the loose).

At Wayne Manor, Alfred answers the phone with "Stately Wayne Manor." He can contact Batman via his emergency Bat Buckle Signal Button (he also assists Batman in the field by donning various disguises). Batman wears a gray/black costume with a black cape and black hood mask; Robin has a red and green costume with a gold cape and black mask; Batgirl wears a tight purple costume with a dark purple hood and a gold and purple cape. She also wears a red wig to conceal Barbara's natural black hair. Bruce and Dick have spare costumes in their limo; Batman invented a dance called "The Batusi"; Batman can't abide being called a coward; Robin's catchphrase is the word *Holy* followed by a term (for example, "Holy Crucial Moments" or "Holy strawberries, Batman, we're in a jam" — the one phrase Burt Ward wanted to use but was never permitted).

The principal villains plaguing Gotham City were: The Archer (Art Carney), Cat Woman (Julie Newmar, Eartha Kitt, Lee Meriwether), Clock King (Walter Slezak), Egghead (Vincent Price), The Joker (Cesar Romero), King Tut (Victor Buono), Lola Lasagna (Ethel Merman), Louie the Lilac (Milton Berle), The Mad Hatter (David Wayne), Marsha, Queen of Diamonds (Carolyn Jones), Minerva (Zsa Zsa Gabor), Mr. Freeze (Eli Wallach, George Sanders, Otto Preminger), The Penguin (Burgess Meredith), The Riddler (Frank Gorshin, John Astin) and The Siren (Joan Collins). Based on the comic strip by Bob Kane. William Dozier does the narrating; Neil Hefti composed "The Batman Theme"; Billy May and Wally Mack, "The Batgirl Theme."

15. *BeastMaster* (Syndicated, 1999–2002)

"In an age when magic and nature rule the world there is an extraordinary legend; the story of a warrior who communicates with animals, who fights sorcery and the unnatural. His name is Dar, last of his tribe. He is also called BeastMaster." Dar (Daniel Goddard), as the opening theme narration says, is the last of his tribe, the Soulas. An invasion by the evil King Zad (Steve Grives) and his Terron warriors ravaged Dar's village in the Midlands. It was only with the help of a beautiful demon named Curupira (Natalie Mendoza, Emilie DeRaven) that Dar manages to escape. Curupira needs a champion for her cause; someone to protect her forests and animals if anything should happen to her. She believes that Dar can fulfill that quest. When Dar passes Curupira's test of silence and nonmovement for three days, she grants him the power over animals (it is later learned that Dar's father made a promise to Curupira to protect her animals; she made a promise to him: to save his son and make him a BeastMaster).

Tao (Jackson Raine) is from a land called Xinca (pronounced Chinka) that is located in the Middle of the World — "where the earth touches the sky"; his people are called Eirons. Tao is embarked on a mission by the Elders to spread the word of his people and bring followers to his village. He is in a forest and under attack by Terrons when Dar saves him. When Dar learns that Tao is attempting to map his world, he agrees to help him. Together they set out on a mission that also involves battling the evil that seems to exist everywhere.

Dar is also accompanied by his animals helpers: Ruh (a tiger), Koto and Poto (ferrets) and Sharak (an eagle) through whose eyes Dar can see what he sees. Dar can command animals, think as they do and he has learned to fight through them. It doesn't bother Dar that Ruh (which means "headstrong") kills other animals ("He's got to eat"). Dar fights his enemies with a white staff (he will not carry a sword) and claims that Poto is always eating while Koto prefers the safety of the duffle-like bag Dar carries them in.

Tao means "The Way." He is a natural sorcerer (makes potions from herbs and plants) and studies weapons "because you can learn a lot about a man by the way he fights." He also believes that being a warrior requires not only strength but intelligence. He feels that the future holds many promises for mankind (by studying Sharak, Tao believes "that man will one day fly like a bird in a machine").

Curupira rules the forests. If a man kills her animals, she kills him. Tao calls her "The Little Demon." She is most fond of her white tiger (Mohan) and "cares only about her animals and some humans." Curupira is incredibly strong. She has blonde hair, a normal flesh face but she is green from the neck down. Her feet are backwards and to kiss her means death (she drains the life force from any human who kisses her). She can burn with her breath and control the weather to protect her forests. Her enemy is Iara (Samantha Healy), an enchanting demon who wants to destroy Curupira and take over her world. Iara considers Curupira "an immature, unpleasant little girl." She has the power of the mist (a white, fog-like mist to trap her victims) and derives strength from water (she lives beneath the water and uses it to project false images of herself). In mid–second season episodes, Iara imprisons Curupira beneath her waters and assumes her powers (Curupira is later said to be "imprisoned neck deep in snakes"). Iara is now the guardian of the animals and controls the balance between man and beast. She oversees Dar's activities as the BeastMaster and is now called "The Demon Who Rules the Animal Kingdom."

Arena (Marjean Holden), called "The Demon Who Lives in the Forest," is actually a good demon Dar and Tao befriend. She is from the Great Desert in a place called Narmead. When the Terrons attacked her village, her mother hid her in a field of wild flowers. Arena grew up alone and now battles the Manlinks, the missing link between man and ape, who rule the Rain Forest. She rides a horse named Cittia. Arena's role gradually changed to help Dar stop the evil King Zad from taking over the land. Zad believes he is "the one and only king" and only Voden (David Paterson), another evil king seeking to rule the land, stands in his way. Voden has set his goal to conquer Zad and build his empire. A confrontation between Voden ("The Mad King") and Zad ("The Savage King") occurred in the last episode of the second season. Zad defeated Voden, who escaped before he could be killed by Zad.

The Apparition (Leah Purcell), called "The Demon of the Burning Forests," is another unnatural being Dar and Tao had to face. The Apparition "is a Hell on Earth" says Dar. She has red eyes and "rules in the Dark Ways" (receives her powers from the Rulers of Darkness).

The Sorceress (Monika Schnarre) is a beautiful woman, known only as the Sorceress, who seeks Dar's ability to control the animals. She lives in a mountain cave and appears and disappears in a purple mist. She uses what she calls "My Third Eye" (a telescope she acquired from Baha the Slave Trader) that lets her see what others cannot through a human female eye. The Sorceress is controlled by the Ancient One (Grahaeme Bond), the magical ruler of the land, who is teaching her how to use her developing powers "to keep the world from sinking into darkness." The Ancient One calls her "My Assistant" and "My Sorceress." He is often furious with Iara because she interferes with magic and could jeopardize magic for everyone.

Midway through the second season Monika Schnarre's Sorceress was imprisoned by the Ancient One in clear stone for abusing her powers. She was replaced by a new, kinder and gentler Sorceress (Dylan Bierk) who "is not supposed to have a heart and is not supposed to fall in love" but did when she became fond of Dar. Neither Sorceress could interfere with human destiny without her teacher (the Ancient One) present. The new Sorceress is unaware of who she really is or where she came from. She is not aware of the full extent of her powers and uses what powers she has for good.

The episode of 10/7/01, "The Legend Reborn," begins the series' third season and drastically changes the previously described concept. Dar is not who or what he appears to be. Monika Schnarre returns to the role of the Sorceress. Marc Singer joins the cast as Dartanus, the Spirit Warrior. The recurring role of King Zad has been upgraded to a series regular.

To establish the new storyline, evil has to be dealt with first. King Zad is now said to have made a bargain with Balcifer, the Lord of Darkness, for eternal life and the power to rule the world. In turn, Zad has vowed to destroy all goodness and plunge the world into turmoil. One man, however, stands in Zad's way—Dar, a force for good that is also a threat to Balcifer's wickedness. For Zad to become ruler of the world, he must destroy Dar, a task that becomes much more difficult because of who Dar really is.

Dar believed he was a member of the Soulas tribe in a village called Dimor. His father, Eldar, was actually the true king, not the village chief as Dar was led to believe. Dar was born in a forgotten land called Ericon, which defied the ways of Balcifer. When Zad invaded Ericon, Eldar and his faithful friend, Dartanus, led the fight against the Terrons. To protect the infant Dar, the future king, from Balcifer, Eldar sent him to the village of Dimor to be raised by its chief until he was old enough to assume his destiny. Eldar then created a crystal ark and transformed five of his family members into animals to protect them. Before King Zad kills Eldar and destroys Ericon, Dartanus is entrusted with a mission: to find Dar when the time is right and pass a magic sword onto him. It is also apparent by this new storyline that Curupira did not save Dar and that Dar's father was not a BeastMaster (although Dar's ability to communicate with animals is not dropped).

Dar encounters Dartanus shortly after the new story begins. Dar is reluctant to believe Dartanus when he is told of his real past and his future destiny. He is convinced when his birthright, the symbol of an X materializes onto the palm of his hand (the symbol magically appears in times of stress to guide Dar on the right path to goodness). Dar is then given Eldar's sword (the sword is magical and will appear only when needed. It disguises itself as Dar's white staff when not in use. Dar summons the sword by twirling the staff and returns it to a staff by twirling the sword). Dartanus, who appears in various disguises, assists Dar and Tao in their battle against King Zad.

The second episode, "The Crystal Ark" (10/14/01), reveals that Dar must find his family and return each of them to the ark. Once all five members have been found, they will become human and evil (Zad and Balcifer) will be defeated and Dar will become king. However, before Zad will allow peace and harmony to be returned to the world, he has vowed to find and destroy Dar's animal family before they can be returned to the ark (it is revealed that Dar's mother is a bird, his sister a white lion and his brother a horse).

Before Dylan Bierk became the Sorceress, the Ancient One became displeased with Monika Schnarre's Sorceress and imprisoned her in a crystal rock. When King Zad finds the imprisoned Sorceress (Monika), he releases her (the fate of Dylan's Sorceress is not revealed). The Sorceress (Monika) can now do as she pleases (the Ancient One is not present to discipline her). While still possessing an evil streak, the Sorceress will help Dar when she feels he is facing difficult circumstances. Graeham Coleman composed the theme.

16. *The Bionic Woman* (ABC, 1976–1977; NBC, 1977–1978)

Jaime Sommers (Lindsay Wagner) is one of the world's top five women's professional tennis players. She has the potential to beat then top seed Billie Jean King and is scheduled to play against her in a tournament in Barcelona. Jaime is also the girlfriend of Colonel Steve Austin (Lee Majors), the world's first bionic man (see *The Six Million Dollar Man*). Shortly before she is to leave for Spain, Jaime and Steve decide to go sky diving. They jump from a single engine plane (I.D. number N5794A) and are descending to earth. When Jaime's altimeter reads seven, she (and Steve) pull their respective ripcords. Both parachutes open but Jaime's malfunctions and sends her plunging to the ground. Perhaps it was the fall through tree branches that spared her life, but the results were devastating: "Her legs have so many breaks that we can't count them; her right ear is hemorrhaging and her right arm and shoulder are crushed beyond repair."

In 1973, Dr. Rudy Wells (Martin E. Brooks) saved Steve's life through a bionic operation that replaced his legs, arm and eye when he was critically injured in a plane crash. Oscar Goldman (Richard Anderson), head of the O.S.I. (Office of Scientific Intelligence) arranges for Jaime to have a similar operation. In a cost-classified operation that saves Jaime's life, Jaime's legs, arm and ear are replaced with bionic substitutes. They are:

1. Bionic Audio Sensor (catalogue number 6314-KAH). Amplification 1400; .081 Distortion, Class BC.
2. Bionic Neuro Link Forearm (Upper Right Arm Assembly), catalogue number 2822/PJ13.
3. Neuro Feedback Power Supply: Atomic Type AED-4 (catalogue number 2821 AED-4), 1500 watt Continuous Duty.
4. Bionic Neuro Link Bi-Pedal Assembly (catalogue number 914-PAA).
5. Neuro Feedback Terminal Power Supply: Atomic Type AED-9A, 4920 Watt Continuous Duty.
6. Overload Follower, 2100 Watt Reserve, Intermittent Duty, Class CC.

Jaime's new bionics make her the world's first female cyborg (a cybernetic organism). She has incredible strength and speed (she can run the mile in 58 seconds) and super fine hearing. Jaime feels she owes Oscar and the government a debt and becomes an agent for the O.S.I., an organization that performs hazardous missions.

The O.S.I. provides a cover for Jaime (who relinquishes her tennis career): school teacher (grade levels seven, eight and nine) at the Ventura Air Force Base in California. Jaime lives in Ojai, California, in a home on the ranch of Steve's parents, Jim and Helen Elgin (Ford Rainey, Martha Scott); Jim is Helen's second husband. Jaime's phone number was given verbally as 311-555-2368, but seen on camera as 311-555-7306. NBC episodes find Jaime working with a bionic dog she calls Max (Oscar named him Maximillion — after a cost of the operation needed to replace his legs and jaw when he was injured in a fire).

Peggy Callahan (a.k.a. Janet Callahan; played by Jennifer Darling) is Oscar's secretary and Jaime's best friend (she lives at 22 Land Cliff Drive). Lindsay Wagner also played Lisa Galloway, a woman surgically altered to look like Jaime by enemy agents seeking to infiltrate the O.S.I. and learn the secret of Jaime's strength. Jerry Fielding composed "The Bionic Woman Theme."

17. *Black Scorpion* (SciFi, 2001)

Darcy Walker (Michelle Lintel) is a second generation police officer. Her father, Lieutenant Stan Walker (David Groh) was a maverick cop who took the law into his own hands. When Darcy (Elizabeth Huett) was a child in the late 1970s, Stan would allow her to monitor the police radio band and tell her a strange bedtime story about a scorpion who wanted to cross a river. The scorpion, unable to swim, asked a frog for a ride on his back. The frog was hesitant, fearing to get stung. The scorpion assured the frog she would not sting him because if she did they would both drown. "I won't hurt you, I promise," she said. The frog permitted the scorpion to ride on his back. Halfway across the river, the scorpion stung the frog. "Now we're both going to drown. Why did you sting me?" asked the frog. "Because I'm a scorpion," she said. "I don't understand the story," said Darcy. "Someday you will," replied her father.

In 2001, Darcy is a detective with the 21st Precinct in Angel City (2962 is her car code). Her father, discharged from the force for being a rogue cop, is working as a security cop when he is shot and killed. In an attempt to solve the case, Darcy takes the law into her own hands and is suspended for doing so (later reinstated). Bitter and disillusioned, Darcy retreats to her apartment. There she sees an unopened birthday gift from her father. She opens it to find a black ring with a silver scorpion as its stone (representing her Scorpio birth sign). Suddenly, the story her father told her begins to make sense "but sometimes the world doesn't make sense" she says to herself. "I need it to." Although she has only her skills in the martial arts as her initial weapon, Darcy creates a sexy and revealing black leather costume and mask not only to avenge her father's murder, but to bring all criminals to justice. Her first act as the Black Scorpion occurs at the Donkey Bar, where she deals justice to a pimp for roughing up her snitch, a prostitute named Tender Lovin'. Darcy is first called the Masked Vigilante by people, then the Masked Marauder by police. It is when Darcy saves Tender Lovin' from a mugger that she receives the name Black Scorpion (Tender described her as dressed in black with her hair in a braid like a scorpion's tail).

Darcy monitors the police band to learn of crimes. She also modifies her father's stun gun to create an immobilizer (laser-like rays that emanate from the ring) and bursts of electricity in her black boots that allow her to leap. Soon newspaper headlines read "Criminals Stung by the Black Scorpion." The police also want the Black Scorpion for a long list of priors: leaving the scene of a crime, reckless endangerment, destruction of public property, possession of concealed weapons, and speeding.

When Darcy's orange Corvette (later said to be a red Stingray) is damaged while attempting to escape from the police, she brings it to her friend, Argyle (Brandon Terrill), a former car thief and chop shop owner who runs an almost legitimate business called Argyle's Garage. Darcy also reveals her secret identity to him. Argyle agrees to help Darcy because "if you didn't bust me when you did, I would be doin' hard time with the rest of my gang."

Argyle customizes Darcy's car for crime fighting. He modifies the AM/FM radio to pick up the police band. He installs an onboard computer and polarized (and bulletproof) glass. He also feels the car should have its own secret identity and installs a morphing switch to change to orange Corvette into the black ScorpionMobile ("My boys lifted a transformer box from Angel Tech that was intended for military use ... it reorganizes the atoms at a molecular level and changes color, size and shape"). He later rigs the morph adjustment to transform Darcy from street clothes to the Black Scorpion when the need arises (accomplished through the scorpion on Darcy's ring). By saying Auto

Transfer, the orange car becomes the black ScorpionMobile. Auto Reverse changes the car back to normal (in the pilot, Darcy had to call the computer by the name "Yo" then give a command).

Darcy's apartment is also her headquarters. She has a pet black scorpion (kept in a fish tank) and an array of weapons (knives and guns) that she rarely uses. Her costume is secured behind a secret wall in the living room and she hides her car in the garage of an adjacent building. In later episodes, Darcy's car (now the red Stingray) is destroyed by a villain. Argyle reconstructs the car as a white Stingray that morphs into the faster and deadlier black ScorpionMobile. The car now has a magnetic field to protect it from gunfire, an auto-visual system (to allow Argyle to monitor Darcy's activities) and stingers (metal tire destroyers shaped like scorpions).

Detective Steve Rafferty (Scott Valentine) is Darcy's partner at the 21st Precinct. He feels a strange attraction to the Black Scorpion and believes he and Darcy should keep their personal and private lives separate. He enjoys video games and sharing a drink with Darcy at O'Brien's Bar.

Tender Lovin' (Enya Flack), real name Veronica, is Argyle's girlfriend. She was a former street walker (and Darcy's information girl) who has turned her life around and now owns a fashion boutique (she designed a line of illuminated attire called Plug Intimate Lingerie). As Tender Lovin' she would say "My name is my fame, they don't call me Tender Lovin' for nothin'." Press material states that Tender Lovin' designed Black Scorpion's costume. This is simply not true. It is clearly shown that Darcy designed her own costume while Tender Lovin' was still a hooker.

Arthur Worth (Robert Pine) is the corrupt mayor of Angel City (also called City of Angels). He is a former criminal, "knows lots of criminals" and uses his position as a means of finding new schemes to raise money for his re-election campaign. Babette (Shae Marks), Arthur's secretary, is a "bouncy bimbo" who knows little about secretarial work but is a pro when it comes to wearing seductive, slinky dresses. Babette says she and "Artie" have been having an affair for five years ("It began on Valentine's Day").

Prisoners are sent to Pearl Gate Penitentiary (although they always manage to escape). The series presents the most diabolical (if not comic book–like) villains since *Batman*: Aerobicide (Renee Allman), After Shock (Sheri Rose), Breathtaker (Adam West), Clock Wise (Frank Gorshin), Firearm (Martin Cove), Flashpoint (Alan Scott), Hurricane (Athena Massey) and Stunner (Allison Armitage). David G. Russell composed the theme. The program opens with these words: "In the light of day, Darcy Walker is a cop. But in the dark of night she becomes Black Scorpion — doing with a mask what she can't do with a badge."

Note: Showtime produced a 1995 TV movie called *Black Scorpion* with Joan Severance (Darcy Walker/Black Scorpion), Garrett Morris (Argyle), Terri J. Vaughn (Tender Lovin'), Ashley Peldon (Young Darcy) and Rick Rossovich (Stan Walker). Steve, the mayor and Babette were not part of the program.

18. *Buck Rogers in the 25th Century* (NBC, 1979–1981)

In the year 1987 Captain William "Buck" Rogers (Gil Gerard) is chosen to pilot the *Ranger III*, the last of NASA's deep-space probes. The *Ranger III* is launched from the John F. Kennedy Space Center and appears to be a successful flight until cosmic forces cause a freak accident that freezes Buck's life support system and alters the craft's planned trajectory. *Ranger III* is sent into an orbit a thousand times more vast and a perfect combination of gasses (oxygen, ozone and methylene) seeps into the ship. The gasses are instantaneously frozen and preserve Buck.

As Buck drifts through endless space, the Earth Buck knew will cease to exist. A futuristic holocaust ravages the planet and the Earth is now dependent upon trade with other planets for survival. People now live in cone-protected cities as the atmosphere still has traces of radiation from the holocaust. New Chicago is now the capital of the United States and headquarters of the Earth Federation, the new system of government. It is now the year 2491. Dr. Elias Huer (Tim O'Connor) is head of the Earth Federation and Wilma Deering (Erin Gray) is commander of the Earth Defense Force, an organization that protects the planet from alien invaders. Princess Ardella (Pamela Hensley) of the planet Draconia, poses the biggest threat to the Earth. The Draconian Empire has conquered three-quarters of the universe and Ardella has plans to add Earth to that total. After drifting in space for 504 years, the *Ranger III* is found by Ardella, commander of the king's flagship, the *Draconia*. Buck is taken to sick bay and revived, but not told about his fate. He believes he is still on *Ranger III* and having hallucinations. Ardella is on a supposed mission of peace to the Earth (to sign a trade agreement) and believes that Buck is an Earth Directorate spy. Rather than expose Buck and cause friction, Ardella allows Buck to leave (the *Ranger III* has been repaired and refueled).

The *Ranger III* soon comes within Earth Directorate air space and Delta Sector fighters are dispatched to intercept it. When Buck fails to comply with orders given by Colonel Wilma Deering, she takes control of his ship and guides it through the defense shield (unauthorized ships are disintegrated if they are not properly cleared). Buck, still unaware of what has happened to him, now believes he has been captured by the Russians. Buck, called a "barbarian" by Wilma for defying her, is brought to Dr. Huer for interrogation. It is when Buck speaks to Dr. Theopolis (voice of Eric Server), a member of the Computer Council that runs the Inner City, that he learns of his fate. Wilma believes Buck is a threat to their safety. Her mind is changed when Buck proves Ardella's supposedly unarmed ship is carrying weapons and helps Wilma foil Ardella's plans to conquer the Earth. Buck is assigned a silver ambuquad named Twiki (voice of Mel Blanc; played by Felix Silla) to help him adjust to life in this new world.

Buck can't go back; his past is gone. He becomes a member of the Third

Force of the Earth Directorate to help the Earth battle its enemies. "Flight 711 to Houston Control" was Buck's code for *Ranger III*. As a kid Wilma was called "Dizzy Dee"; Twiki has the serial number 2223-T; Buck calls Dr. Theopolis "Theo." The Capitol Building in New Chicago is the headquarters of the Earth Directorate; the national retirement age has risen to 85.

Princess Ardella, the daughter of King Draco the Conqueror (Joseph Wiseman) is the eldest of 29 children (all girls). Ardella measures 34-24-34 (by Buck's calculations) and is determined to become her own ruler. She wants to marry Buck "and begin a magnificent new dynasty" with him. Ardella is assisted by the evil Kane (Henry Silva, Michael Ansara) but was unable to complete her objectives due to a second season format change (that dropped Ardella, Kane and Dr. Huer). Wilma and Buck are now members of *Searcher*, a spaceship that is seeking the lost tribes of Earth. Admiral Ephraim Asimov (Jay Garner) commands the ship (he is also called Isaac Asimov); Dr. Goodfellow (Wilfred Hyde-White) is the head scientist; Hawk (Thom Christopher) is their ally, an alien man-bird. The role of Twiki has been cut back to add Crichton (voice of Jeff Davis), the robot who refuses to believe that he is man-made. Glen A. Larson composed "The Theme from Buck Rogers: Suspension" (sung by Kipp Lennon in the pilot).

Note: There were two prior versions, both titled *Buck Rogers in the 25th Century*. The first was an apparently now non-existent unaired pilot with Earl Hammond (Buck Rogers) and Eva Marie Saint (Wilma Deering). The second, which aired on ABC (1950-51) starred Kem Dibbs then Robert Pastene (Buck Rogers), Lou Prentis (Wilma Deering) and Harry Sothern (Dr. Huer). The format here finds Buck Rogers as a young Air Corps veteran who is trapped in a cave-in while surveying an old mine in Pittsburgh. He is soon rendered unconscious by a peculiar gas that places him in a state of suspended animation. Five hundred years later, the earth shifts and Buck is awakened by the fresh air that enters the mine. He emerges from the mine and meets Wilma Deering, a lieutenant on the Space General's staff. He learns that it is the year 2430 and the place is no longer Pittsburgh but Niagara, America's new capitol. Buck eventually becomes a member of the Space General's staff to help Wilma and Dr. Huer battle the enemies of Earth.

19. *Buffy, the Vampire Slayer* (WB, 1997–2000; UPN, 2001)

Buffy Anne Summers (Sarah Michelle Gellar) is a 16-year-old sophomore at Sunnydale High School in California. She was born May 6, 1979 (later given as October 24, 1980), and lives with her mother, Joyce (Kristine Sutherland) at 1630 Rubella Drive in Sunnydale. Buffy likes cheese, eats Sunshine Crisp cereal for breakfast and has a 2.8 grade average. As a child Buffy had a plush pig (Mr. Gordo) and a security blanket she called Mr. Pointy. Buffy was fascinated with Dorothy Hamill and dreamed of becoming an ice skater. She also imagined herself as a super crime fighter she called Power Woman. Buffy is also "The Chosen One," the one girl in all the world with the power to slay vampires and other evil creatures. It is when Buffy turns 16 that she discovers she is "The Slayer" and the latest in a long line of female avengers fate has chosen to protect the people of her generation from evil. By day Buffy is a student (although she does not live up to her potential); by night she patrols as the Slayer, a martial arts expert with superhuman strength who disposes of evil wherever she finds it (particularly vampires, which she kills by plunging a stake into their hearts or with an arrow from her crossbow).

Sunnydale, which is two miles from Los Angeles, is a Hellmouth, a mystical portal that attracts evil. Guiding Buffy is her Watcher, Rupert Giles (Anthony Stewart Head), a man who has been chosen to help a Slayer defeat whatever evil a Hellmouth dispenses. Giles, who works as the school's librarian, is from a long line of Watchers (his father and grandfather were both Watchers) and relies on the prophecies of ancient books and writings to determine how to defeat evil (his most important book is the *Codex*, a text of prophecies concerning the Slayer). Giles can speak five languages and previously worked at the British Museum.

Joyce is at first unaware of Buffy's activities as the Slayer. It was Joyce who decided to move to Sunnydale after Buffy was expelled from Emery High School for burning down the gym (to destroy a nest of vampires). Joyce is single and divorced from Hank (Dean Butler). She runs an art gallery and only accepted Buffy's secret life after she inadvertently invited a vampire into her home and witnessed Buffy's slaying of it (a vampire can only enter a home if it is invited in). Joyce later dies (2001) from a post-complication after an operation to remove a brain tumor.

At her prior school Buffy was voted "May Queen." At Sunnydale High School, the senior class awarded her a special honor "Class Protector" for "showing up when things got weird and protecting us." Instead of that special award Buffy would have liked to have been a normal teenage girl. Her strange behavior kept her out of the "in crowd" and, instead, bonded her with Willow Rosenberg (Alyson Hannigan) and Alexander "Xander" Harris (Nicholas Brendon), two outsiders who became her allies in the fight against Hellmouth.

Willow is a pretty computer whiz who helps Giles search through the volumes of lore for answers on how to battle demons. She is shy and sensitive and has feelings for Xander but knows they will never be more than just friends (which they have been since childhood). Willow later discovers she has the powers of an apprentice witch (third season) and in the episode of 5/5/00, Willow professes that she is a lesbian. She bonds with Tara (Amber Benson), a lesbian who is also a witch, and together their developing powers prove beneficial to Buffy. Willow gets headaches and nosebleeds when she uses a transformation spell and is very protective of Tara when evil threatens her

(Tara becomes extremely jealous if Willow even looks at another pretty girl. The audience is not teased. Willow and Tara do hug and kiss).

Xander is an only child and comes from a family of blue collar workers. He is sensitive but hides those feelings with a jovial outlook on life. He originally had a crush on Buffy but realized a relationship could never be. He later dates Anya (Emma Caulfield), an 1100-year-old former demon who is now trying to adjust to being mortal. During the summer of 1999, Xander worked as a kitchen helper at a nightclub called Fabulous Ladies.

Cordelia Chase (Charisma Carpenter) is a fellow schoolmate of Buffy's and the kind of girl she might have been if she was not the Slayer. Cordelia, considered the most beautiful girl at Sunnydale High, only associates with the most popular girls. She was originally self-absorbed and self-obsessed and thought of Buffy as "that weird girl." Cordelia's license plate reads QUEEN C and she has her dresses specially made for her "because off-the-rack clothes give me hives." This all changes when Buffy saves Cordelia from an invisible female demon who sought to disfigure her. Cordelia then becomes part of Buffy's circle. Giles broke a Watcher tradition by bringing in Xander, Willow and Cordelia (he felt there is strength in numbers). See *Angel* for additional information on Cordelia.

Buffy and her friends hang out at the Bronze (later the Grotto), a nightclub for teenagers ("It's in the bad part of town which is a block away from the good part of town"). Buffy's weakness is her inability to leave anyone behind — even if it means risking her own life. Buffy calls a new grouping of vampires "a fang club." When Buffy left Sunnydale at the end of the second season to find herself, she worked as a waitress (using her middle name, Anne) at Helen's Kitchen. On 10/5/99, Buffy begins a new life at the University of Sunnydale (she occupies dorm room 214 in Stevenson Hall). Willow shares room 217 with Tara; Xander chose not to attend college. He becomes a carpenter and works at various construction sites. It was at this time that Giles also found a new calling — as owner of the Magic Box at 1524 Maple Court, a store that deals in the occult. It also becomes the new hangout for Buffy, Willow, Tara, Xander and Anya. Giles' license plate reads 250-32 and he had a brief romance with Jenny Calendar (Robia La Morte), Sunnydale High's computer teacher. She believed the internet can be just as useful as books with information on the mystical world. She had knowledge of mystical events and ancient creatures but was killed by a demon before Buffy could save her.

Buffy was first romantically involved with Angel (David Boreanaz), a vampire who helped her defeat evil (see *Angel* for more information). She next falls for Riley Finn (Marc Blucas), a member of the Initiative, a government organization that hunts vampires and demons. Riley has captured 11 vampires and six demons (the organization uses scientific methods and weapons to banish demons or neuter them by implanting a chip in their brains so they cannot harm humans). In the episode of 2/8/00, Buffy joins the Initiative and becomes part of Riley's Alpha Team. Shortly after, Buffy discovers the real purpose of the Initiative: to create demons so their energy can be used by the military. Buffy and Riley's relationship ends when Buffy destroys the Initiative and Riley is recalled by the military.

William the Bloody (James Marsters) is a vicious vampire known as Spike (for his habit of torturing people with railroad spikes). He is an escapee of the Initiative (called Hostile 17) who now helps Buffy "out of the evilness of my heart" (he was captured by Riley and a chip implanted in his brain to make him incapable of feeding on humans). Spike originally came to Sunnydale with Drusilla (Juliet Landau) a beautiful vampire who is suffering from a mental disease (she was driven to madness by Angel—who killed her family for fun and turned her into a vampire). Spike and Drusilla lived in Prague and Spike now hopes the Hellmouth will provide a cure for Drusilla. Spike has already killed two Slayers and planned to make Buffy the third. Drusilla is not only evil but she is insane and it was she who turned Spike into a vampire moments after meeting him a hundred years ago. Spike later developed a crush on Buffy and called her "Love," "Blondie" and "Sunshine."

The Master (Mark Metcalf) was the first real demon Buffy faced. He is the oldest and most powerful vampire the world has ever known. He is determined to destroy mankind and reclaim the earth for his people, "The Old Ones." The Master has been imprisoned in a mystical portal beneath Sunnydale by an earthquake and needs to open the Hellmouth to achieve his goal. He attempts to do this through human sacrifice and ancient prophecies but is killed by Buffy in a violent confrontation shortly after he manages to escape.

Darla (Julie Benz) is the vampire who bit Angel and turned him into a creature of the undead. She and Angel ravaged Europe, leaving a trail of death and horror (Darla seduces her victims by wearing a seductive Catholic school girl uniform). She is now seeking to kill Buffy and win back Angel (by turning him into evil once again).

Dawn Summers (Michelle Trachtenberg) is Buffy's 14-year-old sister. She mysteriously appeared as a member of the family beginning in 2000. She is actually the Key, an unknown power source that operates beyond a normal reality. The Key is old and its origins are unknown. The Key was found by the monks of the Byzantium Order who thought they could harness its power for good. For centuries the monks guarded the Key—until an evil goddess named Glory (Clare Kramer) sought it. To protect the Key, the monks transformed that power into human form—as a sister for Buffy to protect. Dawn's energy made her appear that she has always been a part of Buffy's family.

Dawn attends Sunnydale High School. She enjoys salami and peanut butter sandwiches and eats Sugar Bombs cereal for breakfast. She invented a not-so-tasty peanut butter and banana waffle and is called "Dawnie" by Willow and Tara. At first Dawn is unaware that she is the Key. She often wonders "who or what am I" and keeps a diary (which Xander calls "The Dawn Meister

Chronicles"). She believes Buffy thinks of her as "a dumb little sister" and "Little Miss Nobody." "It doesn't matter where you came from or how you got here, you're my sister and I love you," says Buffy.

Dawn likes to hang out with Spike (he lives in a crypt in the cemetery); Dawn thinks "he's cool" (Buffy thinks "he's a monster") but he helps protect Dawn and that is what matters most to Buffy (Buffy also worries about what will happen if the chip is ever removed from Spike). Dawn has memories of growing up with Buffy and her mother (taken from their minds) but no memory of the Key (Joyce supposedly called Dawn "Pumpkin Belly" as a kid).

Dawn learns she is the Key when Glory finds her and tells her. Buffy has never feared a foe — until Glory. Glory is actually Glorificus, a beast that was banished from Hell. She seeks the Key to become all powerful and return to Hell. To achieve her goal, Glory must bleed the Key at a specific time in a specific place. Once Dawn's blood is spilled, the portal to her world will open and all dimensions will collide creating unrelenting havoc on earth ("Blood flows, the gates will open; blood flows no more, the gates will close" — when Dawn is dead).

The monks made Dawn out of Buffy. With that knowledge, a finale was filmed for the WB that changed when the series moved to UPN. In an attempt to save Dawn, who was captured and is about to be bled by Glory, Buffy and Glory engage in a fierce battle. With the help of Willow's powers, Buffy defeats Glory — but not before Dawn is slashed across the stomach. As Dawn's blood drips from her body, a portal is opened and evil is unleashed on the earth. Dawn is about to sacrifice herself to save the world when Buffy stops her — "I'm part of you. My blood is on your blood." Buffy jumps into the portal of energy and reverses the ritual. Buffy is next seen lying on the ground (apparently dead). At this point, the WB had been expected to renew the series. Two final scenes are shown: a gravestone with Buffy's name on it and Willow in Los Angeles waiting in an office to see Angel. When Angel enters and sees Willow with tears in her eyes, the screen goes to black. That was on 5/22/01. When the episode was repeated (7/26), the scene with Willow and Angel was cut as UPN had acquired the series and a proposed crossover of series (*Buffy* and *Angel*) was now not possible.

During the transition, UPN promoted the series as "Buffy is reborn on October 2nd." The first UPN episode, "Bargaining," establishes the new storyline. The demons of Sunnydale are unaware that the Slayer is dead. To convince the demons that Buffy is still alive, Willow activates what she calls the Buffy Bot, a remarkably life-like mechanical version of Buffy that Spike had built for him when he was in love with Buffy but knew he could never have her (Buffy deactivated her when she discovered what Spike had done). Willow has reprogrammed the robot with Buffy's personality, slayer fighting abilities and a chip that compels her to seek out Willow if she becomes damaged.

Dawn is no longer the Key. Buffy's sacrifice has given her human life. She is now cared for by Willow and Tara (with the help of Spike, Xander and Anya). Giles feels that his job as a Watcher has ended and decides to return to England (exactly what to do is not said). Anya takes charge of the Magic Box for Giles. The Buffy Bot is prone to damage. During a confrontation with a vampire, the robot is damaged and reveals that the Slayer is a machine. The word spreads to other demons who now feel Sunnydale is open territory. A rogue gang of motorcycle-riding demons set out to overtake Sunnydale.

Buffy did not die of natural causes. She died by mystical energy. Willow believes that her soul, her essence, could be someplace else and that she can raise her from the dead. In a midnight ceremony, Willow, Tara, Xander and Anya perform a ritual before Buffy's grave. The incantation seems to be working — until their circle is broken by demons. The four manage to escape. Moments later, the real Buffy awakens to find herself trapped inside her coffin. Buffy claws her way out of her grave but becomes traumatized, unsure of who or what she is. As Buffy wanders into town, she sees the demons destroy the Buffy Bot, but is spotted and chased. Buffy runs into an alley where she sees Willow, Tara, Xander and Anya attempting to fight off demons. Buffy's instincts kick in and she destroys the demons. Willow tries to tell Buffy who she is, but it is not until Buffy sees Dawn, who had been protected from the rampage by Spike, that she remembers who she is (Dawn runs to Buffy, hugs her and cries "You're alive and you're home, you're home").

Buffy was gone for 147 days. Willow and Tara have been living in Buffy's home and taking care of Dawn (Willow and Tara occupy Joyce's former bedroom). Willow calls Giles, who returns shortly after to help guide Buffy and run the Magic Box. He is, at first, angry with Willow for doing what she did (being an inexperienced witch, she could have unleashed evil) and is not sure where Buffy was or if she returned from the dead unscathed. Dawn and Tara now assist Giles in doing research on demons (Dawn is determined to learn everything she can about them).

Dawn is still attending Sunnydale High School. Tara and Willow are at the University of Sunnydale and Xander continues to work at various construction sites. Buffy left school when her mother became ill and found it was too late to register for the fall term. She also learns from Willow that her finances are very low (money going to pay for Joyce's hospital bills). Giles comes to the rescue and offers her an undisclosed amount of money. Giles then decides to return to England (episode of 11/13/01) leaving Buffy without a Watcher. Xander and Anya announce their engagement (episode of 10/30/01) and Anya becomes manager of the Magic Box for Giles (after she closes the cash register, Anya places the money in her hands and does what she calls "The Capitalist Dance"). The band Nerf Herder performs "Buffy's Theme." The program opens with these words: "As long as there have been demons, there has been the Slayer. One girl in all the world, a Chosen One, born with the strength and skill to hunt vampires and other deadly creatures, to stop the spread of their evil. When one Slayer dies, the next is called and trained by the Watcher."

20. *Captain America* (CBS, 1979)

Pilot. Two attempts were made to bring the comic book hero to television. The first one (11/19/79), establishes the storyline. It is during World War II when scientist Steve Rogers develops FLAG (Full Latent Ability Gain), a special serum taken from his cells that produced superhuman strength and transformed him into the red, white and blue costumed Captain America, a daring and courageous war hero. In 1979, Rogers' son, Steve Jr. (Reb Brown), is seriously injured in a motorcycle accident. When all attempts to save his life fail, he is given the special serum developed by his father. FLAG not only saves Steve's life, but endows him with amazing powers that he uses to battle crime as a modern day Captain America. The pilot story finds Steve battling a madman who is threatening to destroy the world with a neutron bomb. Dr. Simon Mills (Len Birman) is the scientist in charge of FLAG research; he is assisted by Dr. Wendy Day (Heather Menzies).

In the second pilot (11/23 and 11/24/79), Steve searches for a kidnapped scientist who possesses the ability to accelerate the aging process. Reb Brown recreated his role as Steve Rogers/Captain America; Len Birman played Dr. Simon Mills and Connie Sellecca was his assistant, Dr. Wendy Day. Mike Post and Pete Carpenter composed the theme for both versions.

21. *Captain Midnight* (CBS, 1954–1956)

The Secret Squadron is an organization designed to battle the enemies of the free world. It is located in a secret mountain retreat and is commanded by a mysterious man known only as Captain Midnight (Richard Webb). He is assisted by the mechanical genius Ichabod "Icky" Mudd (Sid Melton) and Aristotle "Tut" Jones (Olan Soule), his scientific advisor. How Icky and Tut became a part of the Captain's team is not explained, but Captain Midnight's destiny began one night in a bomb shelter in France during World War II. The war has reached a moment of crisis and the Allies are in danger of a devastating defeat. Suddenly a man, whose name the general in charge does not want to know, enters the room. The man, Captain Jim Albright, is told "that only two people in the world know the mission to which you have been assigned, myself and the President of the United States. The odds are 100 to 1 against you. If you fail tonight, it will be the end for all of us. If you succeed tonight, you will have started a long and dangerous task that may require a lifetime to complete" (protect the world from evil). Albright's assignment is to exterminate Ivan Shark, the most dangerous criminal in the world (a traitor who has cost the lives of many Americans). As Albright is about to leave, the general tells him, "Henceforth, until you complete your final task, you will not be known by your true name. What name you will be known by rests in the hands of fate." "Sir," the captain says, "If I have not returned by twelve o'clock you will know that I have failed." The hours pass slowly. It is 15 seconds to midnight and it appears as though Albright has failed. Suddenly, the faint sounds of an airplane are heard. "Listen to that," the general tells his aide. "We're saved and it's just twelve o'clock. To me he will always be known as Captain Midnight."

Captain Midnight flies a plane called the *Silver Dart*. Members of the Secret Squadron are assigned and referred to by a number (for example, SQ 7, SQ 3). Viewers could become squadron members by mailing in coupons found inside the lid of the show's sponsor, Ovaltine (chocolate milk-flavoring crystals). Viewers received a decal and a patch identifying them as members of the Secret Squadron plus a special pin for decoding the secret message given at the end of each episode.

Ovaltine cancelled the highly rated series in 1956 after 39 episodes were filmed due to a lack of sales (kids were removing coupons from the jars but not buying the product). Ovaltine, which originated the program on radio, refused to sponsor the program in syndication and reserved its right to the name "Captain Midnight." The title was changed to *Jet Jackson, Flying Commando* and through voice-over dubbing, Jet Jackson was said in place of Captain Midnight.

When a Secret Squadron member needs to contact the Captain, they send a telegram that is received by the Captain at his headquarters via a special receiving unit. Each member of the squadron has a microfilm file that the Captain can use to determine who is contacting him. "Squadron members never send unimportant messages" says the Captain. Secret Squadron uniforms are simple (military gray) outfits with the insignia of the *Silver Dart* on shirt pockets and flying helmets. Icky carries a rabbit's foot for luck ("I'm packin' a little insurance") and, after he is introduced to someone by the Captain, he says, "That's Mudd with two d's." The *Silver Dart*, which carries extra fuel tanks for extended flights, is credited as "Courtesy of the Douglas Aircraft Company and the U.S. Navy." Don Ferris composed the theme; the program incorporates the same uncredited stock background music as used on *The Adventures of Superman*. The program opens as follows: "It's Captain Midnight, brought to you by Ovaltine, chocolate flavored Ovaltine. Delicious! Nutritious! Instant Ovaltine, the fortified food drink that tops them all!"

22. *Captain Nice* (NBC, 1967)

Carter Nash (William Daniels) is a mild mannered chemist for the police department of Big Town, U.S.A., a metropolis of 112,000 people, that is located "somewhere in the Midwestern part of North America." Carter lives at 0306 Prescott Lane with his mother, Esther (Alice Ghostley), and his father, Harvey (Byron Foulger). Carter works in the City Hall Building (door number 1908) and was hired not only because he is a good chemist "and the police department needs good chemists" but because his uncle, Mayor Fred Finney (Liam Dunn) promised Carter's mother (his sister) that he would hire him ("I'm terrified of your mother").

At home Carter is mother dominated and his father, who has trouble remembering his name, calls him "Spot" (Harvey's face is never fully seen and his main purpose in life appears to be reading the local newspaper, the *Chronicle*, which obstructs his face). Carter is shy, timid and helpless. He believes he is ordinary and doesn't stand out. He is afraid of the dark "in the daytime" and thinks of girls as "round men." When Carter tried to join the army they burned his draft card; when he enrolled in a self-defense class "They said I should carry an axe." At work, the beautiful and sensuous police sergeant, Candy Kane (Ann Prentiss) has a crush on Carter. Carter feels Sergeant Kane (as he calls her) "is quite attractive and a credit to her uniform" but hasn't the courage to ask her for a date.

Life changes for Carter when Candy Kane is accosted by thugs and he feels it is time for him to take action. Carter has just created a liquid power source he calls Super Juice. Although he is unsure of what effects it will have on humans, he tests it on himself. The liquid causes him to hiccup; from out of nowhere he is struck by a bolt of lightning and transformed into a super hero he calls Captain Nice (after the initials on his belt buckle — C.N.). Although he is not in costume, Carter rescues the unconscious Sergeant Kane and quickly vanishes after he dispenses justice to the thugs. At home Carter tells his mother what happened and is about to destroy the formula when Esther convinces him to use his invention to battle crime: "This place we live in is a typical American town jam full of crooks, hoodlums and gangsters. It's up to you to do something about it." When asked by Esther why he chose the name Captain Nice "and not Wonder Man or Muscle Head" Carter says "Captain Nice was the first thing that came to my mind." Esther makes him a red, white and blue costume, mask and cape and Captain Nice becomes the heroic savior of Big Town.

As Captain Nice, Carter has incredible speed and strength, the ability to fly and an immunity to harm. The apparently foul tasking Super Juice has effects that last about one hour. When Carter decides to become Captain Nice, he first finds a place of seclusion. He takes off his jacket and hangs it up (he carries a hanger in his briefcase). He then loosens his tie, drinks the juice and transforms into Captain Nice.

Citizens describe Captain Nice as "The man who flies like an eagle," "The man with muscles of lead" and "The masked enemy of evil." "From now on," Carter says, "the forces of evil will have to watch out for Captain Nice!" The theme was written by Vic Mizzy.

23. *Captain Scarlet and the Mysterons*
(Syndicated, 1967)

Spectrum is a 21st century international organization that protects the security of the world. It is headquartered on Cloudbase and all its agents are men (named after the colors of the spectrum; women assist as glamorous, skillful and daring pilots called Angels). Spectrum is attempting to explore the planet Mars when its inhabitants, the Mysterons, mistake their efforts as an unprovoked attack and declare a war of revenge on the Earth.

The Mysterons, who are never seen (only heard) have the ability to recreate any person or object once it has been destroyed. Hoping to recruit Spectrum agents Black and Scarlet to their side, the Mysterons cause an accident that claims their lives. When life is restored to captains Black and Scarlet, Captain Black retains Mysteron characteristics and becomes their agent on Earth; Captain Scarlet, Spectrum's top agent, fails to succumb to the Mysterons and instead becomes their indestructible enemy (he can be killed yet survive. Whatever happens to him, his body is able to repair).

Captain Scarlet is a Supermarionation series and the first of its kind to feature "television's most unusual hero" as well as realistic marionettes. Each of the figures is made to correct human proportions (discarding the tradition that heads should be bigger than bodies). Eyes are remarkably real (replicas of staff members' eyes) and can move in all directions. Male agents have wigs; the female pilots have human hair individually applied to the heads to build up the tresses and give them individualistic style. Faces are made up just as if they were human stars and all clothing is hand-made and perfect right down to the smallest button hole. Producer Sylvia Anderson creates most of the characters' personalities. Experts then mold the figures to the patterns she has created.

THE AGENTS

Captain Scarlet (voice of Francis Matthews) was born in England in 2036 and is from a family of distinguished soldiers. He has degrees in math, history and technology and a brilliant army career (trained as a field combat soldier). He is a professional agent and carries out orders immediately and efficiently. He is popular with all the Spectrum agents, especially the Angels.

Colonel White (voice of Donald Gray) is Spectrum's commander-in-chief. He was born in England and is proficient in computer science, navigation and technology. He served with the World Navy and Universal Secret Service and enjoys playing war games with Captain Scarlet. Because of his daring escapades, ability to handle tricky situations and extraordinary leadership, he was chosen to lead Spectrum.

Captain Grey (voice of Paul Maxwell) was born in Chicago. He served with the World Aquanaut Security Patrol and was in charge of the submarine *Stingray*. He enjoys swimming and developing new strokes.

Captain Blue (voice of Ed Bishop) is the oldest son of a wealthy Boston financier. He has degrees in applied math, aerodynamics, computer control, economics and technology. Before joining Spectrum he was a test pilot with the World Aeronautic Society, then a member of its security department.

Captain Ochre (voice of Jeremy Wilkins) is an American but does not have outstanding academic qualifications. He loves flying and acquired his pilot's license when he was 16. He served with the world Government Police Corps and broke up one of the toughest crime syndicates in the U.S. When he turned down a promotion because he preferred action to paper work, he was approached by Spectrum to become an agent. He is quick-witted and a brilliant conversationalist but loves to play practical jokes.

Captain Magenta (voice of Gary Files) was born in Ireland. After his parents emigrated to America he was brought up in a poor New York suburb in an environment of poverty and crime. He worked hard at school, earned a scholarship to Yale and graduated with degrees in physics, electrical engineering and technology. This, however, did not satisfy him. He yearned for a life of adventure and big money and turned to crime. He soon became a big time operator and a ruthless mastermind who controlled two-thirds of New York's crime organization. Spectrum's selection committee realized they would need a man, trusted and respected in the underworld, in their security organization (someone to work on the inside and get into the heart of criminal activity). He was offered the job and accepted.

Lieutenant Green (voice of Cy Grant) was born at the port of Spain in Trinidad and is Colonel White's right-hand man. He holds degrees in music, telecommunications and technology and served with the World Aquanaut Security Patrol, Submarine Corps Division. He was sole commander of communications at the Marineville Control Tower before joining Spectrum.

Dr. Fawn (voice of Charles Tingwell) is an Australian who serves as Spectrum's supreme medical commander. Prior to this, he developed robots for the World Medical Organization.

THE PILOTS

Destiny Angel (voice of Liz Morgan) was born in Paris. She was educated in both France and Rome and first worked for the World Army Air Force, then in its Intelligence Corps and finally as commanding officer of the Women's Flight Squadron. Three years later she started her own firm of flying contractors and was approached by Spectrum to become leader of the five Angels. On duty she is utterly ruthless and totally efficient; off duty she is feminine, charming and sophisticated. She is also fashion conscious and a wizard at designing and making her own clothes.

Symphony Angel (voice of Janna Hill) was born in Cedar Rapids, Iowa. She holds seven degrees in mathematics and technology and first worked for the Universal Secret Service where, after five years, she revolutionized the spy game with her methods being copied all over the world. During training as a pilot for special U.S.S. missions, Symphony fell in love with flying. She later joined a charter company and was asked to join Spectrum. She enjoys creating new hairstyles for herself and the other Angels.

Melody Angel (voice of Sylvia Anderson) was born on a cotton farm in Atlanta, Georgia. She was a tomboy as a child and later took up professional motor racing. It was during her stay at a Swiss finishing school that she developed an interest in flying. After being expelled for unruly behavior, she joined the World Army Air Force where she displayed amazing courage and nerves of steel. This determination and ability led Spectrum to hiring her as a pilot.

Rhapsody Angel (voice of Liz Morgan) was born in Chelsea, England, to aristocratic parents. After earning degrees in law and sociology at London University, Rhapsody joined the Federal Agents Bureau and later became its commander. She next became chief security officer for an airline before starting her own airline company. She joined Spectrum when they asked her to become a pilot. Her pastime is playing chess.

Harmony Angel (voice of Lian-Shin) was born in Tokyo, Japan. She is the daughter of a wealthy flying taxi owner and grew up in a world of high speed jets. She was educated in Tokyo and London and was a member of the Tokyo Flying Club. When she flew around the world nonstop and broke all records, she was asked to join Spectrum. Harmony loves sports and spends her spare time teaching the Angels judo and karate.

The Mysterons themselves are never seen. An eerie shot of the planet Mars is seen with a Mysteron voice (by Donald Gray) alerting the viewers to what the next plan of attack is. Paul Maxwell doubles as the voice of the World President and Jeremy Wilkins voices many of the supporting characters, including the occasionally seen Captain Black, the Mysterons' agent on Earth. Barry Gray composed the theme, "Captain Scarlet," which is sung by the British group the Spectrum.

24. *Captain Video and His Video Rangers* (DuMont, 1949–1957)

On June 27, 1949, a daily series called *Captain Video* premiered in New York City on the DuMont network's flagship station, WABD-TV, channel 5. It was simply a showcase for old western theatrical films with Captain Video (Richard Coogan) serving as the host. As the network began to grow, the format was changed to focus on a crime fighter known as "The Guardian of the Safety of the World." The Captain was given an assistant, the Video Ranger (Don Hastings) and the program opened with these words over Wagner's "Flying Dutchman Overture": "Master of Space! Hero of Science! Captain of the Video Rangers! Operating from his secret mountain headquarters on the planet Earth, Captain Video rallies men of goodwill everywhere. As he rockets from planet to planet, let us follow the champion of truth, justice and freedom throughout the universe. Stand by for Captain Video and His Video Rangers."

Only a handful of *Captain Video* episodes appear to exist; press release information is very scarce; and the pre-national *TV Guide*, *TV Forecast*, is extremely sketchy. It is difficult to determine when in 1949 the new *Captain Video* format emerged and when the words "and His Video Rangers" were added to the title. At this time, and until 1951, Jack Orsen played the Captain's superior, Commissioner Bell. In 1951 (and until 1957) Al Hodge took over the role of Captain Video; Ben Lackland became Commission Carey, the Captain's new superior, from 1951 until 1955. The evil Dr. Pauli (Bram Nossen, Hal Conklin, Stephen Elliott) also became a regular at this time.

Hoping to cash in on the show's popularity, DuMont added a Saturday morning version of the series called *The Secret Files of Captain Video* (9/5/53–5/29/54). Although that original DuMont station is still broadcasting in New York (now WNYW) it has no records of its time as a DuMont station. The *TV Forecast* listings were mostly generic, listing only the series title; if program information was given, it was the star or a statement (for example, "Scientific adventures in the world of the future"). *TV Guide* lists program notes for a number of *Secret File* episodes, although many state "No program information available at press time." It is possible, however, to determine that the Saturday shows were complete in one episode, not serialized adventures characteristic of the daily series.

On March 28, 1955, the daily series came to an end. On July 10, 1955, the format changed again; it was now an hour-long series wherein Captain Video was the host to old theatrical serials and movies. On September 25, 1955, *Captain Video* was incorporated into *Wonder Time*, a six-hour series that ran from noon to 6:00 P.M. Sandy Becker served as the host and Al Hodge, as Captain Video, hosted a series of cartoons and documentaries. On August 16, 1957, *Captain Video* ended with the demise of the DuMont network.

The series itself was set in the future (the 21st then 22nd centuries). Captain Video is a scientific genius who heads the Video Rangers, an organization that battles evil throughout the universe (only the best candidates at Video Ranger Training Academies are chosen to become Video Rangers). The Space Federation appears to be the governing force on Earth (orders are given by the Space Council). Commissioner Bell (then Carey) is its leader and the Federation is based on the 144th floor of the Public Safety Building in Planet City. Captain Video first pilots a rocket ship called the *X-9*, then the *Galaxy* and *Galaxy II*; the Video Ranger had his first command as captain of a ship called the *Cormorant*.

Captain Video's code to his secret base is 398 and he has invented such devices as the Atomic Rifle, the Atomic Collector Screen, a cathode gun, the Cosmic Vibrator, the Opticon Scillometer Astro Viewer, a pocket radio and the Solenoid Assentuator. Copter Cabs escort people through space; prisoners are sent to the moon, which has been turned into a penal colony. Travel to Mars, Venus and other planets (such as Torion, Nemos, Cosmo and Lyra) has been accomplished. It is mentioned in the episode of 11/14/53 ("Blaster Master") that the first attempt to land on Jupiter was made in 1990. The 21st century is also the start of an intergalactic sporting event called the Olympic Rocket Meet.

Dr. Pauli, the Captain's enemy, is president of the Asteroidal Society and inventor of the Cloak of Invisibility. He ruled from the manmade metallic Planet of Dr. Pauli (from which he plans to conquer the universe). Clipper Evans (Grant Sullivan) was another enemy of the Captain's who often sided with Dr. Pauli. Before he was able to control it for purposes of good, the evil robot Tobor (Dave Ballard) was also a threat to the Captain (see *Here Comes Tobor* for a proposed series based on this character; Tobor is robot spelled backwards).

Early episodes that were broadcast live contain scenes from old theatrical films. The stars of these films were called Video Rangers and the action scenes were said to be the adventures of other Video Rangers fighting elsewhere for justice (they were seen via Remote Carrier Delayed Circuit TV Screens and their code was KRG-L6). On episodes broadcast without a sponsor, viewers saw a "Video Ranger Message," a public service announcement geared to children. Fred Scott, who later played Ranger Rogers, announced and narrated.

25. *C.A.T. Squad* (NBC, 7/27/86)

Pilot. The Counter Assault Technical Squad, C.A.T. for short, does not officially exist. It is an elite team of special U.S. agents that was formed to battle international crime. It is supervised by Mr. Director (Barry Corbin), the Assistant Secretary for Law Enforcement. Richard "Doc" Burkholder (Joseph Cortese) is a veteran special agent who heads the team in the field. He is assisted by Nikki Blake (Patricia Charbonneau), a forensics and computer expert; Bud Raines (Steve W. James), an intelligence and interrogation expert; and John Sommers (Jack Youngblood), a weapons and demolitions expert. The pilot story finds the squad seeking terrorists who are killing NATO laser defense scientists.

A second pilot, called *C.A.T. Squad II*, aired on NBC on May 23, 1988. Joseph Cortese, Steve W. James and Jack Youngblood reprised their roles of Richard Burkholder, Bud Raines and John Sommers. The character of Nikki Blake became Nikki Pappas and was played by Deborah Van Valkenburgh. Mr. Director was dropped. The story finds the team traveling to South Africa to stop the illegal exporting of plutonium. Ennio Morricone composed the theme for both versions.

26. *Chameleon in Blue* (Unaired, 1990)

Pilot. Before Dr. Samantha Waters became a fixture on television (see *Profiler*), there was an attempt to bring a profiler to the medium via Sally Peters (Loryn Locklin), a young woman who works as a criminal psychologist with the Los Angeles Police Department. As a young girl, Sally witnessed the horrifying murder of her family by a psychotic killer. Although she survived, the events left her with a unique ability — a special psychic sensitivity that allows her to "see" how crimes were committed after they happen. Stories were not only to focus on Sally as she uses her abilities to find killers, but help the victims of the crime as well. Frank McCarthy played Police Commissioner Nathan David and James Remar was Detective Tom MacKey. The project, produced for NBC, was written (with Thomas Baum), produced and directed by Wes Craven.

27. *The Champions* (NBC/Syndicated, 1968)

Sharron Macready, Craig Stirling and Richard Barrett (Alexandra Bastedo, Stuart Damon, William Gaunt) are agents for Nemesis, an international organization based in Geneva, Switzerland, that tackles extremely dangerous matters. W.L. Tremayne (Anthony Nicholls) heads the organization.

Sharron, a shapely blonde, lives at 36 Bristol Court, Richard at 101 Barrington Place and Craig at 487 Hampton Avenue.

When it is learned that Chinese scientists in Tibet have developed a deadly bacteria, Sharron, Richard and Craig are assigned to obtain the specimens. During the assignment, the Nemesis agents trigger an alarm. Craig, Richard and Sharron make it to their awaiting plane, but the craft is hit by gunfire and crashes moments later in the Himalayan Mountains. Shortly after, a mysterious white-haired old man (Felix Aylmer) appears and takes the apparently lifeless agents to his city, which is inhabited by the survivors of an unknown race. Here, Richard, Sharron and Craig's wounds are healed and they are endowed with super powers: "Their mental and physical capacities fused to computer efficiency; their sight, sense and hearing raised to their highest futuristic stage of mental and physical growth."

Sharron, Craig and Richard awaken at the site of the crash, amazed that they are apparently unharmed. Richard, however, is not convinced of their miraculous escape from death. He tells Sharron and Craig about a dream he experienced — "about an old man and a mysterious white light" (that was used to heal and enhanced them). Unable to shake the feeling that something extraordinary happened to them, Richard decides to pursue his "dream" while Craig and Sharron continue with the mission.

A short time later, Richard's dream confronts him — he meets the mysterious old man and learns that he and his friends have been endowed with special powers to help keep the world safe. Richard vows that he and his friends will keep the secret of the lost city and that he, Sharron and Craig will use their gifts to benefit mankind.

Sharron was a former operative for the C.I.D. (Criminal Investigation Division) of England's New Scotland Yard whose outstanding series of arrests prompted her to be drafted by Nemesis. While seductive in any outfit, Sharron prefers not to use her sex appeal as a part of her assignment (although some assignments find her doing just the opposite—like wearing a miniskirt to focus attention on her and create a distraction for Richard and Craig). Richard, the son of a former Nemesis agent, is British, well versed in the martial arts, and the unofficial head of the group (it is his plans that Craig and Sharron often follow). Craig, a former operative for the Secret Service, is impetuous and often takes chances to ensure the success of their missions. Ten episodes aired on NBC; 20 additional episodes aired in syndication.

28. *Charmed* (WB, 1998)

Prue, Piper and Phoebe Haliwell (Shannen Doherty, Holly Marie Combs, Alyssa Milano) are the Charmed Ones, three beautiful witches who protect innocents threatened by evil. Prue, short for Prudence, has the power to move objects with her mind. Piper can freeze time and Phoebe has the ability to see the future. Their legacy began with Melinda Warren ("The girl who started it all," says Phoebe), a 17th century witch. Melinda had three powers: the ability to see the future, the power to move objects and the ability to freeze time. When Melinda was discovered to be a witch, she was burned at the stake. Before she died, she willed her spirit to carry the Power of Three from century to century until it culminated in three sisters who would become the most powerful good witches in the world.

Prue, Piper and Phoebe are the sisters through which Melinda's spirit lives in the present-day world. The sisters, however, are not witches when the series begins. Prue and Piper are living in Los Angeles, Phoebe in New York. When Phoebe learns that she, Prue and Piper have inherited their late mother's house, she moves to San Francisco to join her sisters as the home's new owners. It is when Phoebe finds the spirit board she played with as a child that their lives suddenly change. When the board spells out the word *attic*, the sisters become curious and decide to investigate. In the attic, Phoebe finds *The Book of Shadows* and reads the incantation from the open page ("...bring your powers to we sisters three"). Suddenly, Prue, Piper and Phoebe are endowed with Melinda's powers—powers they must learn to control and only use to help people in trouble (using their powers for personal gain is prohibited). They are assisted by the mysterious *Book of Shadows* (which can only be touched by the sisters and contains spells to banish evil that have been written by their ancestors through the centuries) and Leo Wyatt (Brian Krause), their Whitelighter (a witch's guardian).

Prue, Piper and Phoebe live at 1329 Prescott Street (also given as 7511 and 1829 Prescott); 555-0198 is their phone number. The sisters attended Baker High School, played at Kenwood Park and attended Camp Skylark. They had an imaginary fairy friend they called Lily.

Prue is 28 years old. She originally worked as a curator at the American Museum of Natural History but quit when her partner took credit for an exhibit she designed. She next works as an appraiser for the Buckland Auction House (she resigns when she identifies a Monet painting as a fake but her superiors opt to auction it off as an original). With an interest in photography, Prue became a photographer for *4-One-5*, a trendy magazine. Prue channels her powers through her eyes and developed the power of astro projection (be in two places at once) three years later. Prue wears a 36C bra and drives a car with the plate 2WAC 231.

Piper, the middle sister, is 26 years old and most resembles their mother, Patty (Finola Hughes), who was killed in 1978 by a warlock at Camp Skylark shortly after Phoebe was born. Piper was originally a chef at the Restaurante (later changed to Quake), a stylish bar-restaurant. She quit to pursue her dream of opening her own eatery. She does so with the Industrial Zone, a failed club she purchases from S.W.A. Properties and turns into a fashionable nightclub called P-3 (for herself and her partners, Prue and Phoebe). Piper has type AB negative blood and drives a car with the plate 26A3 123. She calls Prue "an Einstein with cleavage." When Piper becomes nervous (which is often) she babbles and waters flowers. Unnatural forces have turned Piper into a Windago ("a werewolf but only worse") and a furrie (a demon who kills anyone she fears is evil). Piper buys the herbs she needs to make spells in Chinatown.

Phoebe, the youngest sister (20 years old) was the only one born in the house and can go either way — stay good or become evil. She is the only one of the sisters with a passive power and must take self-defense classes to protect herself. Phoebe fears the basement because as a child she saw "The Woogie Man," an evil force that thrives in the dark. Phoebe is unemployed when the series begins. She is enrolled at the College of the Humanities and takes whatever temporary jobs she can find (from receptionist to secretary). Shortly after Prue acquired her new power, Phoebe received one also — the ability to levitate. When speaking to Prue, Phoebe calls her "Honey," "Sweetie" or "Darling." Phoebe wears a 36D bra and drives a car with the plate 3B58 348. In New York, Phoebe held jobs as a hostess at the Rainbow Room and the Chelsea Bar. Phoebe composes the spells they need to vanquish demons. Evil has transformed Phoebe into a Banshee and was later possessed by the Woogie Man she feared. Lori Ram played Phoebe in the original unaired pilot.

Leo is a guardian angel for good witches. He was born in 1924 and works for the Founders (later called the Elders), who watch over witches. Leo disguises himself as the sisters' handyman and became a Whitelighter during

World War II (he was a medic and tending to a soldier when he was chosen). He has the power to heal — but not himself or animals. His enemies are Darklighters, who seek to destroy witches and create evil. A romance developed between Leo and Piper and they married in the episode of 2/22/01. Leo also refers to his superiors as the Others.

The sisters have a white cat they call Kit that magically appeared when they occupied the house. The cat wears a collar with the symbol of the Triquetra — which also appears on the cover of the *Book of Shadows* and supposedly transferred Melinda's powers to the sisters. When the *Book of Shadows* is seen, the pages appear to be turning by themselves. It is revealed that the spirit of the sisters' grandmother, whom they calls "Grams," is responsible (she called them "My Darlings") — her way of looking after them.

The house in which the sisters live is also mystical. It was built on a spiritual nexus and a pentagram — as a battleground between good and evil (the house serves as an instrument to reclaim good). Because Phoebe was born in the house she is most connected to it and is more susceptible to possible evil.

Prue, the most powerful of the sisters (considered "The Power of One"), had a relationship with Andy Trudeau (W.T. King), a homicide inspector with the S.F.P.D. He learned the sisters were witches shortly before he was killed while helping Prue fight the demons of the Triad (an evil organization behind demon attacks in San Francisco).

Phoebe's love interest is Cole Turner (Julian McMahon), a powerful demon known as Beltizor, who poses as the assistant D.A. Cole, a member of the Brotherhood, is on a mission from Hell to destroy the Charmed Ones and has begun his quest by getting close to Phoebe. Now, considered a betrayer to the forces of darkness, he is sought by the Source (the embodiment of evil) who has dispatched bounty hunting demons to destroy him. Cole now helps Leo and the Charmed Ones battle demons to protect innocents (it is mentioned that Cole has been a demon for 1000 years).

Darryl Morris (Dorian Gregory) is the S.F.P.D. inspector who worked with Andy and is aware that the sisters are witches. He keeps their secret and calls on them for help when he feels a case is related to a demonic happening. James Read appeared occasionally as the sisters' father, Victor.

The episode of 10/4/01, "Charmed Again," introduces Rose McGowan as Paige Matthews, the half-sister of the Charmed Ones. In a cliffhanging third season finale, the sisters battle a fierce demon named Shacks. Although Shacks doesn't kill Phoebe or Piper, the fate of Prue is unknown (Shannen Doherty wanted to leave the series — and did. Rather than replace Shannen with another actress and continue the role of Prue, a long-lost half-sister, Paige, was added). The fourth season premiere finds Piper and Phoebe mourning the death of Prue. Now, without Prue, they are no longer the Power of Three. Piper tries casting several resurrection spells, but all fail to bring Prue back to them. Unknown to Piper and Phoebe, they have a fourth sister named Paige.

Paige is the result of an affair Patty had with her Whitelighter (Sam) after her divorce from Victor. At this time it was unnatural — and forbidden — for a witch and her Whitelighter to be together. Patty and Sam kept the affair a secret because Patty feared repercussions (her daughter would be denied Melinda's legacy). Prue, Piper and Phoebe were toddlers at the time "and thought mommy was just getting fat." Patty wanted to keep the baby but couldn't. She took her to a church and gave her to a nun (Sister Agnes). Patty said, "Let her name begin with a *P*" and orbed out (vanished in a sprinkling of white lights). The nun, who believed she was a heavenly visit, named the baby Paige and found her a good home, knowing that one day she would fulfill a preordained destiny.

Paige, now grown, is the youngest of the sisters. She is working at South Bay Social Services when she is first seen by viewers. At this time, Phoebe has visions of a girl being attacked by the same demon who killed Prue. With Cole's help, Phoebe saves the innocent from the demon but is astonished to see the girl "orb out" to safety.

Phoebe tells Piper about the girl. Leo is unable "to pick up on her" because she is not a witch yet. It has to be assumed Paige is drawn to the Haliwell house. Just as Piper and Phoebe are setting out to find her, she walks in ("The door was open..."). But she is not alone — Prue's killer is right behind her. Phoebe instructs Paige to follow her and Piper upstairs to the attic. There, at the *Book of Shadows*, Paige is instructed by Piper and Phoebe to chant a spell with them. The spell vanquishes the demon but leaves a bewildered Paige remarking, "What are you guys, witches?" "So are you," responds Phoebe. At that moment the Power of Three is reborn. (When Phoebe learned that their unknown sister's name was Paige, she remarked, "Image that, another *P*.")

Paige is actually half witch and half Whitelighter. She has Prue's power to move objects by concentrating but can also do it by "orbing the object" (making it vanish from one place and reappear in another place). Paige has the ability to sense evil and is being taught by Piper how to develop and control her powers. Leo is also Paige's Whitelighter.

Paige originally lived in an apartment (3) across town. She moved in with Piper and Phoebe when Piper convinced her they need to be together to evoke the Power of Three (strongest when together). In a past life, Paige learned she was an evil Enchantress (episode of 11/1/01). In the episode of 11/15/01, Cole becomes human when Phoebe creates a power-stripping potion that kills the demon in him (Beltizor).

After Prue's death, Piper changed the name of her club to The Spot. It became hipper and more active, but she now had another sister and changed it back to P-3.

29. *Cleopatra 2525* (Syndicated, 2000-2001)

The theme tells us that "in the year 2525 three women keep hope alive, joining forces to reclaim the Earth, looking ahead to humankind's rebirth." The women are Sarge (Victoria Pratt), Hel (Gina Torres) and Cleopatra (Jennifer Sky), resistance fighters who are battling to reclaim the Earth's surface from the Bailies, diabolical, alien machines that have destroyed most of mankind and forced its survivors to live underground. The resistance fighters are led by the unseen, mysterious Voice (Elizabeth Hawthorne) and use weapons called Gauntlets (which attach to the arm and possess amazing power). The underground world is seemingly made up of a series of endless (and bottomless) shafts and travel to the various corridors is accomplished by special propulsion gear.

Hel, short for Helen, is the woman Voice has chosen to communicate with (through a voice recessor implanted behind Hel's left ear). Voice, who can only be heard by Hel, informs Hel of Bailey activities and issues instructions on how to stop them (Bailey robots that infiltrate the underworld are called Betrayers). "The Voice," Hel says, "is fighting a noble cause — to liberate us all and the people who obey her are just as dedicated."

Sarge, real name Rose, was originally a soldier with the Black Watch Resistance Fighters. She is impulsive and plunges into violent confrontations with the enemy without thinking first. She has been wounded "and repaired" many times and if not for Cleopatra, would not be alive. When Sarge was a child, the Bailies were a symbol of the future and hope; now they are her deadly enemy.

Cleopatra, called Cleo, is a "thaw." She was born in 1980 and "thawed out" in the year 2525. Cleo, a graduate of Glendale Community College, worked as a stripper under the stage name Cleopatra (real name not revealed). At age 21, Cleo felt larger breasts would benefit her act and checked into a hospital for the necessary operation. During the enhancement process "something went wrong" and Cleo was cryogenically frozen "until a cure can be found." During a battle with the Bailies, Sarge is seriously wounded and requires a new kidney. She and Hel enter a medical unit and learn they can bargain for a kidney. Hel trades her most treasured possession — a wood tube that holds a picture of her father — to save Sarge's life (wood is said to be extremely rare and valuable. Although trees are seen in above the ground sequences, it is apparently not possible to harvest them for wood due to the war). The lab has just acquired "some cryogenically frozen bodies from the 21st century" and Cleo's genetic makeup is found to be a perfect match for Sarge. Following the operation Cleo awakens, looks down at her breasts and says "good work." Within seconds the lab is attacked by a Bailey betrayer and Cleo quickly learns of her fate. She is now a part of Sarge and becomes, at first, a reluctant member of their team.

Cleo was born in Phoenix, Arizona. As a kid she had a dog named Mr. Pants and has a scar on her elbow (at age eight she received 12 stitches after she fell off her rollerblades). She studied acting in college and had a Mustang (car) she called Maggie. Cleo is an excellent mimic and uses terminology that no one understands (for example, "One for all and all for one," "Make my day"). Cleo tends to scream, cry and whimper when the team involves itself in perilous situations. Cleo wears a pink miniskirt and low-cut pink blouse. Sarge wears an orange and black bikini-like top with tight, color-matching pants. Hel wears a silver and black tube top and tight black shorts. Cleo gave Sarge her first facial and introduced Hel and Sarge to the concept of a slumber party.

Mauser (Patrick Kake) was a robotic power reactor engineer who was captured by the Bailies and cybernetically programmed to kill. Hel and Sarge captured him and reprogrammed him to assist Voice's Flagship Team (Hel and Sarge). As a present, Mauser made Cleo a mechanical dog he called Mr. Pants Two.

When the Bailies capture humans they are taken to a Betrayer Factory. Here, the subject is cloned and programmed to duplicate the original exactly. To detect Betrayers, Mauser uses a Crono-Molecular Scan to determine age (Betrayers would be in minutes or days, not years old).

Creegan (Joel Tobeck) is the man responsible for the Earth's plight. His real name is George Bailey and 500 years ago he created the Bailies as environmental control units to help save the Earth (which was infected and dying "from a swarming plague of humanity"). In due time the Bailies became sophisticated and declared that humans were the problem and should be eliminated. Creegan, whose longevity is not explained, agreed with them.

Shaft Defense Cannons protect humans from Bailey ship attacks. The series was cancelled abruptly and an ending was not filmed. The last episode (3/9/01) was filmed as a season finale cliffhanger and showed the humans and Bailies in a fierce battle with the human forces waging rather successful attacks against the Bailies.

The program opens with these words (spoken by the Voice); "Five hundred years into the future she will enter a world where machines rule the Earth. Mankind has been driven underground and Cleopatra is about to discover there's no place like home." Joseph LoDuca composed the theme.

30. *Command 5* (ABC, 8/5/85)

Pilot. Command 5 is a special unit of the U.S. government that is designed to battle crime in a manner as unorthodox as the criminals themselves. Blair Morgan (Stephen Parr), a retired naval intelligence chief, heads the group. He is assisted by Christine Winslow (Sonja Smits), a former police department psychiatrist; J.D. Smith (William Russ), a former champion racing car driver;

Jack Coburn (Wings Hauser), a tough, maverick street cop; and Nick Kowal-ski (John Matuszak), a weapons and demolitions expert. The pilot story finds the group attempting to rescue private citizens from a gang that is holding them hostage to exchange for convicted felons. Lalo Schifrin composed the theme.

31. *Commando Cody, Sky Marshal of the Universe*
(NBC, 1955)

A ghost town called Graphite is the secret headquarters of a U.S. government scientist known only as Commando Cody (Judd Holdren), and his associates, Joan Albright (Aline Towne) and Ted Richards (William Schallert). Ted is later transferred and replaced by Dick Preston (Richard Crane).

Commando Cody works for an undisclosed organization headed by Mr. Henderson (Craig Kelly). The government insists that Cody wear a black mask (like the Lone Ranger's) at all times to protect his true identity. Cody, the inventor of the Rocket Flying Suit, has come to be known as "The Sky Marshal of the Universe" for his tireless efforts of protecting the Earth from the evils of outer space. Cody, Joan, Ted (and Dick) communicate with each other via their identification patches, which contain miniature two-way radios and operate on a frequency assigned only to Commando Cody. Cody's Rocket Flying Suit (which he wears over his gray suit) has a silver helmet, a backpack with two rockets for power and a front panel with the controls: On/Off, Up/Down, Slow/Fast. Cody needs to take a running start and then jump to be able to fly. Cody also has a space ship that is equipped with a ray gun that can be used to fire a normal round or as a heat-seeking ray when a target is out of firing range. Other than being scientists, nothing else is known about Joan, Ted or Dick. Joan and Ted originally joined Cody to adapt atomic power for rocket ship propulsion.

Only 12 episodes were produced and very little is done to explain things. When the series began, Cody has perfected the Cosmic Dust Blanket to protect the Earth from a missile attack by Retik (Gregory Gray), an evil extraterrestrial who must conquer the Earth to use it as a staging platform for his conquest of other planets. The serial-like chapters chart Cody's efforts to stop the Ruler. Dr. Varney (Peter Brocco) first assisted Retik; he was replaced in episode four by Baylor (Lyle Talbot). How the Ruler came to Earth or how he acquired his aides is not shown. Hydrogen hurricanes, the Magno Force Ray, radioactive gas, the Magnetic Drag Ray and the Refraction Field Force were some of the obstacles Cody had to battle to stop Retik (whose home base was the Moon).

The series is based on three Republic theatrical serials: *King of the Rocket Men* (1949), *Radar Men from the Moon* (1952) and *Zombies of the Stratosphere* (1952). In the first serial, Tris Coffin played Jeff King, Director of Security for Science Associates, who invented the flying suit, and was known as Rocketman. In the second serial, the Rocketman character became Commando Cody (George Wallace). The final theatrical entry starred Judd Holdren as Larry Martin, alias Commando Cody, and Aline Towne as his associate, Joan Albright (both of whom appeared on the TV series; Holdren, however, did not wear a mask here). Commando Cody was not a super hero. He was depicted as having no special powers in movies and on TV; the only weapon he carried was a gun.

32. *Conan* (Syndicated, 1997-1998)

Conan the Samarian (Rolfe Moeller) is a warrior and savior of people threatened by evil in a time of ancient myths and legends. He carries the ruby-handled Sword of Atlantis and seeks to establish hope wherever he goes (he was enslaved as a boy, escaped and now fights anyone who seeks to deprive innocent people of their freedom). He is assisted by Otli (Danny Woodburn), Bayu (T.J. Storm) and Zzeben (Robert McRay), three adventurers who not only fight injustice, but help Conan battle Hissah Zul (Jeremy Kemp), an evil wizard who seeks to become king by killing Conan before he can fulfill his destiny — to become the rightful king of the land. Conan is following a destiny he does not understand (he had a mystical encounter that led him to the Sword of Atlantis and told him of his destiny. He believes the sword is meant to kill Hissah Zul and lift his evil curse from the land. At this time, the powers of darkness will be defeated and Conan will become king). Hissah Zul rules from a mountain cave. His accomplice is the Skull, a cursed demon who seeks to regain his former self by helping Hissah Zul defeat Conan. Hissah Zul summons the Skull, who lives in a pond of water, by dropping rubies into it. The Skull then rises to the surface of the water to tell his master about Conan's current activities.

Zzeben, a Viking-like warrior, is mute; Bayu, proficient in the art of swordplay, rides a horse named Thunderbolt. Otli, the diminutive member of the group (stands four feet, one inch tall), rarely engages in physical confrontations with the enemy. He often remains behind in camp (to cook) or in a village (to protect someone) when Conan and the others need to be someplace else. Also assisting Conan is Karella (Ally Dunne), a beautiful female thief and warrior who sides with Conan against his enemies. She rides a horse named Indio. Charles Fox composed the theme.

33. *Condor* (ABC, 8/10/86)

Pilot. Condor is a futuristic (1999) U.S. government organization that battles terrorism at home and abroad. In an unusual move, the scientists of Condor create Lisa Hampton (Wendy Kilbourne), a beautiful female android that has been programmed to battle crime but protect human life. To test Lisa in the field and hopefully pave the way for additional "molecular computers," Lisa is teamed with Christopher Proctor (Ray Wise), a Condor agent whose partner has just been killed during an assignment. The pilot story finds Lisa and Proctor attempting to stop Rachel Hawkins (Carolyn Seymour) from stealing the Pentagon's computer codes and selling them to a foreign enemy. Cyrus Hampton (Craig Stevens) is the head of Condor; Sumika and Cass (Cassandra Geva, James Avery) are agents who work for Hampton. Ken Heller composed the theme. See also *Mann and Machine.*

34. *Dangerous Curves* (CBS, 1992-1993)

Based in Dallas, Texas, Personal Touch is a security firm that is 90 percent female and caters to individuals, P.R. firms, insurance companies and European royalty. The company is owned by Marina Bonelle (Diane Bellego). Gina McKay (Lise Cutter) and Holly Williams (Michael Michele) are her main operatives.

Most people believe Personal Touch is a call girl service. Marina started the company as a means by which to help people and to create an organization that employs women and incorporates the best female operatives in the field. Unlike Vallery Irons of *V.I.P.* (see entry) who is an amateur but heads a high profile protective agency, Marina is totally professional, intelligent and serious in her approach to protecting clients (not comical like Vallery). Another striking difference between the girls of Personal Touch and the girls of V.I.P. is modesty—"*V.I.P.* blatantly shows cleavage (especially Vallery's) while the Personal Touch girls cover more than they show. The token male at V.I.P. is Quick Williams, a bodyguard, while at Personal Touch, the girls work with Holly's boyfriend, Oscar "Oz" Bird (Gregory McKinney), a lieutenant with the Dallas Police Department.

Holly was a street cop with the N.Y.P.D. who quit "when I got tired of spinning my wheels" (arresting suspects only to have them back on the street before a conviction). She lives at 310 Mandarin Place; 555-0213 is her phone number. Gina, a former officer with the San Remo, Arizona, Police Department, quit the force after she was reprimanded by her captain for stopping fellow officers from beating up a suspect. She hates what she calls "macho man assignments" (men who need babysitting and hire women so no one will know they need protection). She and Holly are often assigned to undercover work. Holly jokes about it; Gina takes it seriously and feels undercover assignments are the most dangerous aspects of the job. Gina lives in an apartment on Hennessy and drives a car with the plate INB 68A. The Blue Cat Bar is their favorite hangout.

The premise changed shortly after the premiere when Marina was dropped and François Gendron was brought on to play Alexander D'Orleac, head of the Paris Personal Touch Bureau who is actually an undercover agent for Interpol (the International Police Force). Gina and Holly like it better when they can make something happen (as opposed to being reactive and waiting for something to happen). They get the opportunity when Marina sends them to Paris to help Alexander find a culprit who is distributing a deadly drug called Ink. After a successful operation, Alexander recruits them as Interpol agents when he discovers they are not only ex-cops but "attractive, well trained and you're women. There always seems to be a shortage of women here." The girls continue to work for Personal Touch as a cover for their new control, Alexander D'Orleac. Michael Parnell, Larry Weir and Tom Weiss composed the theme.

35. *Dare Devil* (CBS, 5/7/89)

Pilot. Matt Murdock (Rex Smith) and Krista Klein (Nancy Everhard) are partners in the New York law firm of Murdock and Klein. The firm is unusual in that Matt is blind but possesses an amplified sense of hearing and the ability to read normal print with his fingers. Together he and Krista form a perfect team of criminal attorneys. For Matt, his life changed when he was 14 years old. He was walking down a street when he saw a speeding truck about to hit an old man. Without thinking, Matt pushed the old man aside. The truck swerved to avoid hitting them, but a steel drum from the back of the truck came loose and its radioactive contents splashed Matt in the face (blinding him but giving him extraordinary powers). In the years that followed Matt studied to become a lawyer. One day, while listening to Police Captain Anthony J. Tindelli (Joseph Mascolo) talk about crime in the city and the need for a lone crusader to ferret out corruption, Matt decides to become the crusader Tindelli is seeking—the mysterious Dare Devil (Matt uses his heightened senses to "see"). The pilot story finds Matt attempting to nail Wilson Fisk (John Rhys Davies), a madman who is seeking to become the head of a crime ring. Lance Rubin composed the theme.

36. *Dark Angel* (Fox, 2000–2002)

Manticore is a secret genetics lab in the mountains of Gillette, Wyoming, that is seeking to produce superior humans for the military. Women are used to produce the children whose DNA will be altered by scientists. The mother and child, however, are never permitted to meet. One snowy night in the year 2009, a group of 12 children escape from Manticore. One of them, a nine-year-old girl named Max (Geneva Locke), is found by Hannah Sukovic (Eileen Pedde) and given shelter. The series begins ten years later. The world is in a depression. Computers have been wiped out by "The Pulse" and the U.S. is now a third world country. Max (Jessica Alba), now 19, has taken up residence in Seattle, Washington, and is "living a life on the run and always looking over my shoulder." She fears Donald Lydecker (John Savage), an army colonel assigned by Manticore to apprehend Max and the other escapees. At this time, machines called Hover Drones patrol the city.

One man, Logan Cale (Michael Weatherly) is attempting to change things. Cale, a cyber journalist, secretly operates a nontraceable cable broadcast called *Streaming Freedom Video* wherein he reveals information to authorities to help them catch criminals (Cale's video is "the only voice of freedom for the city. It cannot be traced or stopped." They last for 60 seconds).

Although Max has a job (bike messenger for Jam Pony-X-Press Messenger Service) she says, "I steal things in order to sell them for money. It's called commerce." One night, while attempting to rob Logan, Max is caught in the act. Logan, however, does not call the police. He notices a barcode on the back of Max's neck (her Manticore label) and offers to help her find her roots if she will help him. Max refuses until Logan is shot and crippled by one of the criminals he is seeking to catch. Logan, an expert cable hacker, calls himself "The Eyes Only Informant" when broadcasting his video. Logan has AB negative blood, hates needles, spiders and heights and drives a car with the plate DHL 1426. He is able to walk when he gets a blood transfusion from Max (her cell-enriched blood enables new tissue growth, but the effect is not permanent as it will not fuse his severed spinal cord). Logan receives additional help from Dr. Adrianna Veretes (Brenda Baake), a physio therapist who is trying to stabilize his cells through a process called osteo-regeneration (she charges $10,000 initial visit, $5,000 each additional visit). Logan was born on November 11, 1998, and 748-93-2308 is his Social Security number.

Max was designed to be the perfect soldier. Although she is a genetically engineered killing machine, she is opposed to guns. She can see in the dark, prowl like a cat, and doesn't need to sleep. She rides a Kawasaki motorcycle (plate JG154) and breaks the law to get what she wants; she steals, cheats and lies without any remorse. When Max gets set to ride her cycle, she says, "Gotta bounce."

At Manticore Max was housed in Block 12 (her group was called X-5). Mothers were kept out of the lab. Once they gave birth they were sent away and the infants used for experiments. The barcode on the back of Max's neck reads 332960073452; her file is X5452. Max is athletic, very strong and agile. She excelled in telecommunications as a child and the pupils in Max's eyes work like a telescope lens and can pinpoint distant objects. She can dodge a bullet and has a photographic memory.

The technical term for Max is chimera (a mythological creature). She has 11 "brothers and sisters" and feared the Nomilees (supposed creatures who drank blood; actually genetic mistakes in the basement) and found faith in the Lady of the Sacred Heart (whom they called "The Blue Lady"). Max has a genetically engineered flaw — seizures, and must take pills (tryptophan) to control them. She is also haunted by recurring nightmares about the escape (wherein she was hunted by Lydecker and some of her party killed). What Max does now "isn't my regular line of work. I'm making it up as I go along." Max uses cherry lip balm and when she has to be by herself she seeks the serenity of the top of the Seattle Space Needle building ("I look down at the people and think how everybody has problems ... and if I sit up here long enough I start to feel like I'm one of those people, a normal girl").

Lydecker calls Max a Rogue X-5. He considers Max top of the line as some of the other X-5's have been affected by the aging process (an acceleration of the genes that ages them dramatically). Donald Michael Lydecker was born in 1968 and enlisted in the army right after high school. He was accepted to the O.C.S., graduated in the top of his class and was assigned to the Third Ranger Battalion. He was later made captain of the Delta Force. His wife was murdered in 1995 (the case is still unsolved). He went ballistic and was dishonorably discharged. He became an alcoholic, went to rehab and cleaned up his life. He then went to work for Manticore. Lydecker has a plan for Max and others like her: "Instead of sending 1,000 soldiers into battle and losing 100, send in 10 perfect soldiers and lose none."

In one episode, Max teamed with "Phil, just call me Phil" (Rainn Wilson), a self-made superhero called Street Sweeper, to find out who is killing parolees days after they are released from prison. Phil became the Street Sweeper to avenge the death of his sister, Francesca (who was killed by thugs when they broke into their apartment and attempted to rob them). Phil worked in a warehouse as a forklift operator and one day discovered an abandoned Department of Defense crate that contained an experimental suit called an Exo-Skeleton (designed to provide movement to limber limbs). This, coupled with a makeshift eye scanner (made from a camera lens) gave him the courage to rid the street of crime. His secret headquarters was located in a room behind the back door of a pigeon coop.

The season finale (5/22/01) revealed that Lydecker wanted to capture Max and reprogram her. The mysterious Madame X (Nana Visitor), also called Renfrew, headed Manticore and had other plans. She frames Lydecker for a killing in an attempt to capture Max. Her plan backfires when Lydecker teams with Max and Logan to bring Manticore down by destroying the DNA lab. The episode ends with Max being shot in the heart and captured by Renfrew as she attempts to destroy the lab. The second season opener (9/28/01) finds Max fully recovered (heart transplant) but a prisoner at Manticore. She is now a number (X5452) not a name and the year has progressed to 2020. It is now learned that Madame X requires Max's unique DNA to create flawless soldiers and that Manticore is thought of by the outside world as a VA hospital (Max was found to have no junk DNA; each one of her cells is coded for a specific use). The format also changes. Before Madame X can control Max, she escapes through a secret tunnel and not only destroys Manticore, but unleashes a series of genetic mistakes (those Nomilees) that were concealed in the lower level of the building. There is now a threat to the city—unearthly creatures who prey on innocent people. Stories now follow Max and Logan as they attempt to expose Manticore as a government coverup and protect people from the Nomilees.

Chuck D and Gary G-Wiz composed the theme. The program opens with these words: "They designed her to be the perfect soldier—a human weapon. Then she escaped in a future not far from now. In a broken world she is haunted by her past. She cannot run; she must fight to discover her destiny."

37. *Dark Avenger* (CBS, 10/10/90)

Pilot. Paul Cain (Leigh Lawson) is an incorruptible judge whose career is ended when he becomes the victim of an acid bomb placed by an unknown criminal. The bomb fails to kill Cain, but seriously injures him. By chance, Paul is found by Rae Wong (Maggie Han), a beautiful electronics expert who was convicted of a crime she did not commit. Paul believed she was innocent and arranged a prison furlough for her prior to the bombing. She repays the favor by nursing him back to health.

Paul's face, however, is horribly disfigured and he uses a mask to conceal it. He decides to keep his survival a secret from his wife, Karen (Debra Eagle) and daughter Amanda (Jenny Dugan) as well as his sworn enemies. With Rae's help, Paul becomes the Dark Avenger, a mysterious figure who strikes at night to bring to justice the criminals that the system fails to convict. (Rae has converted a warehouse into a high-tech, state-of-the-art crime lab to assist Paul.) The pilot story finds Paul attempting to capture a killer known as "The Grim Reaper." The pilot was originally titled *I Accuse*. Sylvester Levay composed the theme.

38. *Dark Justice* (CBS, 1991–1993)

The Night Watchmen are a secret group of four people who avenge crime in an unnamed U.S. city. Nick Marshall (Ramy Zada, Bruce Abbott) heads the team. He is assisted by Catalana "Cat" Duran (Begona Plaza), Arnold "Moon" Willis (Dick O'Neill) and Jericho "Gibs" Gibson (Clayton Prince).

Nick is now a Superior Court Judge. He was first a police officer, but lost his collars through legal loopholes. He was next a district attorney but lost his cases to crooked lawyers. As a judge he finds his hands tied by a strict interpretation of the law. Nick, however, still believes in the law; that is, until his wife and daughter are killed in a car explosion set by a mobster seeking revenge. With no faith in the system, Nick decides to bring justice to those who are guilty but beat the system as leader of the Night Watchmen (originally called the Secret Vigilante Force).

Nick first researches a case "to see how the scuzz got off" then determines what action should be taken to bring the criminal back to justice. He then sets up an elaborate scam to accomplish that goal. "I can't balance the scales all the time, not even half the time. I do what I can and hope I get a break once in a while." Nick rides a motorcycle with the license plate IHD 469 when avenging crimes; "850 Commando" is printed on the side.

Cat was tired of being mistreated by the system. Nick helped her turn her life around "and gave me a new start, a new identity and a new bra size. I'm half the size I used to be; they got in the way before." Cat, a former forger and counterfeiter, now runs Cat's Liberal Child Care Center. Cat, born in 1963, is replaced by Maria (Viviane Vives) when she is shot twice in the back while saving Nick's life. Maria was born in Barcelona, Spain, and like Cat, met a tragic end (shot while saving the life of a girl she was trying to protect). Maria's replacement is Kelly Cochran (Janet Gunn), a private investigator who joins the team when she and Nick meet during a case probe—finding the corrupt police officers who raped Kelly.

Moon says only "I owe the judge 5,000 hours of community service. That's all there is to it." He was a minor league ball player and spent time in prison for gambling and forgery; he now runs Moon's Gym. Gibs is a special effects expert Nick cleared of a false murder charge. To repay Nick, he uses his talents in elaborate scams Nick requires.

"Justice may be blind," says Nick, "but it can see in the dark." Caitlin Delany played Nick's late wife, Sandy, in flashbacks. Mark Snow and Jeff Frelich composed the theme.

39. *The Dragon* (Syndicated, 5/19/01)

Pilot (segment of *The Queen of Swords*). Kami (Sung Hi Lee) is a beautiful Japanese girl who has come to Santa Helena (Old California, 1817) to begin a new life. She is with her master, Kiyomasa (Burt Kwouk) when they are attacked by bandits. During a fight, Kiyomasa is killed. Kami, injured, is found by Teresa Alvarado (Tessie Santiago), alias the crime fighting Queen of Swords, and taken to the doctor. When Kami recovers she vows to avenge her master's death ("The voices of a thousand ancestors cry out for vengeance"). Kami battles evil with a ceremonial sword ("The Blade of the Samurai") and lives by the code of the Dragon (which represents the power of Kami's order. It is an aura comprising the power of the physical, its fire and the wisdom of the unseen).

Kami is part of a warrior cult called the Shorinji Kimpo (the only sect that allows women but teaches them to fight like men). It is not explained how Kami, born in Japan, speaks perfect, unaccented English. Subplot of the story is the efforts of the evil Colonel Montoya (Valentine Pelka) to rid his life of the Queen of Swords by convincing Kami that she is evil. See also *The Queen of Swords*.

40. *The Dream Team* (Syndicated, 1999)

Zack Hamilton (Jeff Kaake), Kim Taylor (Angie Everhart), Victoria Carrera (Traci Bingham) and Eva Kiroff (Eva Halina) are the operatives for DREAM (Dangerous Reconnaissance Emergency Action Missions), a secret organization that operates out of the basement of a mansion in Puerto Rico. The team is run by J.W. Garrison (Martin Sheen), a mysterious figure who assigns them their missions. Their cover is that of the Dream Team, a company that offers gorgeous models for photographic shoots; Zack poses as Kim, Eva and Victoria's manager.

Zack is a former FBI agent who considers himself "the new sheriff in town" and the girls "my three beautiful deputies." Zack, born in Oregon but raised in Los Angeles, was an L.A.P.D. officer then an agent for the FBI. In Puerto Rico–based episodes, Zack drives a car with the plate CVA 796.

Kim, the toughest member of the group, only models "because it's my cover." Kim had dreams of becoming a Navy SEAL but women were not permitted to join the SEALs at the time. She set her ambitions elsewhere and became a member of the FBI Hostage Rescue Team before becoming part of the Dream Team.

Victoria is an expert on explosives and weapons and can defuse any bomb. She was born in Los Angeles and was a former Freedom Fighter before becoming a fashion photographer (her stunning looks also made her money and fame as a high fashion model). While Victoria does model with the team, she sometimes poses as a photographer to allow her to take surveillance photos rather than "just pictures of pretty girls." Her license plate reads DPX 301.

Eva, born in Poland, is a world-class gymnast who later worked as a spy for the Russian KGB. It is not said how Eva made the transition from spy to model, but she was recruited by Garrison for her knowledge of foreign operations and ability to get into places without being detected. Her training for the KGB made her ruthless and deadly, but she has learned to control that temperament when on assignments with the team.

The Dream Team mansion is located on Lucinda Road in Puerto Rico for a specific purpose: It is a tourist spot and provides the perfect cover ("We hide in plain sight," says Zack). The building is owned by the D.E.A. (Drug Enforcement Administration) and the mansion appears normal, even on the inside. Its secret lies behind the wall to the billiards room. One flight down is the team's operations center. While nothing is said about the equipment, the room is filled with computers and monitors. One specific, large screen monitor became a central part of their work when J.W. Garrison "is booted upstairs" and replaced by Sir Desmond Heath (Roger Moore), a distinguished Englishman who contacts them via closed circuit television (he is seen sipping tea or brandy and in the company of a beautiful girl). The Dream Team provides fashion layouts, commercials, music videos and swimsuit layouts as a cover for its extremely dangerous covert assignments—from stopping terrorists to apprehending diabolical criminals. See also *Acapulco Heat*.

41. *18 Wheels of Justice* (TNN, 2000-2001)

Chance Bowman, alias Michael Cates (Lucky Vanous), and Celia "Cie" Baxter, alias Katherine Spencer (Lisa Thornhill), are crime fighters who have one thing in common: They are both in the Federal Witness Protection Program and both ride the highways of America in a high-tech Kenworth T-2000 18-wheel truck that is the prototype for the Kenworth Project, a trucking program that not only transports goods, but key witnesses in criminal prosecution cases.

For Michael, a former Army Ranger turned Federal agent, it began when he testified against Jacob Calder (G. Gordon Liddy), a notorious crime lord. Shortly after, Michael's wife and child are killed in a retaliation explosion Michael believes was ordered by Calder. To protect Michael, Burton Hardesty (Billy Dee Williams), Chief of the Justice Department, arranges for Michael to have a new identity (Chance Bowman) and a new occupation (longhaul trucker). Hardesty believes that the best address for Chance is no address at all (as a Ranger, Michael had experience operating heavy machinery when he was assigned to clear land for airfields).

Katherine, age 27, was born in Louisville, Kentucky, in 1972. Her father is a law professor; her mother an eighth grade teacher, and she is one of five children. Katherine, educated in a private girls' school in Charlotte, attended Virginia Tech and specialized in micro technology. She was later recruited by the Justice Department for her work in surveillance technology. Katherine was also an instrumental witness in the final stages of a high profile criminal case. When an internal leak revealed her to be a key witness, a contract was put on her life. To protect her, the department gave her a new identity (Cie Baxter), relocated her to California and put her to work on the Kenworth Project. Because the truck is needed by the Justice Department for immediate operations, it is placed in the field before it is actually ready. Not willing to see "my baby" destroyed, Cie becomes Chance's partner to help him with his assignments and care for the truck she created.

Chance is determined to avenge the death of his wife and daughter. He was originally depicted as somewhat passive, hauling goods (and witnesses) and stopping crime wherever he found it. However, when Calder is released from jail on a technicality, Chance becomes more aggressive — now determined to bring Calder to justice and end his ring of organized crime. Complicating matters is the fact that Calder is aware of Michael's new identity and has taken a personal interest in seeing that he (and his hitmen) get Chance before Chance can get the goods on him.

Features of the aerodynamic blue Kenworth T-2000 Advanced Technology Truck include a fingerprint identification system that can identify individual truckers; a navigation system that can talk a driver to a destination; and a safety monitoring system that even detects drowsiness in a driver. See also *The Highwayman*.

42. *Electra Woman and Dyna Girl* (ABC, 1976-1977)

Crime Scope is an ultramodern, highly complex computer system that is programmed to pinpoint criminal activity. It is run by Frank Heflin (Norman Alden), an electronics expert who devised the system as a means of battling the villains who terrorize his unnamed city. Helping Frank in his battle are Laurie and Judy (Deidre Hall, Judy Strangis), reporters for *News Maker* magazine, who are secretly Electra Woman and Dyna Girl, costumed superheroes who battle the city's diabolical villains: the Sorcerer (Michael Constantine), Cleopatra (Jane Elliot), the Pharaoh (Peter Mark Richman), the Empress of Evil (Claudette Nevins) and the Spider Lady (Tiffany Bolling). Background information on how Laurie and Judy teamed with Frank is not given.

As Electra Woman, Laurie wears a reddish-orange costume with a yellow cape, boots and tights (to match her blonde hair). The letters *EW* appear on the front of her costume. Judy, as Dyna Girl, dons a red costume, cape and boots with pink tights (*DG* appears on the front of her costume). Electra Base is the headquarters for Crime Scope. By activating the Electra Change, Laurie and Judy go from street clothes to their crime fighting outfits. They travel in either the Electra Car or the Electra Plane and use the power of electricity to its fullest potential. Devices used by Laurie and Judy are the Electra Comp (their wrist-worn, portable link to Electra Base), Electra Strobe (allows them to perform anything at 10,000 times normal speed), Electra G (adds gravity to their bodies when activated), and Electra Power (a sudden burst of power to help in difficult situations).

Electra Woman is resourceful and fearless in the face of danger. Dyna Girl is a bit impetuous and lunges into situations without thinking. She uses terms such as "What an Electra Mess" or "Electra Wow" when in a jam. Broadcast as a segment of *The Krofft Super Show*. Marvin Miller does the narrating; Jimmie Haskell composed the theme.

43. *Exo-Man* (NBC, 6/8/77)

Pilot. Nicholas Conrad (David Ackroyd) is a physics professor at Wisconsin State College who is working on an experiment to revitalize immobile limbs with a process he calls energy cells. Nicholas becomes his own subject after he sustains a broken back from an attack and creates an exo-suit, an exterior costume made from the energy cells that not only revitalizes his limbs, making him mobile again, but endows him with superhuman abilities (like strength) which he uses to battle crime. The pilot story sets up the potential series storyline as Nicholas creates the exo-suit to get the culprits responsible for his plight. Emily Frost (Anne Schedeen) is Nicholas's romantic interest; Arthur Travis (Harry Morgan) is the government agent Nicholas assists. Dana Kaproff composed the theme.

La Femme Nikita see under L

44. *The Flash* (CBS, 1990-1991)

Central City is a thriving metropolis and famous for being "the place where the corn dog was invented." It has its own newspaper (the *Daily Star*), TV station (WCCN, Channel 6) and its share of crime. In the 1950s, Central City had a hero, the Night Shade, a mysterious, masked crime fighter who rode in a black car, wore a black costume and used tranquilizer darts he called "tranq bullets" as a weapon. The Night Shade was in reality Desmond Powell (Jason Bernard), a doctor at Central City Hospital (also called County Hospital). As time passed, Desmond, now the hospital's chief of staff, had to put Night Shade to rest. Central City is without a crime fighter until fate steps in.

Barry Allen (John Wesley Shipp) is a chemist for the Central City Police Department. One day, while working in his lab, a sudden, fierce electrical storm materializes. A bolt of lightning strikes a shelf of chemicals and Barry is doused with a variety of highly volatile substances (for example, aluminum sulfate, potassium nitrate, hydrochloric acid and phosphorus glycerin). He is taken to Central City Hospital and becomes the concern of Tina McGee (Amanda Pays), a government scientist at Star Labs, who becomes intrigued by the results of tests taken on him. She tells Barry that all his systems have been accelerated with bone and muscle tissues changing to keep the pace. As Tina helps Barry to recover, she discovers that he is capable of fantastic speeds (up to 620 mph; he broke the treadmill at 347 mph). He can run so fast that he can cause sonic booms. However, because of the fantastic amount of energy he uses, Barry needs to consume enormous amounts of food to sustain himself. With the growing crime rate, Barry decides to use his power of speed to battle evil as the Flash. Tina, fearful that the government will want to study Barry, decides to help him and keep his secret. To control and regulate Barry's body temperature, Tina adapts a prototype red friction Soviet-made deep sea suit as a costume for him. She places sensors in the suit (to monitor him), makes a red hood (to conceal his identity), and a lightning bolt symbol (so villains will fear him).

Barry lives in Apartment 34 in an area called North Park. He attended Central City High School and was a member of the science and Latin clubs. He enjoys eating at Burger World and Lucky Dogs, drives a car with the plate DLW 647 (later PRC 358) and has a pet canine named Earl. Barry hides his

Flash car behind a wall in his building (the billboard on that wall reads "Our World in Your Hands—Love It or Lose It").

Tina, a widow, lives at 1530 South Street (her late husband was named David). She follows Barry (when he becomes the Flash) in a Star Labs 05 Field Truck (wherein Panasonic and Sony monitors can be seen). Tina took a walk on the dark side when in the episode of 2/14/91, she was exposed to a lab accident that altered her brain waves and turned her into a criminal (a member of the all-girl Black Rose Gang). The only other people who know Barry is the Flash are Megan Lockhart (Joyce Hyser), a private detective who uncovered his identity and promised to keep his secret, and Reggie (Robert Shayne), the blind newsstand operator who recognized Barry's voice as that of the Flash. Lieutenant Warren Garfield (Mike Genovese) is Barry's superior; Julio Mendez (Alex Desert) is Barry's assistant at the crime lab; Ruth Werneke (Deborah May) is Tina's superior at Star Labs. Danny Elfman composed the theme.

45. *Flash Gordon* (Syndicated, 1953)

The G.B.I. (Galactic Bureau of Investigation) is a 22nd century organization that protects the members of the United Planets from alien invaders. Earth, Mars, Jupiter, Venus and Neptune are mentioned members of the alliance, while planets such as Thor, Eben, Diana, Oden and Zerkes are its enemies. Eben is said to pose the biggest threat as it is closest to Earth and only negative gravity protects the Earth from Eben.

Commander Paul Richards (Henry Beckman) heads the G.B.I. Flash Gordon (Steve Holland), the son of a famous scientist, is its chief operative. Dr. Alexis Zarkov (Joseph Nash) is the agency's chief scientist (inventor of negative gravity) and Dale Arden (Irene Champlin) is his assistant, a scientist almost as brilliant as he. While Dr. Zarkov and Dale always assist Flash on assignments, Dr. Zarkov is always the last one to know what is happening "because my work at my mountain lab keeps me out of touch with what is going on." Flash, who wears a T-shirt with a lightning bolt on the front, originally had a rocket ship called the *Sky Flash*. When it was destroyed in a battle, he had the *Sky Flash II* (Casey the parrot is its mascot).

Although the series is based on the comic strip by Alex Raymond, it differs greatly from the 1936 theatrical serial *Flash Gordon*. As originally depicted in the film, Flash Gordon (Buster Crabbe) was the athletic son of Professor Gordon, a world renowned scientist. He had no special powers and belonged to no organization. Steve Holland was like Buster Crabbe, physically right for the role. Dale Arden (Jean Rogers) was beautiful and sexy; she was not a scientist and always in harm's way. Jean, as Dale, was incapable of defending herself and relied on Flash to save her. Irene Champlin was not as pretty as Jean Rogers and immediately strikes one as being too old for the part. Irene had dark hair (not blonde like Jean) and differed in the fact that she could defend herself and would jump into harm's way to help someone (Flash and Dr. Zarkov often had to restrain her from getting herself killed). Unlike Jean Rogers, whose character meant dangerous rescue missions for Flash, Irene's Dale was a quick thinker and often saved the trio from perishing. Television's Dr. Zarkov was thinner and younger than one would imagine for one who accomplished so much. In 1936, Dr. Zarkov (Frank Shannon) was somewhat older, a bit heavier and was said to have invented Earth's first rocket ship (which he, Flash and Dale used to travel to the planet Mongo to stop Ming the Merciless from destroying the Earth). The television series was filmed in West Berlin (on a rather cheap budget); Kurt Heuser composed the theme.

Note: The only other known attempt to produce a series based on the comic strip is the 1979 animated series *Flash Gordon* with the voices of Robert Ridgely (Flash Gordon), Diane Pershing (Dale Arden) and Alan Oppenheimer (Dr. Hans Zarkov). This series followed the 1936 theatrical serial in that Flash battled Ming the Merciless (Alan Oppenheimer), the evil ruler of the planet Mongo. Other characters from that serial also appeared: Princess Aura (Melendy Britt), Ming's daughter; Thun (Allan Melvin), leader of the Lion Men; Prince Barin (Robert Ridgely), ruler of the planet Aborea; and Vultan (Allan Melvin), king of the Hawkmen.

The TV movie pilot film for the series, titled *Flash Gordon — The Greatest Adventure of Them All*, was filmed in 1979 but didn't air until 8/21/83. Billed as "The first full length adult animated space fantasy ever produced for television," it showed how Flash Gordon (Robert Ridgely), an Olympic medalist, and Dale Arden (Diane Pershing), a reporter, met Dr. Zarkov (David Opatoshu). In 1939 in Warsaw, Poland, Flash receives a cryptic one word message — Mongo — from a dying scientist with instructions to seek out Dr. Zarkov, a brilliant scientist. En route, Flash meets Dale, who is seeking a story on Dr. Zarkov. Suddenly, the plane on which they are traveling is bombarded by meteors. With only one parachute between them, Flash and Dale jump and are rescued by the man they both seek. Flash learns from Dr. Zarkov that Mongo is a warring planet that is threatening to destroy the Earth. When Flash and Dale learn that Dr. Zarkov has built a rocket ship and plans to travel to Mongo to stop the evil Ming the Merciless from destroying the Earth, they join him. The series picks up at this point with the trio's endless efforts to stop Ming (Bob Holt). *Other voices:* Melendy Britt (Princess Aura), Ted Cassidy (Thun), Vic Perrin (Vultan), Robert Douglas (Prince Barin).

46. *Forever Knight* (CBS, 1992)

Detective Nicholas Knight (Geraint Wyn Davies) of the 37th Precinct of the Toronto Metro Police Department, is the city's most unusual crime fighter — an 800 year old vampire who uses his strength, ability to fly, night vision and sensitive hearing to help him defeat evil (making him television's first good vampire, not Angel from *Buffy, the Vampire Slayer*).

Nicholas, called Nick, is single and lives at 7 Curtis Avenue. He drives a 1962 Cadillac (plate 358 VY5) and doesn't kill for blood; he has a supply of cow's blood in his refrigerator to sustain himself. Nick works the night shift (he told his captain he was allergic to sunlight) with the obnoxious Don Scanke (Gary Farmer). While Nick's year of birth is not revealed, it was in 1228 that he wished for immortality. A master vampire named Lucien LaCroix (Nigel Bennett) arranged for Nicholas to have his wish. Nicholas, unable to kill anyone, turned his back on vampirism and used his powers to help good defeat evil. Nick can become mortal by facing his fears (for example, looking at a cross, which weakens him, or facing the light of day, which can destroy him). LaCroix, who seeks to keep Nick a vampire, possesses the one item he needs to become mortal—the jade glass of the Mayan Indians (European legend states that if blood from a sacrificed victim is consumed from the glass it will cure vampirism). Natalie Lambert (Catherine Disher), the police department's medical examiner, is aware of Nick's affliction and is seeking a way to help him become mortal without the jade glass (he begged her to help him see the sunrise and regain his mortality).

The Raven, Nick's favorite nightclub, is run by Janette (Deborah Duchne), a beautiful vampire Nick met in 1228 and who now warns him when LaCroix is near. Fred Mollin composed the theme.

Note: The original pilot, *Nick Knight*, aired on CBS on August 20, 1989. Rick Springfield was Nicholas Knight; Michael Nader, LaCroix; John Kapelos, Don Schnake; and Cec Verrell, Janette. Dr. Jack Barrington (Robert Harper) was the police chemist attempting to help Nick (changed to Natalie for the series).

47. *Freedom* (UPN, 2000-2001)

It is the near future. War has broken out in the Middle East. Domestic terrorism has become a serious problem. In an effort to stop the violence, the President tours the country, urging peace and calm. Then unexpectedly, the President's plane, *Air Force One*, crashes and the President is presumed dead. Martial law is declared and the United States is turned into a police state. Curfews are enforced and identity papers are required for all. Penalties for unlawful behavior are harsh and certain. Two years later, stability and peace are returned to the country. But the military personnel from those special operations units used to impose martial law now pose a threat to the new order. Owen Decker (Holt McCallany), Becca Shaw (Scarlett Chorvat), James Barrett (Darius McCrary) and Londo Pearl (Bodhi Elfman) are four such specialists who are captured by U.S. Special Forces and sent to the William Jefferson Clinton Federal Prison. The charge: treasonable acts against the U.S.

Fifteen months later, a secret government organization, the Resistance, arranges for them to escape. They first meet their mysterious female contact, Jin (Francoise Yip) and learn "that the world isn't what you remember when you went in. Everything has changed." Half the country accepts the idea of a military takeover; the other half desires a freedom like before. A civil war has broken out and the Resistance needs their help to restore freedom by overthrowing the powers that reject it. Decker is given an encrypted cell phone (good for one use only). "When it rings it means the Resistance needs you."

The program is all action and devotes little dialogue to the character's backgrounds. Decker, a captain, was assigned to a top secret military unit called Covert Operations 10 Zulu. When his unit was assigned to kill the President and blame it on domestic terrorism, he refused and was arrested. The military leader, Colonel Devon (James Morrison), killed his wife and kidnapped his son when Decker resisted arrest. Decker's mission is also a personal one: get Devon and find his son. He believes that "My country betrayed me."

Becca, a lieutenant with the Army Rangers, is well trained in the martial arts. She refused to carry out a mission against innocent civilians and was arrested. Londo, a first sergeant with the U.S. Army's Special Intelligence Forces, has the serial number 34622595. He becomes tense and uneasy if he has to go without coffee for long periods of time. Londo, like Becca, was arrested for refusing to betray his country. James, nicknamed Jake, was a Navy SEAL arrested on the same charges (he says "They gave me orders and I refused to obey them"). He enjoys Big 'n' Chunky candy bars, is claustrophobic and says "I can't stand rodents." The series ended without any conclusions. Eddie Jobson composed the theme.

48. *The Gemini Man* (NBC, 1976)

Intersect is a U.S. government research organization that specializes in sensitive and often classified work. When an unidentified satellite loses orbit and crashes into the ocean, Intersect assigns special investigator Sam Casey (Ben Murphy) the task of finding it in a mission called "Operation Royce Explorer." While attempting to recover the satellite, it explodes and renders Sam invisible when heavy radiation affects his DNA structure.

Abby Lawrence (Katherine Crawford) is an Intersect doctor who saves Sam's life by fitting him with a DNA stabilizer to control his visibility. Abby later develops a sophisticated subminiature stabilizer in an atomic battery powered wristband (top secret file 487384). The stabilizer, which looks like a wristwatch, has three gold contacts on its back. When these contacts touch Sam's skin, he remains visible. When Sam presses the stem of the watch, he can change the frequency and become invisible, but only for 15 minutes a day; any longer and he will disintegrate. While Abby searches for a permanent solution to Sam's problem, Sam uses his power of invisibility to fight crime by performing hazardous missions for Intersect.

Sam was born on April 16, 1948, in New York City. He received a juris doctor's degree from Harvard Law School in 1973 and has a clearance level of A-6 at Intersect. He lives as 3210 Driscoll. Abby, a graduate of Harvard Medical School (class of 1975) lives at 173 Northern Boulevard and also has a clearance level of A-6. Leonard Driscoll (William Sylvester, Richard Dysart) is the head of Intersect (International Security Technics). The series ran for only six episodes; Lee Holdridge composed the theme.

49. *Generation X* (Fox, 2/20/96)

Pilot. Emma Frost (Finola Hughes) and Shawn (Jeremy Ratchford) are adult mutants who run the Xavier School for Gifted Children — a front for teaching mutant teenagers how to become superheroes. In a futuristic time, humans are at risk of becoming genetic mutations due to activity by the X-factor in certain glands. The X-factor causes bizarre powers and people affected with them are declared "nonhuman" and denied human rights. Mutants must register as such and are subject to reeducation or forcible confinement. Emma and Shawn rescue mutant teens from official custody and teach them to understand and develop their powers for good.

Emma, alias the beautiful White Queen, has the power to create illusion while Shawn, alias Banshee, can create powerful sound waves. Their students are: Jubilee (Heather McComb), Buff (Suzanne Davis), Refrax (Randall Slavin), Mondo (Bumper Robinson), Skin (Augustin Rodriquez) and Monet (Amarilis). Their nemesis is Russell Tresh (Matt Frewer), a "mad scientist" who seeks to harvest the X-factor in mutant brains to create his own mutants and control the world.

Jubilee can discharge energy from her fingertips; Buff possesses super strength; Refrax has x-ray vision; Mondo can take on the properties of any substance; Skin has "thermo flexibility" (can stretch his skin); Monet is a strikingly beautiful girl who possesses advanced brain functions and is immune to everything. The pilot story finds Trench developing a dream machine that enables him to enter a person's mind to control them for his own bidding. Based on the Marvel comic book. J. Peter Robinson composed the theme. See also *Mutant X.*

50. *Ghost Writer* (PBS, 1992–1994)

Ghost Writer is an unknown entity that appears in a glowing light and can only communicate through words. It appears to be very old (not familiar with modern technology) and has no recollection of a past life. No information is given as to where the spirit came from or how it came to be. The first episode relates only how the spirit gets its name and how it was discovered by Jamal Jenkins (Sheldon Turnipseed). While moving an old trunk in the basement of his home, Jamal unknowingly knocks over an old book. The pages open as the book falls and a glowing light emerges from it. The light scans the house and takes refuge in Jamal's computer. Later, when Jamal attempts to use his computer, he finds that he is receiving messages from an unknown source. Through questions typed into the computer, Jamal learns that the spirit can speak but only through typed or written words. Jamal contacts his friend, Lenni Frazier (Blaze Berdahl), and shows her what he has found. They name the spirit Ghost Writer and learn that it is dedicated to helping children (and can only be seen by the children it is helping). A short time after, when their friend Gabriella "Gaby" Fernandez (Mayteana Morales, Melissa Gonzalez) becomes the victim of a crime at school (her money and school bag stolen), Jamal, Lenni and Ghost Writer decide to investigate. They recruit Gaby's brother, Alejandro (David Lopez) and their friend Tina Nuen (Tran-Ahn Tran). Together they uncover the culprits as the members of a gang who wear two faced masks called THABTO (Two Heads Are Better Than One). They now work as amateur detectives to solve crimes.

Ghost Writer is not bound to a computer. It can rearrange any word it sees and communicate with team members in this manner (a question can be written on a piece of paper; Ghost Writer will rearrange the words to respond). Each team member carries a felt-tip pen necklace and uses the word *Rally* with an initial (for example Rally G — G for Gaby) to arrange a meeting (Ghost Writer picks up on this and alerts the other team members).

Jamal lives at 11 East 39th Street with his widowed father, Reginald (Dean Irby), sister Damitra (Samaria Graham) and grandmother, C.C. Jenkins (Marcella Lowery), a postal worker. Their phone number is 555-9648. As a kid Jamal had two plush toys: Bernie the bear and Melvin the duck. He attends the Zora Neale Hurston Middle School (as do Lenni, Alex, and later Tina) at 347 Baltic Street, Brooklyn, New York.

Lenni is a talented musician and song writer who lives at 361 East 46th Street (also given as Cumberland Street) with her widowed father, Max (Richard Cox); her late mother was named Colleen. Lenni wrote the song "Friends Forever" but it was her performance of the song "You Gotta Dance" at the School Jam Talent Show that brought her to the attention of Jade Morgan (Annabelle Gurwitch), the owner of Smash Records, who produced a music video of that song for MTV.

Gaby and Alex live with their parents, Eduardo (Shawn Elliott) and Estella (Cordelma Gonzalez) over a bodega they own at 6629 Cumberland Street (over which Lenni is later said to live); 555-8943 is their phone number. Gaby and Alex share a room. Gaby's favorite TV show is *Galaxy Girl* and when they lived in El Salvador, three-year-old Alex had a pet chicken named Naomi. Gaby, the youngest member of the team, attends Washington Elementary School.

Tina first attended Washington Elementary, then the Hurston School (where she is a reporter for its newspaper, the *Hurston Herald*); in her prior school, she worked on the school newspaper with Gaby (Gaby did the reporting; Tina was the videographer). Tina, brought up by strict Korean parents (played by Ginny Yang, Richard Eng), worked as a Girl Friday to Lana Barnes (Patricia Barry), a once famous movie star. See also *The New Ghost Writer Mysteries*. Peter Wetzler composed the theme.

51. *The Great Merlini* (Unaired, 1951)

Pilot. The Great Merlini (Jerome Thor) is a master illusionist and escape artist who uses the wizardry of his craft to solve baffling crimes. "Magic and crime have one thing in common," he says, "deception. And when criminals use deception to commit crimes it also takes deception to solve them." The Great Merlini (no other name given) is assisted by Julie Boyd (Barbara Cook), a beautiful girl who sighs, "I'm supposed to be working in a magic act, not in a detective agency." They assist Inspector Gavigan (Robert Noe) of the N.Y.P.D. The pilot story, titled "The Transparent Man," finds the Great Merlini and Julie attempting to solve a jewel theft committed by a supposedly invisible thief. See also *Mandrake* and *The Magician*.

52. *The Greatest American Hero* (ABC, 1981–1983)

Ralph Hinkley (William Katt) is a special education teacher at Whitney High School in Los Angeles. He has integrity, a strong moral character and a healthy idealism. William "Bill" Maxwell (Robert Culp) is a dedicated but hot headed FBI agent attached to the Los Angeles bureau. He is idealistic, noncorruptible and obsessed with bringing criminals to justice. The two are strangers, but unearthly forces soon bring them together. In Palmdale, Ralph becomes separated from his students during a field trip while Bill's car is made to drive to a predestined spot. As Ralph and Bill meet, an alien spacecraft appears and engulfs them in a circle of light. An alien leader (John Zee) from an unspecified planet, tells them that crime on Earth must be stopped to save the planet from destroying itself. Because of their qualities Ralph and Bill have been chosen for the job. Ralph will become the fighter and Bill his assistant. Ralph is presented with a special costume (red tights, black cape, silver belt) that endows him with superhuman powers and an instruction manual on how to use the costume (which Ralph calls "The Suit"). Complications set in when Ralph, walking away from the site, unknowingly drops the instruction book. With no knowledge of how to use the Suit or the powers it beholds, Ralph has to play being the Greatest American Hero by ear (the circle insignia on the front of the costume is a symbol of the alien society).

The Suit (or "the Red Jammies" as Bill calls it) makes Ralph impervious to harm. He can deflect bullets, run at incredible speeds and possess great strength. He can fly (although this is difficult and awkward without the instruction book) and appear and disappear at will. Ralph also has visions (called "holographs" by Bill) that allow him to see a past or future event associated with a crime they are investigating. Bill believes "The job takes 110 percent of what you have 25 hours a day." He calls women "skirts," enjoys snacking on Milkbone dog biscuits and says "Life used to be so simple for me, an ordinary, card-carrying FBI agent trying to do the best job I knew how ... doing everything by the book until they teamed me up with a school teacher named Ralph Hinkley..." Bill's car license plate reads 508 SAT (later 293 X45) and his two "worst case scenarios" are that Ralph's true identity will be revealed and that his superiors will find out about his secret crime fighting activities. He calls the aliens "The Little Green Guys."

Pamela "Pam" Davidson (Connie Sellecca) is a lawyer with the firm of Carter, Bailey and Smith (later the firm of Selquist, Allen and Minor). She is also Ralph's girlfriend (later wife) and the unwitting assistant on most cases that involve Ralph and the Suit (Bill calls Pam "Counselor"). Pam is a brilliant attorney but often questions her thinking when she places herself in danger by joining Bill and Ralph. Pam, the daughter of Harry and Alice Davidson (Norman Alden, June Lockhart), lives in an apartment at 2871 Bryer. Ralph, who lives in a home on Meadow Lane, is divorced from Alicia (Simone Griffeth) and is the father of Kevin (Brandon Williams). Ralph's phone number is 555-4365, later 555-0463.

The *Daily Galaxy* was the first paper to publish a picture of Ralph flying. Although this upset Bill, who becomes a bit crazy when Ralph's activities threaten to reveal his secret identity, his "worst case scenario" came true when Ralph was revealed as being the Greatest American Hero. (In a rather vague sequence, Ralph saves the life of a girl who, in turn thanks him as "Mr. Hinkley." Ralph appears to be a bit surprised—"How did she know?" He and the viewer are never told.) This sequence is from an unaired network episode (seen only in syndication) that was a pilot for a female version of the series called *The Greatest American Heroine*.

The time is 1986 (although the episode was filmed in 1983). With the world aware of who the Greatest American Hero is, Ralph becomes a celebrity. Pam and Bill object to all the publicity—as do "The Little Green Guys." The aliens summon Ralph and Pam to their Palmdale site to tell them their plan will not work and the Suit must be given to someone else so crime can be battled in secret. Once the Suit is given to another person, the world will forget that Ralph was a super hero. He and Pam, however, will be allowed to keep their memories.

Ralph suggests giving the suit to Bill, but the aliens refuse ("He is not the type. Mr. Maxwell was meant to serve as an associate. You will find someone and when you do you will know it"). The alien leader thanks Ralph and Pam for all they have done and Ralph begins a quest to find his replacement.

Holly Hathaway (Mary Ellen Stuart) is a young woman devoted to helping others. She is the foster parent of seven-year-old Sarah (Mya Akerling), works in a day care center, is founder of the Freedom Life Foundation and owner of an animal shelter called Anything's Pawsable. Holly cares, is honest and has a strong moral character. She is the girl Ralph chooses to become the Greatest American Heroine (Bill's reaction: "You did it to me Ralph, you picked a skirt ... you paired me with Nancy Drew"; Pam's reaction: "She's not a skirt, she's a woman").

Holly faces the same problems as Ralph: an inability to fully understand the powers of the Suit without the instruction book (Ralph tried to convince the aliens to give him another book but failed). Holly tells only Sarah about her secret identity: "You are the most important thing in my life... I don't want you to ever think that anything would ever come between us, not even a magical suit. I also want you to help me and Bill, we'll be a team ... and the most special thing you could do as our special little partner is never to tell anyone about this." Sarah promises and, if the series had sold, Sarah would have played an active role as their "special little partner."

Holly is never in a bad mood — something she feels Bill will like about her. She also has two pets — Roosevelt and Churchill; but what kind of pets? As Sarah told Bill, "You don't want to know." Holly drives a car with the plate 5Q8 HPO and believes the assignments are going to be fun. "They're not supposed to be fun," says Bill. Holly and Bill's only assignment was to investigate the illegal killing of whales in Newfoundland. Bill's closing scene with Holly ends the episode: "As I always said, we're gonna make a terrific team." Joey Scarbury sings the theme, "Believe It or Not."

The Greatest American Heroine see *The Greatest American Hero*

53. *The Green Hornet* (ABC, 1966-1967)

The *Daily Sentinel* is considered the greatest crusading newspaper in America. It is published by Dan Reid, a man who uses the paper as a means by which to bring criminals to justice. Dan, however, is past retirement age and his only heir, his son Britt Reid (Van Williams) is a playboy who squanders money and has no sense of responsibility. In an effort to change Britt, Dan hands over ownership of the paper to him. He then hires Mike Axford (Lloyd Gough), an ex-cop turned reporter, to secretly watch over Britt's activities.

Britt is, at first, reluctant to take the job until he learns about his great-grand-uncle, John Reid (alias the Lone Ranger). Britt's carefree attitude suddenly changes as he becomes instilled with a desire to help people in trouble and bring criminals to justice.

Believing that criminals are superstitious and cowardly, Britt devises a scheme to become the mysterious crime fighter, the Green Hornet. He chooses the symbol of the green hornet (which appears in the center of the eye cutouts in his mask) because it is the insect that is most deadly when aroused. His costume, however, is nothing extraordinary — a black suit, black hat and green mask. He reveals his secret identity to Kato (Bruce Lee), his Asian houseboy, who assists him as the Hornet's aide (Kato's outfit is a black chauffeur's costume and black mask); his secretary, Lenore Case (Wende Wagner); and Frank Scanlon (Walter Brooke), the D.A. The Green Hornet and Kato, however, are considered criminals and wanted by the police. To avoid capture they avenge crimes as semi-fugitives, rather than a law enforcement organization, and always disappear before the police arrive.

As Britt Reid, Britt drives a white sports car; as the Green Hornet, he and Kato ride in the Black Beauty, a 1966 Chrysler Imperial (plate V 194) that is equipped with a number of gadgets (rocket firing capabilities front and rear; a smoke screen button and a knockout gas emissions control). The Hornet's weapon of choice is a knockout gas gun to subdue suspects; Kato incorporates his skills in the martial arts.

The floor below Britt's living room is the secret headquarters of the Green Hornet. Little information is given and it appears far less sophisticated than, for example, Batman's Batcave. There is a secret button in the living room that allows Britt and Kato to enter their secret room via an elevator in the fireplace. To allow the D.A. or Miss Case access when Britt is below, Britt lowers three books on the library shelf behind his desk. This activates the fireplace elevator and allows them to enter. Britt pushes the books back to normal to raise the elevator. Britt's home has a white garage door that allows entry for Britt's normal car via a remote control device (presumably in the car). The back of the building has a secret garage door for the Black Beauty. This entrance is concealed by a billboard that covers sliding double doors. To the left (of the screen) is a girl and the words "Candy Mints." To the right is a boy and the words "How Sweet They Are." When the doors are closed, the girl and boy appear to be kissing; when opened, the kiss is interrupted.

When the Black Beauty is needed, Kato presses hidden buttons next to a pegboard wall of tools. The first button places clamps on special bars that protrude from the undercarriage of the car. The second button allows the floor to revolve to reveal the Black Beauty. The clamps are released from the Black Beauty when the third button is pressed.

D.A. Scanlon's phone number is 555-6789. If he has to contact Britt, he can call him either at home or at his office (where he has a special phone with a scrambler attached). When crime doesn't make sense, as to the why or the how, Britt feels it is time for the Green Hornet to act. Al Hirt performs the theme, "The Flight of the Bumblebee." The program opens with these words (spoken by William Dozier): "Another challenge for the Green Hornet, his aide Kato, and their rolling arsenal, the Black Beauty. On police record, a wanted criminal, the Green Hornet is really Britt Reid, owner/publisher of the *Daily Sentinel*. His dual identity, known only to his secretary and the district attorney. And now, to protect the rights and lives of decent citizens, rides the Green Hornet."

54. *Hercules: The Legendary Journeys* (Syndicated, 1994–2000)

Hercules (Kevin Sorbo), the legendary hero of ancient Greece, is a half-god (the son of the god Zeus and a mortal woman named Alcmene), who uses his mighty strength to help those the gods have turned away. He is assisted by Iolaus (Michael Hurst), his friend and traveling companion.

Zeus (Anthony Quinn, Peter Vere-Jones, Charles Keating) is the King of the Gods. He rules from Mount Olympus and is married to Hera, the all-powerful Queen of the Gods. Based on the ancient Greek myth (which was adapted to TV), Zeus was unfaithful and had an affair with Alcmeme (Jennifer Ludlam, Elizabeth Hawthorne, Liddy Holloway), a beautiful mortal woman. The tryst resulted in a half mortal son (Hercules) and angered Hera who frowned on infidelity and set her goal to kill Hercules, a constant reminder of Zeus's infidelity. When Hera attempts to kill Hercules with a fireball but misses and destroys his home, killing his wife, Deianeira and his three children, Hercules begins a quest to avenge their deaths by destroying Hera (Hera is only seen in human form in the last episode, "Full Circle." She is played by Meg Foster and was previously only heard and usually represented by an animated pair of all-seeing eyes).

Hercules has chosen to live among mortals. He believes the Earth is round and that the sun revolves around it ("It is the reason why there are seasons"; Iolaus believes, like others, that the Earth is flat). Hercules can sew and make clothes ("My mother taught me") and devised the first Olympic games (as a means to avoid a bloody conflict between the Spartans and Eleans). Hercules has a certain knack for arriving just as a crisis erupts and, being of kind heart, feels honor bound to resolve the conflict.

Being a halfgod means Hercules is also related to full gods. His half-brother, the devilishly evil Ares (Mark Newham, Kevin Smith), the God of War, is his most troublesome relative (Ares seeks only to create havoc; Hercules despises Ares for this and risks his life to stop him and restore the peace).

Although Deianeira has been killed (her spirit lives on in the Elysian Fields), Hercules has vowed to remain faithful to her. The Golden Hind is a female deer with large hooves and golden horns. It can also take human form — that of the beautiful woman Serena (Samantha Jenkins). A Golden Hind also possesses something that Ares fears—blood that can kill a god. In the episode "When a Man Loves a Woman," Hercules marries Serena in an attempt to protect her. He fails, however, when Strife (Joel Tobeck), Ares's impish nephew, kills her with an arrow. In a later episode, "The End of the Beginning," a crystal that controls time thrusts Hercules back to the moment when Serena is shot and lies dying. He confronts Ares and forces him to make Serena human so she can live. When Hercules is returned to his own time, he sees that Serena is still human. She is also married and has children. Serena (now played by Kara Zediker) and Hercules never actually married. "The snake in Ares cavern" was the first monster said to have been killed by Hercules.

Iolaus considers himself to be a great comedian (he tells jokes and is often the only one who laughs at them). He is two years older than Hercules and was a thief (as a child he would steal donuts from villagers). It was Hercules who turned his life around. Iolaus is the son of Skouros, a professional soldier who spent little time at home and was later killed in a battle. Although Iolaus does not possess the strength of Hercules, he often becomes offended when Hercules thinks he cannot defend himself and steps in to help. Iolaus believes he and Hercules find trouble without looking for it (Iolaus is a mortal and must use his skills and wits to survive).

Hercules also assisted Jason (of "Jason and the Argonauts" fame) as he sought the Golden Fleece. Jason (Jeffrey Thomas), the ruler of Corinth, later becomes the stepfather to Hercules when he marries Alcmene. After his marriage, Jason named Iphicles (Kevin Smith), the mortal half-brother of Hercules, Corinth's new ruler.

Salmoneus (Robert Trebor) is the fast-talking toga salesman who befriends Hercules and Iolaus and involves them in his various get-rich-quick schemes (that always seem to fail). Autolycus (Bruce Campbell) is the self-proclaimed "King of Thieves," a master cat burglar whose crimes often mean trouble for Hercules. Aphrodite (Alexandra Tydings) is the beautiful Goddess of Love (in one episode she called Hercules her brother, although in mythology they are not related). She is very protective of her shrines and often causes trouble when her love spells backfire. Callistro (Hudson Leick) is an evil warrior condemned to the hell of Tartarus (the underworld's place of punishment). She is used by Hera in plans to kill Hercules. Xena (Lucy Lawless) is the evil and ruthless warrior princess reformed by Hercules to use her skills to help people besieged by evil. See the spinoff series *Xena: Warrior Princess* for additional information. Joseph LoDuca composed the theme. The program opens, in part, with these words: "He journeyed the earth battling the minions of his wicked stepmother, Hera, the all-powerful Queen of the Gods. But, wherever there was evil, wherever an innocent would suffer, there would be Hercules."

Note: A series of five-minute cartoons, *The Mighty Hercules*, appeared in 1960 (syndication) with the voices of Jerry Bascombe (Hercules), Helene Nickerson (Helena, the maiden), and Jimmy Trapp (the evil Daedalus; and Newton and Tweet, friends of Hercules). *The Sons of Hercules* was a syndicated 1962 series of edited European theatrical films that dealt with the adventures of the various sons of Hercules. On 9/12/65, ABC aired an unsold pilot called *Hercules* with Gordon Scott as the Greek hero. Diana Hyland was Diana; Martin Hulswit, Ulysses; and Paul Stevens, Diogenes.

55. *Here Comes Tobor* (Unaired, 1955)

Pilot. A proposed spinoff from *Captain Video and His Video Rangers* that was to use the once evil (but now reformed) robot, Tobor, as a U.S. government secret weapon against crime. Tobor (robot spelled backwards) is now owned by Bruce Adams (Arthur Space), a professor at the Adams Research Center (exactly how Tobor came to be in Bruce's possession is not explained). Assisting the professor is his nephew, Tommy (Tommy Terrell), a boy who was born with one of the highest ESP quotient's ever known. Tobor has built-in Extra-Sensory Perception. Tommy has been cleared for top secret material and because of his gift, controls Tobor through thought transferences. Together they work with Professor Adams to thwart evil. The pilot story finds Tobor and Tommy helping the U.S. Navy locate a missing atomic submarine. The credit for Tobor reads "Tobor played by Tobor." Howard Jackson composed the theme.

56. *Highlander* (Syndicated, 1992–1998)

Duncan MacLeod (Adrian Paul) and Tessa Noel (Alexandra Vandernoot) are co-owners of an antique store in an unspecified city (the store is referred to as The Antique Shop and only the words "Antiques" and "Appraisals" are seen on the window). Tessa and Duncan are lovers and Tessa is one of the two people who know Duncan's secret: he is an Immortal. Although he looks to be 35, Duncan was born in the Scottish Highlands 400 years ago. He knows only that he was brought to his father as an infant by a midwife when the baby that was born to his mother died at birth. It was not until Duncan was a young man that he learned he was an Immortal. During a battle with a rival clan Duncan was mortally wounded. Duncan's father praised him as a brave warrior; but when Duncan's wounds healed and he returned to life, his father condemned him, saying he was in league with the devil. Although cast out by his parents, Duncan kept the only name he knew. Now, as a representative of the Clan MacLeod, Duncan is seeking to become the last Immortal and acquire the power of all Immortals to rule the world for good. Legend states that all knowledge is contained by the Immortals. When one Immortal encounters another, the Gathering is held. This is followed by the Quickening (combat by sword) to acquire additional strength. An Immortal can only be killed by beheading. When this happens, the surviving Immortal acquires the other's knowledge and strength. If a virtuous Immortal delivers the final blow, goodness triumphs; if the last surviving Immortal is evil, darkness will reign forever. "In the end there can be only one." There is no information given as to where the Immortals come from or how they came to be. As Duncan seeks to fulfill his destiny, he helps people who have become victims of crime and dispenses justice with his ornamental Japanese sword (he also seeks to prevent evil Immortals from harming people and has become a vigilante of sorts).

Duncan and Tessa live in a loft over the antique store. Before her career as a sculptress proved financially sound, Tessa worked as a tour guide on a sightseeing boat. It is here that she met Duncan when he boarded at the last moment. Duncan's assistant, Richie Ryan (Stan Kirsch) is a young hoodlum Duncan reformed and the only other person who knows Duncan's secret.

In the episode of 10/23/93, "The Darkness," Tessa and Richie become involved in a struggle with car thieves and are shot; Tessa is killed and Richie seriously wounded. Richie miraculously recovers and learns from Duncan that he is an Immortal. Richie, however, has no recollection of his past. The following episode, "An Eye for an Eye," finds Duncan selling what is now called The Art Gallery and purchasing controlling interest in DeSalvo's, a gym run by Charlie DeSalvo (Philip Akin). Duncan remains basically behind the scenes; Charlie and Richie conduct the daily operations. The following episode, "The Watcher," introduces an additional regular — Joe Dawson (Jim Byrnes, the owner of Joe's Bookstore at 27 North Jay Street). Joe is a member of the Watchers, a secret society of mortals who observe and record the deeds of Immortals. Joe also helps Duncan in his quest (which has been changed somewhat to destroy the evil Immortals).

First season episodes also feature Randi McFarland (Amanda Wyss), a television reporter for KLCA, Channel 8 News, who covers the incidents that just happen to involve Duncan. Tessa dislikes Randi because she feels Randi is only interested in air time and does not care about the victims of the crime. Amanda (Elizabeth Gracen) is a beautiful Immortal who is not only Duncan's romantic interest (after Tessa) but a cunning thief who is drawn to the good things in life (see the following title for additional information).

Duncan's Thunderbird license plate reads 827 KEG (later 427 KEG); Tessa's license plate is RC8 737. Queen performs the theme, "I Am Immortal," based on the 1985 feature film of the same title.

57. *Highlander: The Raven* (Syndicated, 1998-1999)

There is a mysterious Eskimo legend about a raven who stole the sun, the moon and the stars to protect them from an evil thief who wanted to rob them and plunge the world into darkness. When the evil was defeated, the raven returned light and goodness to the world.

A mysterious, modern-day woman named Amanda (Elizabeth Gracen) is the human incarnation of that raven. She is an Immortal and, like the raven, a creature of the night who steals only the most fabulous treasures— "from jewels to paintings to fine cigars."

Nick Wolfe (Paul Johansson) is a detective with the South Police Precinct, 52nd Division, in an unidentified city. He is a dedicated, skilled investigator who believes in what he is doing.

Amanda (called Amanda Montrouse in the pilot) is a "Princess of Thieves." She lives in a plush hotel suite with her friend, Lucy Becker (Patricia Gage), and is spending three times more than she steals (she fences her goods through Basil Morgan [Julian Richings], an Immortal who gives her twenty cents on the dollar). Amanda targets only the rich and famous. She never kills "I only steal." Nick, assigned to investigate a recent series of robberies, feels that Amanda is the culprit but can't prove it. Believing Amanda will make the perfect suspect, a dishonest cop frames Amanda when she convinces him that she is innocent. An investigation leads Nick to the real thief. In an ensuing confrontation, two people are killed: the real culprit and Nick's partner, who died saving Amanda. Amanda cannot forget what Nick's partner did for her. She is suddenly developing something she has never known before—a sense of responsibility. Nick, on the other hand, brought down a crooked cop, something he thought was good for the department—until he finds his superiors unwilling to admit that one of their own was a killer. Now, feeling betrayed, he begins to question his definition of right. When he is offered a promotion to lieutenant to forget about the incident, he quits. Nick, however, cannot abandon his right "to protect and serve." While working outside the law to solve crimes and defend people, Nick finds unexpected help from Amanda—her way of trying to pay back Nick for what he has done for her. Rather than work as separate entities, they join forces to return light to the world by waging a private war against evil and injustice. Nick carries a 9mm gun and was said to have worked for the bomb squad for six months.

Amanda cannot die, except by beheading (which is her ultimate death. Other methods can kill her, but she will be reborn again). Like Duncan MacLeod (of the series *Highlander*; see prior title), Amanda fights injustice with a Samurai sword. Amanda, said to be 1200 years old in dialogue (but 1000 years old in the theme), has lived for centuries as a roguish beauty who is attracted to the good things in life. She is never malicious and not without scruples. Some episodes are set in Europe and find Amanda and Nick becoming detectives to return stolen art objects for a percentage of their value. OSW 676 is Amanda's license plate from the pilot episode. Joe Dawson (Jim Byrnes), the Watcher from the prior series, appears only once in the third episode. Like Duncan, Amanda's history is a mystery; there is no explanation given as to who she really is or where she actually came from. Amanda says only that she belongs to a privileged class called the Immortals. She has lived and died many times and recalled her first birth as a young peasant girl in Normandy in A.D. 850. This life was cut short when she was killed for stealing a loaf of bread. She was reborn that same day, but was unaware of her destiny. She was found and taken in by a mysterious woman named Rebecca Horne. It was Rebecca, who is assumed to be a good Immortal, who cared for Amanda until she became a young woman. At this time, Amanda was taught the martial arts and the art of swordplay. She was also told that she was an Immortal and that to survive, she must defeat the evil Immortals who seek to plunge the world into darkness (when a good Immortal meets her evil counterpart, the Quickening is held — a fight to the death by sword. The Immortal who is victorious acquires the strength and powers of the defeated Immortal). Amanda has been a duchess, a slave and a woman of nobility (what she has mentioned). If Amanda cuts herself, the wound heals immediately. She fears that modern technology could expose the secret of her eternal life if a sample of her blood made its way to a laboratory. Amanda mentioned that six minutes, fourteen seconds was her best time in opening a safe. Simone Cloquet composed the theme.

58. *The Highwayman* (NBC, 1988)

In an effort to battle crime and corruption in areas where laws often terminate (at county lines on long stretches of highway), the Justice Department institutes a test program called the Stealth Project and creates a new breed of lawmen called Highwaymen who work in secret. Our mysterious Highwayman (Sam J. Jones) is known only as "Highway" or "Highwayman." He uses a high tech 12-ton black Mack truck and an awesome handgun (capable of firing grenades like bullets) to battle crime in those legal blackouts. His field code is "Highway One"; "Master Key" is the code for his base of operations. The message "If You Love Something, Set It Free" is posted on the back of Highwayman's truck (along with these license plates: 29-3588, PC 6045, 12 8R41, PC 2986, 76R 8E2, T-28032 and 7GR 8E2). The cab, which has "The Highwayman" printed on the doors, is actually the cockpit of a helicopter which can operate independently of the truck. The truck can also become invisible when full Stealth Power is ordered. Although the opening theme narration tells us that "Highwaymen work in secret and alone," Jetto (played by Jacko), an Australian-bred Highwayman, assists our hero.

A girl known only as Dawn (Claudia Christian) was Highway's original contact (she was a government agent who posed as a disc jockey; she hosted "The Dawn Patrol" on an unnamed 50,000 watt clear channel station—"The Mighty 690 from New Orleans"). She was replaced by Tanya Winthrop (Jane Badler), an agent who met with Highway in the field (as opposed to over the airwaves). Highway's superior is Admiral Conte (Jack Ging), who supervises operations for the Control Center as Master Key.

Highway has no other name. If someone asks "Who are you?" he responds with "Someone who may be able to help." We are told the Highwayman is a legend: "They say his mother was born of fire and his father was born of wind... You hear a lot of legends told when you ride the long hard slab. Some who say the man is good and some who say he is bad; but all agree who try to play a cheatin' hand, you only get one chance to draw against the Highwayman." William Conrad narrates; Glen A. Larson and Stu Phillips composed the theme. See also *18 Wheels of Justice*.

59. *Honey, I Shrunk the Kids: The TV Series* (Syndicated, 1997–2000)

Matheson is a small town in Colorado that is also the home of Wayne Szlinski (Peter Scolari), an ingenious inventor whose creations often backfire. Wayne is married to Diane (Barbara Alyn Woods) and is the father of Amy and Nicholas (Hillary Tuck, Thomas Dekker). They live at 6808 Bonnie Meadow Court and have a dog named Quark.

Wayne works as a research scientist for Jen Tech West Labs, a company whose motto is "Exceptional Living Through Expensive Technology." While Wayne enjoys the scientific challenges of his job, he finds pure satisfaction at home in his private attic lab where he has invented such devices as the Shrink Ray, the Time Hopper (for travel through time) and the Igloo of Health (a plastic isolation bubble). He has also invented FRAN (Felon Repeler Accident Neutralizer), a computer that protects the house, the Fido Feeder (an automatic dog feeder), the Cloud Buster (to make rain), the Artificial Personality Chip (to make a plush toy a child's friend), the Universal Remote (to find lost remote controls), and the Three I-D-ER (to produce a holographic image of a person or object).

Matheson appears to be a peaceful town. However, when crime threatens its citizens, Wayne comes to the rescue, using one of his inventions to secretly help the police apprehend the bad guys. When Wayne decided that Matheson needed its own super hero, he donned a costume (tights, cape and jet pack) and called himself Captain Astounding. However, because Wayne chose to wear a metal bucket as his helmet, the Matheson *Daily Times* dubbed him "Bucket Head" and the name stuck (not only did the bucket impair

Wayne's vision, but he had trouble controlling his flights due to a faulty jet pack).

It was when Wayne was in college that his life changed. He was exploring a cave as part of a science project when he discovered a strange, glowing metal. After experimenting with the metal, Wayne determined that it was alien in nature as it produced extraordinary power. He called his find "Szlinskism" and it enabled him to invent items no one else could. Wayne has a lab hamster (Herkimer) and his license plate reads PAT PNDG. In college Wayne was with a comedy improv group called the Mexican Jumping Beans. When Wayne gets upset, he uses the phrase "Cheese and Crackers" or "Jiminy Christmas."

Diane is a successful lawyer with Coleman and Associates who often becomes the "victim" of one of Wayne's inventions when it backfires (for example, becoming a gorgeous but evil Egyptian queen; reverting back to a 16-year-old girl; aging far beyond her years; speaking in rhymes). Diane wears a 36D bra and became a spy (of sorts) when the Canadian Secret Service recruited Wayne to develop his inventions as part of a project called ND3 (Wayne's code was "P" and he required Diane's assistance to help him foil the baddies seeking his inventions. He called himself "Papa Bear" and Diane "Mama Bear" when he and Diane had to communicate with each other via their wrist communicators). Diane is also president of the Matheson School Board. When Quark was a puppy, Diane would play the theme song to the TV series *Lassie* to get him to come to her (or come home when he was out; Quark's favorite movie is *Lassie Come Home*).

Amy, called "Ames" by Wayne, is a pretty 16-year-old girl who attends Matheson High School (where she is a member of the Spartans' basketball team). Amy worries that her father's wacky inventions are ruining her reputation. When Amy tinkered with Wayne's Neuron Nudger (a device to improve mental power) she acquired amazing powers and sought to become Mistress of the Universe. Amy also became a victim of Wayne's Suntan Block (made from fish oils) that slowly turned her into a mermaid.

Nicholas, called Nick and "The Nick Meister" by Wayne, attends Matheson Elementary School. He is very smart and seems to be following in Wayne's footsteps (as he understands the logic behind what his father invents). He is a member of the Science Club at school and Copernicus the rabbit is its mascot. Nick has invented a device to track extraterrestrials he called the Alien Locator. He has his own lab hamster (Alvin) and if he doesn't get an *A* on a test, he feels he will be living in disgrace.

When Wayne saw his family reading trashy novels (they rarely watch TV) he decided to write his own bestseller — *Wayne Wolf, Private Eye* (in a dream sequence Wayne was Wolf and Amy his sexy but dumb blonde secretary, Lola. Diane was his client, Jamie Wyatt, a bombshell seeking her missing sister; and Nick was Mr. Whoo, "a deranged little man with a cane").

The series is based on the theatrical feature *Honey I Shrunk the Kids*; Christopher Stone composed the theme.

60. *Human Target* (ABC, 1992)

The *Wing*, a huge, highly technical black plane that resembles the wings of an airliner, is the mobile headquarters of Christopher Chase (Rick Springfield), a man who steps into the lives of people marked for murder to become a human target until he can restore that person's safety. It was an incident from Chris's past that led him to become a human target. During the Vietnam War, Lieutenant Chase was in charge of a special unit that went into villages to destroy them. During one such raid Chris was captured by the Vietcong and placed in a tiger cage. Chris spent ten days in the cage before he was rescued (he now has a fear of small places). When he was discharged from the service, he realized what he had done and it all came crashing in on him; so much so that he spent 19 months in the psychiatric ward of the Walter Reed Hospital. When he was released he knew the only way to keep sane was to somehow balance it all out and right wrongs through his unique abilities. He begins by commissioning construction of the *Wing* (although it is not made clear, Chris is apparently wealthy). He then hires three highly skilled people to assist him: Libby Page (Signy Coleman), Philo Marsden (Kirk Baltz) and Jeff Carlyle (Sami Chester).

Chris has an amazing ability to impersonate voices and through the use of highly advanced computer makeup (masks) Chris becomes the person he is seeking to protect. The fee varies depending on the job (usually ten percent of a client's yearly income) and the client remains in safety on the *Wing* until Chris completes the job. The *Wing* has worldwide television reception and an advanced audio and visual communications system. Chris can also communicate with the *Wing* from any part of the world via a special disk that he carries; he uses the RX 7000 ("the Squirrel") to scramble calls.

Libby has known Chris for several years. She previously worked for the Company, a secret U.S. government organization, in a top level security position. When the project she was working on collapsed, she found employment with Chris, who required her expertise to operate his high tech telecommunications equipment.

Philo is a movie special effects makeup expert who impressed Chris with his computer-generated masks for the film *Zombies on Holiday*. Philo now incorporates his computer skills to make the target masks for Chris (which combine Chris's general features with special features of a target's face).

Jeff served with Chris in Vietnam; he now pilots the *Wing*. The team also assists in the field if necessary. When a woman is marked as a target, Chris goes undercover as the male closest to her. An unaired pilot version exists with Frances Fisher as Libby and Clarence Clemmons as Jeff. The series is based on the D.C. comic book character. Anthony Marinelli composed the theme.

61. *Hunter* (Syndicated, 1968)

COSMIC, the Commonwealth Office of Security and Military Intelligence Co-ordination, is a branch of the Australian government that has been established to combat the evils of CUCW (the Council for the Unification of the Communist World). John Hunter (Tony Ward) is COSMIC's top operative. He is attached to Division SCU-3, which works behind a front organization called Independent Surveys.

Hunter, a veteran of the Korean War, combines the elements of commando, spy and detective. He works above the law and knows the law offers him no protection "and no exemption. If necessary, his country will deny his existence." Eve Halliday (Fernande Glyn) is an undercover agent and Hunter's partner on assignments. Her cover is as a stenographer for Independent Surveys. Blake (Nigel Lovell) is the stern Security Chief and head of SCU-3.

A man called Mr. Smith (Ronald Morse) is the scheming local representative of CUCW. It is his job to disrupt the inner workings of COSMIC and pick the targets his agents must destroy or sabotage around Australia and South East Asia. Kragg (Gerard Kennedy) is Smith's chief operative, an expert killer with no conscience. The 26 episode series was produced in Australia.

62. *I-Man* (ABC, 4/6/86)

Pilot. The *Galaxy I* is a U.S. space probe that has returned to Earth with a sample of an alien atmosphere. The sample is being transported by truck to a NASA research center when it is involved in an accident. Jeffrey Wilder (Scott Bakula) is a cab driver who attempts to help the injured truck driver when he is exposed to a canister that is leaking the alien atmosphere. The unknown gas reacts with his molecular structure and endows him with superhuman powers (strength and indestructibility). Immediately, he is recruited by the International Security Agency to use his unique abilities as an agent for the U.S. government. Jeffrey is teamed with agent Karen McCorder (Ellen Bry) and together they set out to perform dangerous missions for the benefit of mankind.

The pilot story finds Jeffrey and Karen attempting to stop Oliver Holbrook (John Anderson) from using a government laser weapon to destroy San Francisco. Herschel Bernardi plays the agency's supervisor, Art Bogosian. Craig Safan composed the theme.

63. *I Spy* (NBC, 1965–1968)

Kelly Robinson (Robert Culp) and Alexander Scott (Bill Cosby) are U.S. government undercover agents who pose as a tennis pro (Kelly) and his trainer/masseur (Scott, called Scotty). Their exact affiliation is not mentioned by name; they call their "boss" "our people," "our superiors" or "Washington."

Kelly, called Kel by Scotty, is a graduate of Princeton University. He is skilled in karate but still manages to take a beating from the enemy. He loves fishing, golfing and duck hunting and has a bad habit of repeating what the person he is speaking to says. He also enjoys eating (especially steamed clams) and Scotty warns him to curtail his culinary pursuits "or you'll look like a lox on the court." Kelly calls himself a "tennis bum" and has won two Davis Cup trophies (when asked why he chose such a life, he responds with "It's better than digging ditches"). Although he travels around the world to compete, he doesn't always win (for example, he lost in five sets at Forest Hills).

Scotty is a Rhodes scholar and can speak eight languages. He was born in Philadelphia and mentioned he would have become a basketball coach at Allentown High School had he not become a spy (he also mentioned, when under the influence of truth serum, that his name was Fat Albert, referring to Cosby's real life friend in South Philly). Scotty, a black belt in the martial arts, has the instincts of an alley cat and is an expert on explosives. He has training as a chemist and can make a bomb out of almost anything (for example, dry ice, ammonia, fertilizer and a cigarette). Scott will also shoot to kill.

While they work well as a team, Scotty and Kelly constantly argue, usually about how a case should progress. They also bicker about who saves who the most (Scotty claims to have pulled Kelly out of a lot of "close shaves" and Kelly promises "I will do the same thing when the situations arise." In one episode, Kelly claims that he rescued Scotty on a number of occasions, but Scotty claims "Yeah, but you're always too late or too early").

In the opening theme, a closeup of Kelly's eyes is seen in the top portion of the screen in color while the bottom portion of the screen shows him viewing black and white scenes from that particular episode. Earle Hagen composed the theme.

64. *The Immortal* (Syndicated, 2000-2001)

Rafael "Rafe" Caine (Lorenzo Lamas) is an Immortal, a man who has sworn an oath of vengeance to send demons back to hell. It was while on a trip to Japan in the year 1638 to acquire silk and spices for his father, an importer, that destiny would change young Rafe's life. An unexpected encounter with a severe storm sinks the ship on which Rafe is traveling. Rafe manages to swim to shore and after three days of wandering, meets a man named Yashiro (Robert Ito). Yashiro welcomes Rafe into his home. Rafe remained and eventually married Yashiro's daughter, Mikko (Grace Park). They built a home near a small stream and were blessed with a child. One day, in 1643, evil demons named Mallos (Keith Martin Corday) and Vashista (Kira Clavell) kill Mikko and steal Rafe's child. An enraged Rafe burns his house to the ground, forges a sword of revenge and swears an oath: "I'll hunt them forever and never rest until they're dead. With this sword I seek an oath of vengeance. The evil ones will know my name and fear it. I will send them back to hell with this blade and never stop until it's done." "Me too," says the man who is at his side, Rafe's companion, who is known only as Goodwin (Steve Braun). Just then, Rafe raises his sword to the heavens. Thunder sounds and he and Goodwin are encircled in a sphere of light. Their destiny has begun. Rafael is the Chosen One and Goodwin his Squire.

It is not until the year 2000 that Rafael and Goodwin acquire a companion — Dr. Sarah Beckman (April Telek), a paranormal physicist who specializes in psychokinetic exploration (Sarah was threatened by a demon when Rafe came to her rescue. When Sarah saw Rafe dispose of the demon by using his sword to behead it and send it back to hell, she became intrigued and attached herself to Rafe and Goodwin in the hope of acquiring material on demons for her studies).

Rafael doesn't eat or drink. He can smell demons when they are near and has a plan for everything ("We make it up as we go along"). Rafael doesn't make mistakes when it comes to demons—"I make decisions." Demons call Rafe "The Vengeful One." Rafe can be killed, but Yashiro taught him how to survive. "If the demons win," says Rafe, "the world would be plunged into darkness." Rafe has one treasured keepsake from his daughter — a doll she played with that he keeps in a wooden box. In addition to his sword, Rafe carries other "demon fighting equipment" with him at all times: three guns, two large knives, a small knife, and a small rapid-fire gun.

Goodwin enjoys Trix cereal for breakfast. His favorite TV show is "Barbie: College Girl Temp" and he hates to be called "Kid." Rafe says "He's a good companion but don't turn to him for help in a fight — he's a coward." Goodwin contends "I'm not a coward, I'm practical." Although Rafe believes "Goodwin makes cowardice look like an art form," Goodwin is the only person who can awaken Rafe when he goes into "a vapor lock" (meditation). This is difficult, he says ("Like the time we were in the Alps and I rolled him down a mountain into a frozen stream to wake him"). He also has an emergency kit (that contains various bottles of odors—"Like monkey extract") to help him wake Rafe.

Sarah previously lived at Parkchester and 20th but now rides with Rafe and Goodwin in a mobile home (plate 441 RLI). Sarah has invented the Sonic Transponder to study subjects believed to be suffering from demonic possession (they react to the ultrasonic stimulus and Sarah has determined that a demon's body temperature is 150 degrees). Rafe calls the invention "a dog whistle for demons"; Goodwin, called Goodie by Sarah, refers to it as "a creature screecher" (when Sarah activated the device for the first time, it attracted a demon who threatened her life. Now Sarah is not safe—"People you can hide from, demons you can't." "I'll find 'em," Sarah says. "You destroy 'em," she tells Rafe). Rafe keeps the key to the mobile home in a Ming Dynasty vase.

Sarah was skeet shooting champion in summer camp and was called "Pumpkin" by her parents as a kid. She thinks she, Rafe and Goodwin make an excellent team ("With your experience and my research, we're going to kick some serious demon butt"). Sarah also insists on "more ammo" when they go out on a mission ("You know how I like to shoot things"). She likes nonfat veggie pizza and calls Vashista "a malicious skank who dresses like a Vegas cocktail waitress." (Vashista's partner, Mallos, has a thousand year plan to defeat good and let evil rule the world.)

While Rafe seeks to destroy evil and find his daughter, he must also content with Randall (Bret Harte), a demon hunter known as "The Collector." Randall comes from the fifth level of Hell hunting. He is relentless and his mission is to find demons who have strayed from the darkness of evil to the goodness of light and return them to evil by beheading them. G. Tom Mac composed the theme. These words are heard as the theme plays: "An oath sworn is an oath answered. An oath of vengeance for a life taken, a past destroyed, a future threatened. Enemy of darkness, eternal, he walks the earth relentless. His mission is to hunt the messengers and drive them back to hell. Now the light of earth depends on the Immortal."

Note: There was a prior series called *The Immortal* (ABC, 1970-71) that dealt with Ben Richards (Christopher George), a man who possessed a rare blood type that made him immune to old age and disease. Richards, however, did not fight evil; he was on the run from Jordan Braddock (Barry Sullivan), a dying billionaire who wanted Ben's blood to sustain life.

65. *The Infiltrator* (CBS, 8/14/87)

Pilot. Dr. Paul Sanderson (Scott Bakula) is a research scientist at the Stuart Institute of Technology. During an experiment in teletransportation, a freak accident occurs that links his cells and atoms to an experimental space probe called Infiltrator. The power generated by the probe has been absorbed by Paul's molecules. Now, when he becomes angered or enraged, a startling metamorphosis occurs: Paul becomes the Infiltrator, a metal, robot-like defense mechanism that the U.S. government uses for its most hazardous assignments. The pilot story finds Paul and his partner, Dr. Kerry Langdon (Deborah Mullowney) attempting to retrieve Infiltrator's blueprints from its creator, Richard Markus (Michael Bell), who is holding them for ransom. Charles Keating plays John J. Stewart, Paul and Kerry's supervisor. Stan Jones composed the theme.

66. *Invincible* (TBS, 11/18/01)

Pilot. Os (Billy Zane) is a 2,000-year-old mystic and evil warrior whose fate changes when he encounters a greater force for good in the form of a White Angel. The angel places a sword to his head and offers him a choice: "Love or die." Os accepts love and is transformed into a mighty warrior who must now battle all the evil in the world — specifically Slate (David Field) and his league of Shadowmen. Os, however, is unable to battle evil alone. He is told of the Chosen, people born with a birthmark that resembles a tattoo shaped like an ornate lattice. Each of the Chosen is found by Os and trained in the art of Wushu, the ancient form of Chinese military combat. The Chosen are Serena Blue (Stacy Oversier), a police officer; Ray Jackson (Tory Kittles), an ex-soldier; Michael Fu (Byron Mann), a bodyguard; and Keith Grady (Dominic Purcell), a professional thief. Each is then named after elemental signs: Earth (Ray), Fire (Michael), Metal (Grady) and Air (Serena). The pilot story finds the Chosen attempting to stop the Shadowmen from using an ancient tablet to open a portal that will unleash evil and destroy the world. The pilot is produced by Mel Gibson and Jet Li.

67. *The Invisible Avenger* (Unaired, 1960)

Pilot. A proposed television version of the radio series *The Shadow* that deviates greatly from the original format to focus only on Lamont Cranston (Richard Derr), a wealthy man-about-town who secretly helps people as the Shadow, a mysterious figure for justice. Lamont has the ability to cloud men's minds so they cannot see him (an art for TV he learned in the Orient from a mystic named Jogendra). When Lamont concentrates he sends a powerful image into the minds of others. The affected person does not see Lamont — only his image in a shadow. Missing from the TV version are the Police Commissioner and Margot Lane, Lamont's "lovely traveling companion" (a vital part of the radio series). Margot has been replaced by Jogendra (Mark Davids), who uses the power of hypnotism to help Lamont. In the pilot story, Lamont and Jogendra travel to New Orleans in search of an old friend and become involved in a plot to overthrow the foreign government of Santa Cruz. This opening, from the radio version, best explains the difference in concept. It begins with the voice of the Shadow: "Who knows what evil lurks in the hearts of men? The Shadow knows" (laughs menacingly). An announcer speaks: "The Shadow, Lamont Cranston, a man of wealth, a student of science and a master of other people's minds, devotes his life to righting wrongs, protecting the innocent and punishing the guilty... Cranston is known to the underworld as the Shadow — never seen, only heard... The Shadow's true identity is known only to his constant friend and aide, Margot Lane... These dramatizations are designed to demonstrate to the old and young alike that crime does not pay."

68. *The Invisible Man* (Syndicated, 1958–1960)

Peter Brady is a scientist employed by Castle Hill Laboratories in England. He is conducting an experiment on the problems of optical density (the refraction of light) when reactor number three begins to leak and sprays Peter with a gas. His body absorbs the gas and renders him invisible. Brady, however, lacks the knowledge to become visible (he wears facial bandages, dark glasses, clothes and gloves to be seen). Peter mentions that his clothes will become invisible if they are made of animal fibers (such as wool). Before Peter can do anything, he is put under lock and key by the Ministry of Defense (they fear a panic will result if it is known an invisible man exists). Peter escapes and retreats to the home of his widowed sister, Diane Wilson (Lisa Daniely) and her daughter, Sally (Deborah Watling). There, he explains to them what has happened. He concludes with, "It's quite simple. Take a jellyfish, put it in water and you can't see it. That's what happened to me. My reflective index has been lowered to that of theirs."

The situation changes when a rival scientist learns what has happened and attempts to steal Brady's formula for invisibility. The Ministry reverses its decision and allows Peter to continue his research: to find the key to becoming visible again. In the meantime, Peter uses his great advantage of invisibility to assist the British government in its battle against crime. In later episodes, Peter's invisibility becomes known to the general public.

Peter first made his guinea pig, Freddie, invisible. He is called "a state secret" by the Ministry. Before his invisibility was generally known, Peter would appear in public in his bandages. When seen on the street, people would ask, "An accident?" He would respond, "In a way."

Peter has a lab at Diane's home and at Castle Hill. When not working at home he arrives at work at 9:00 A.M. Peter doesn't like to experiment on mice or guinea pigs because they have a different molecular structure. If he is successful at making Freddie visible again, it may take twice as long to find the formula he needs for himself. "I need a human guinea pig," he says, "but the Ministry won't allow it."

Diane, a reporter for the *Morning Star*, lives at 21 Hugo Drive in London. She drives a car with the license plate 2490 PC (later 457 J); Peter's plate reads VON 495 (later VOK 495). When Dee, as Peter calls Diane, goes to the continent, she spends most of her time at the gambling table. Peter's superior is Sir Charles (Ernest Clark, Ewen MacDuff), the British Cabinet

Minister (telephone number Whitehall 7402; later Whitehall 9802). Peter is used by the Ministry "for impossible situations; only something an invisible man can do."

Radar beams can pick up Peter's presence (he is solid although he can't be seen). Baby powder or flour can also make him visible to the enemy (who want Peter "because he is unique; we need him for our experiments"). Before his invisibility was known, Peter had revealed his secret to only one other person — Yolanda (Adrienne Corri), a resistance fighter he helped in the Middle East. Tania (Zena Marshall) became the only girl to kiss Peter in his invisible state when he saved her from kidnappers. When Peter saved the life of Penny Page (Hazel Court), a ventriloquist known as "The Doll with the Dolls," she made a marionette of him she called "Dr. Brady, the Invisible Puppet."

The mystery started in 1958 and is still a mystery today. The identity of the actor playing Peter Brady is unknown. It has been rumored that series producer Ralph Smart played Brady or that actor Tim Turner, who appeared in the episode "Man in Disguise," was actually the uncredited actor behind the bandages. The actor's identity was not only concealed from the public, but also from the cast and crew (the actor wore bandages on the set; his voice was dubbed in after the episodes were shot. This is noticeable at times when the booth recording atmosphere does not match the set atmosphere used for the other actors). Although Peter is supposedly British, the dubbed voice is American (possibly to appeal to U.S. audiences). Based on the story by H.G. Wells.

The original concept for the series exists in an unaired pilot. In it, Peter Brady (same unknown casting) is conducting experiments in optical density when a reactor begins leaking and renders him invisible. Peter is free to leave the lab; in fact, it is known that Peter Brady has become invisible (as television and newspaper reporters constantly annoy him). In this version, Peter lives with his widowed sister, Jane Wilson (Lisa Daniely) and her daughter, Sally (Deborah Watling). It is not possible to predict how this version would have progressed. Peter could have either become a detective and used his invisibility to solve crimes, or follow the series format and continue his work for the British government (which would give him a greater chance of discovering the formula for visibility). There is no ending explaining what Peter would do next. Sydney John Kay composed the theme.

69. *The Invisible Man* (NBC, 1975-1976)

Daniel Westin (David McCallum) is a scientist with the Los Angeles–based KLAE Corporation, who believes it is possible to transfer objects from one place to another via laser beams. After eight months and spending $1.5 million in research, David develops his Tele-Transportation Project.

Although the project is still experimental, Daniel is able to make himself invisible by standing between two laser beams and bring himself back to visibility by injecting himself with a special serum he developed. When Daniel learns that his discovery is being sought by the military, he protests, but fails to convince anyone of his objections. After becoming invisible to escape from the building, Daniel destroys the Tele-Transporter. Later, when he injects himself with the serum, it fails to work and Daniel discovers that he is permanently invisible.

Daniel is able to appear normal looking through the help of his friend, Nick Maggio (Henry Darrow), a brilliant plastic surgeon who has developed Derma Plaque, a lifelike plastic substance that can reconstruct a patient's face. To help Daniel, Nick modifies the process to what he calls Derma Plex, a rubbery liquid plastic that he uses to reconstruct Daniel's face and hands (for his eyes, Nick develops a special set of contact lenses; caps are used for his teeth; and a wig becomes his hair). Daniel, however, must take his new face (the mask) off every six to eight hours to allow his invisible skin to breathe. When Daniel realizes that KLAE Corporation's research center is his only means of finding a way to become visible again, he becomes their chief operative, using his invisibility to tackle dangerous assignments.

Daniel and his wife, Kate (Melinda Fee), live at 40137 Hazleton Road in Los Angeles; 758 CKP is their car license plate. The KLAE Corporation is a highly specialized research center that undertakes government contracts. Walter Carlson (Jackie Cooper, Craig Stevens) is Daniel's superior. Kate calls Daniel "Danny" and Daniel has a lab rabbit named Harvey. Richard Clements composed the theme.

70. *The Invisible Man* (SciFi, 2000)

When petty thief Darien Fawkes (Vincent Ventresca) is caught in the act of robbing an elderly man in a San Diego retirement home, it becomes his third strike and he is sentenced to life without parole in the Bakersfield State Penitentiary. While awaiting transfer to the prison, Darien is approached by his brother, Kevin, a government scientist with the Agency, who feels that he got a raw deal. Kevin offers Darien an option: to become the subject of a secret experiment in lieu of spending his life behind bars. Kevin's experiments on invisibility have been successful on rats; he now needs a human guinea pig.

An artificial gland called Quick Silver is implanted in Darien's brain. When fear is induced, the Quick Silver seals the skin (like Saran Wrap) and makes the subject invisible (the Quick Silver bends light instead of reflecting it). When the subject relaxes, the Quick Silver dissolves and the subject returns to visibility again. The government wants to use Darien to make a difference — to fight for right. This version of the H.G. Wells story adds a drawback to becoming invisible: the procedure drives Darien violently insane and he must be injected with a counteragent every week (which is also how the government continues to get him to do what they want).

Bobby Hobbes (Paul Ben-Victor) is Darien's partner, a government agent who will break the rules and get his hands dirty to accomplish his assignments. Hobbes is smart, street-wise, cynical and jealous because Darien, "the new kid on the block," has a higher security clearance than he does.

A woman, known only as "The Keeper" (Shannon Kenny) is a mysterious figure who represents rationality, control and the established order. She has an uneasy alliance with Darien and is the one who administers the special Quick Silver counteragent that preserves Darien's sanity and keeps his violent temper in check. She is a scientist and intrigued by what has happened to Darien (it appears she may be tempted to learn Darien's secrets and either use them herself or sell them to the highest bidder).

Alexandra "Alex" Monroe (Brandy Ledford) is the Agency's highest ranking agent (a five star A rating). She is an expert in weapons, seduction, surveillance and infiltration. She is in peak physical condition and has something no other agent at the Agency has—her own office. While Alex does help Darien, she has instituted her own personal mission: to destroy Chrysalis, the Agency's arch rival organization. Alex wanted a child without the hassles of a marriage. She used artificial insemination to conceive a child but the fertility clinic that performed the procedure was owned by Chrysalis (they implanted her with a genetically engineered fetus and abducted her son shortly after birth). Alex is now determined to find her son — and destroy Chrysalis for what they did to her.

The Agency is headed by a man called The Official (Eddie Jones). He is a typical bureaucrat and appears to have many hidden secrets. The Official controls all top secret experiments (like the one performed on Darien). He gets others to do what he wants by wielding red tape and paperwork like a Samurai wields a sword. He says, "I'm no mere paper pusher."

Albert Eberts (Michael McCafferty) is the Official's right hand man. He is a by-the-books agent who is often on the receiving end of abuse from Fawkes and Hobbes (they treat him like an annoying kid brother) and from the Official, who constantly tells him "Shut up, Eberts!" when he complains. Eberts is a computer genius and a master of the double ledger (his job is to keep the Agency's paperwork organized and secure); he is also responsible for trying to keep the Agency's meager budget under control despite Fawkes' and Hobbes' tendency to destroy property and cars. See also the two prior *Invisible Man* titles, *The Gemini Man* and *The Invisible Woman*.

71. *The Invisible Woman* (NBC, 2/13/83)

Pilot. Sandy Martinson (Alexa Hamilton) is a reporter for the Washington, D.C., *Daily Express*. Her uncle, Dudley Plunkett (Bob Denver) is a biochemist whose experiments never quite turn out as he expects. One day, while visiting Dudley, Sandy touches a spilled chemical solution that was mixed by Dudley's lab chimp, Chuck. The solution renders Sandy invisible — a situation she must learn to live with when she discovers that Dudley is unable to counteract the mysterious formula Chuck created. While Dudley seeks a way to make his niece visible, Sandy uses her invisibility to solve crimes (she uses makeup, contact lenses, a wig, caps and clothes to appear as a normal girl). Dan Williams (Jacques Tate) is Sandy's boyfriend, a lieutenant with the Washington Police Department; Neil Gilmore (David Doyle) is Sandy's editor. The pilot story finds Sandy attempting to solve a series of art museum robberies. David Frank sings the theme, "She Must Be Around Here Someplace."

72. *Isis* (CBS, 1975–1978)

While on an expedition in Egypt, high school science teacher Andrea Thomas (JoAnna Cameron) uncovers a magic amulet that is possessed of unique powers. The amulet, given to the queen by the Royal Sorcerer, Thuhaupee, endows its possessor with the powers of Isis, the Egyptian goddess of fertility.

Later, when Andrea is at home in California, she decides to use the powers of the amulet to help good defeat evil. Andrea, a teacher at Larkspur High School, is now "The dedicated foe of evil, defender of the weak and champion of truth and justice." Andrea wears the amulet as her necklace. When she holds it and says "O Mighty Isis," she becomes Isis (the skies darken around her, the symbol of Isis is seen and Andrea is magically transformed into the goddess. She is able to soar, has power over animals and the ability to control the elements of earth, sea and sky). As Isis, Andrea wears a white tunic with a short skirt and a tiara that allows her to see beyond her normal vision. Her hair also increases in length —from Andrea's mid-back length to hip length for Isis. Little effort is made to hide JoAnna Cameron's beauty as Andrea. Conservative dress, glasses and a ponytail are the "disguises" Andrea uses to conceal her secret identity. To perform any feat, Isis must recite a special rhyme related to the task at hand; the rhyme most often heard is "O zephyr winds which blow on high, lift me now so I may fly."

Andrea lives at 21306 Baker Place (Apartment 4A) in the town of Larkspur; 555-3638 is her phone number. She has a pet crow (Tut) and drives a red sedan (later yellow, after it is stolen and repainted yellow) with the license plate 69 CBE. Cindy Lee (Joanna Pang) was Andrea's teaching assistant for the first two seasons. Renee Carroll (Ronalda Douglas) replaced her in the final season. Rick Mason (Brian Cutler) was Andrea's friend, a teacher who had a boat called the *Star Tracker*. Last season episodes were broadcast as *The Secrets of Isis*. When broadcast back-to-back with the series *Shazam!*

(see entry), it was titled *The Shazam!/Isis Hour*. Yvette Blais and Jeff Michael composed the theme.

73. *It Takes a Thief* (ABC, 1968–1970)

Alexander Mundy (Robert Wagner) is a cunning cat burglar who is captured in the act but granted a pardon (from the San Jobel Prison) in exchange for performing acts of thievery for Noah Bain (Malachi Thorne), a U.S. government S.I.A. Chief ("Look Al, I'm not asking you to spy. I'm just asking you to steal" as Noah said in the opening theme).

Alexander poses as an international playboy as a cover for his assignments (which include highly dangerous feats of thievery to acquire information the government needs). He is a master pickpocket, escape artist, explosives expert and skilled at posing as someone else. Alexander can recognize style in a thief and "I can spot a pickpocket in the middle of St. Petersburg Square on Easter Sunday." Al, as Noah calls him, is a ladies' man and often dines at the Cheetah Club in Washington, D.C. Alexander lives in a swank penthouse (A) on Washington Square and uses the alias Alexander Barnes, fashion designer, on occasion. Charlotte Brown, nicknamed "Chuck" (Susan Saint James) is the beautiful but "kooky" thief who complicates Al's assignments. Wally Powers (Edward Binns) replaced Noah as Al's superior in last season episodes. Dave Grusin composed the theme. See also *Thieves*.

74. *Jack of All Trades* (Syndicated, 2000-2001)

Pulau Pulau is a small island in the East Indies. The time is 1801. The island is ruled by Governor Croque (Stuart Devenie), the wimpy brother of Napoleon Bonaparte, the emperor of France. Pulau Pulau is also the home of Jack Stiles (Bruce Campbell) and Emilia Smythe Rothschild (Angela Dotchin), secret agents who have been ordered to thwart the French expansion and save Pulau Pulau from French rule.

Emilia works on behalf of the British government and Jack on orders from U.S. President Thomas Jefferson. Emilia is a brilliant scientist and has a secret laboratory in the basement of her home. She has the cover of an exporter and Jack poses as her attaché. Jack lives in that same basement with Emilia's skeleton, Mr. Bones. To protect himself, as well as Emilia, Jack adopts the alias of the Daring Dragoon, a local folk hero who helps good defeat evil (mostly the devious plans of Croque as he sets out to prove to his brother that he is capable of ruling a country). Croque considers the Dragoon a criminal ("He lives to spit in our faces. He strikes and vanishes into the shadows of the night"). He also calls the Dragoon "The Masked Weasel." Although Croque fears the Dragoon, he is more fearful of his wife, Camille (Ingrid Parke), a buxom woman who is seeking to become the ruler of Pulau Pulau.

Jack, as the Daring Dragoon, wears a black mask and hat and a red cape. He rides a horse named Nutcracker and fights for the people—"I am an enemy of all crime." Jack hangs out at a pub called The Drunken Pig and has a scar on his chin (as a young boy in a Catholic grammar school, he cut himself while trying to carve a hole in the stained glass window in the nun's convent) and jokes endlessly about everything. Jack has an eye for the ladies and sizes Emilia to measure 36-24-36 (although she won't admit it). Jack plays the harmonica and is most often skeptical about Emilia's inventions (she tells him "You must have faith in the miracles of science").

Emilia believes that God is a woman and tries to impose her beliefs that Britain is better than America on Jack (Jack tries to prove just the opposite). Emilia takes a daily break for tea time and has invented such military weapons as knock-out gas, ginger spray, bullet-proof clothing (using titanium thread) and a submarine. The secret entrance to Emilia's lab is through the fireplace in the living room (it has an illusionary fire made from candles and mirrors). Emilia is a graduate of Oxford; Jack attended West Point. Jean Claude (voice of Shemp Wooley) is the secret courier, a parrot that delivers messages from the Resistance. When Jean Claude, who sometimes has too much alcohol to drink, departs, he says "Viva La Resistance." As a child, Emilia's father called her "Fu Fu."

Governor Croque is fond of wealth and fancy clothes (that portray him as a "sissy") and secretly runs the Bonaparte family vineyards on the island. He is learning to play the triangle (and after a year of practice he still hasn't mastered it). Croque carries a cow hand puppet with him at all times that he calls Mr. Nippers and is quite fearful of his brother, Napoleon (Verne Troyer), the diminutive (literally here) ruler of France. Napoleon believes Croque is a wimp and will never follow in his footsteps. Napoleon despises the Daring Dragoon and beats on a Daring Dragoon doll to control his rage. Joseph LoDuca composed the theme.

75. *Jane* (Syndicated, 1989)

Jane (Glynis Barber) is a beautiful undercover agent for the British government during World War II. Her mission is to battle the enemies of freedom and protect people who are important to the war effort. Jane is not a superhero; she has no amazing powers and she is not impervious to harm. Her sexuality is her only "weapon" (it appears that the enemy has never encountered a woman as sensuous as Jane and their bedazzlement becomes their downfall). While Jane can fly an enemy plane by instinct, fire complicated weapons accurately by chance, she does have one serious problem: keeping on her clothes. Jane wears only dresses and losing that dress to reveal her sexy lingerie is not her fault: things just happen (for example, snagging the dress on a nail while climbing over a wall; being stranded on a raft and needing a sail). To add further spice for the viewer, Jane often manages to lose her bra (while split second nudity is seen, Jane is most often depicted from the back, side or in a silhouette). Finding outerwear becomes Jane's number one priority (it is typical to hear "By golly Jane, I didn't recognize you with your frock on").

In addition to Jane's lack of wardrobe, the program is unique in its presentation: that of a comic strip come to life. The series is based on the World War II *Daily Mirror* British newspaper comic strip *Jane*. Each scene is a panel and all backgrounds and props (such as cars, trucks and planes) are drawings. Through special effects, the live actors are convincingly placed in comic book–like situations.

All of Jane's serial-like adventures involve her faithful companion, her dog, Fritz, a Dachshund whose thoughts are seen in balloons (the cloud-like areas used for comic book characters' speeches). Fritz wishes he could help Jane "But I'm not a Doberman." When not on assignment, Jane enjoys relaxing in her flat in London. Her superior is Colonel Birdie Ewell (Robin Bailey), a Royal Navy commander who often joins Jane on assignments. He is cared for by Tombs (Max Wail), his ever-faithful butler (Tombs is often displeased with always being so far from home and longs for "the rationing, blitzes and blackouts of England"). When Birdie realizes something has happened, he slaps his forehead and a bell sounds (when Jane gets an idea, a ping is heard followed by a superimposed light bulb over her head). Tombs calls Jane "Miss Jane."

Jane and her boyfriend, Georgie (John Bird), are very much in love and would like to marry but circumstances will not allow it: "There is a war on, man." Georgie, an undercover British army agent, has been assigned to capture Lola and Pola Pagola (Suzanne Danielle in a dual role), deadly spies who are more of a threat to the Allies' success than Hitler. The seductive twins feel that Jane is a threat to their missions and killing her has become their top priority. Detecting that Lola smokes Egyptian cigarettes and Pola doesn't is Jane's way of figuring out which sister is which. Bob Danvers Walker does the narrating; Neil Innes sings the theme.

Jet Jackson, Flying Commando see *Captain Midnight*

76. *Kimbar of the Jungle* (Unaired, 1958)

Pilot. Kimbar (Steve Reeves) is a white "Lord of the Jungle" who, with his pet chimpanzee, Tamba, protects his adopted homeland, Africa, from evil. The program gives no information regarding Kimbar's background and was set to be a fifteen-minute weekly serial. The pilot story, titled "The Lion Men of Tanganyika," finds the Tarzan-like Kimbar helping Joan Winston

(Virginia Hewitt) find her missing father, who disappeared while searching for uranium. Kimbar assists Commissioner Litchfield (James Craven) and can talk to and understand animals. The program ends with "See the next chapter of *Kimbar* on this channel next week."

77. *Knight Rider* (NBC, 1982–1986)

KITT is a Knight Industries Two Thousand black Trans Am car (plate KNIGHT) that was created for the Foundation for Law and Government as a means to battle crime. It is made of a molecular bonded shell and has the serial number Alpha Delta 227529. The car is able to talk (voice of William Daniels) via its ultra sophisticated and elaborate micro circuitry. Microprocessors make it the world's safest car and it has been programmed with a chip to protect human life. KITT has long-range tracking scopes, turbo boost, normal and auto driving and a pursuit mode (that gives it extra speed). KITT is also programmed to avoid collisions and is equipped with a mini-lab and a third stage aquatic synthesizer that allows it to ride on water, a system developed by KITT's engineer, April Curtis (Rebecca Holden). Bonnie Barstow (Patricia McPherson) is a computer whiz and electronics expert who developed SID (Satellite Infiltration Drone), a bugging device that can go where KITT cannot.

KITT's driver is Michael Knight (David Hasselhoff), a former police officer with the 11th Precinct of the L.A.P.D. At this time Michael was known as Michael Long. He wore badge number 8043 and lived at 1834 Shore Road. While on an undercover assignment, Long was shot in the face during a bust that went wrong. Although not expected to survive, he is saved by Wilton Knight (Richard Basehart), a dying billionaire and owner of Knight Industries, who provides life-saving surgery, a new face (patterned after his own when he was young), a new identity, and a mission: apprehend criminals who are above the law. Michael now works for Devon Miles (Edward Mulhare), the head of the Foundation for Law and Government. Michael calls KITT "Buddy." The foundation also has a portable lab that assists Michael in the field: the Roving Knight Industries black with gold trim 18-wheel truck (plate 141 3265; a chess Knight is painted on each side of the trailer).

KITT's prototype was KARR (Knight Automated Roving Robot), an evil car (voice of Peter Cullen) that Wilton designed as the car of the future; he neglected, however, to program it with a respect for human life. KITT's enemy is Goliath, an indestructible truck owned by Wilton's evil son, Garthe (David Hasselhoff). Garthe seeks to kill Michael because he feels he is a living and breathing insult to his likeness. Michael Sloan and Glen A. Larson composed the theme.

A pilot called *Knight Rider 2000* (NBC, 5/19/91) appeared next. When the series ended, Michael Knight quit the Foundation and opened a bass charter service. He now lives in a house by the lake and drives a classic 1957 Chevrolet. It is the year 2000 and the Foundation for Law and Government and Knight Industries have merged to form the Knight Foundation, an independent corporation that helps various police departments enforce the law. Its ultimate weapon is the red Knight Rider 4000, a highly upgraded model of the prior KITT. Although the car is still experimental, Devon Miles (Edward Mulhare), the foundation head, recruits Michael (David Hasselhoff) to help them launch the new car. Michael is bitter when he learns that KITT has been dismantled and his parts sold off. Devon orders the repurchase of KITT's parts; all but one memory chip is recovered and the recycled KITT is placed in the new car.

That missing chip, sold to a trauma center, comes into play when Shawn McCormick (Susan Norman), an officer with the Metropolitan Police Department, is shot at point blank range during a case investigation. The chip is used in an operation to replace the part of her brain that was lost. Shawn, however, has lost all memory of what happened to her and quits when she is assigned to desk duty. She applies for a position at the Knight Foundation and is hired when the new car's designer, Russ Maddock (Carmen Argenziano) discovers that Shawn carries KITT's memory chip in her brain. She is teamed with Michael and the new "Knight Rider" premise was formed (but not sold). Other than wearing a perfume called Desire, no other information is given about Shawn. The Knight Rider 4000 (voice of William Daniels) is a ten million dollar, three liter, 300 horsepower car that can go from zero to 300 mph in a matter of seconds. It runs on nonpolluting hydrogen fuel that is refined from gases emitted by algae fields. KITT now has an aromantor to detect odors and sonic beams to immobilize evildoers. A collision factor analyzer tells Michael when it is safe to run a red light or speed through traffic. Virtual reality allows Michael to look through the windshield to see an enhanced simulation of the road's topography and vehicles in pursuit. Digital sampling allows KITT to analyze voice patterns and duplicate them exactly. The thermal expander heats the air in the tires of fleeing cars and explodes them. Jan Hammer composed "The New Knight Rider Theme." See also *Team Knight Rider*. The program opens with these words (spoken by Wilton Knight): "Knight Rider, a shadowy flight into the dangerous world of a man who does not exist. Michael Knight, a young loner on a crusade to champion the cause of the innocent, the helpless, the powerless in a world of criminals who operate above the law."

Note: *Knight Rider 2010*, a TV movie pilot that aired in syndication (2/4/94) is mistakenly thought to be an attempt to revive the original *Knight Rider* series. It is the story of Jake and Will McQueen (Richard Joseph Paul, Michael Beach), brothers who use a high tech car to battle crime in the year 2010. The car, which has no name, is a 1969 Ford Mustang that is equipped with weapons and a special coating to protect it from fire and bullets. It has an electronic helper — Hannah (voice of Heidi Leich) — that helps Jake and Will uphold the law.

78. *Kung Fu* (ABC, 1972–1975)

Kwai Chang Caine (David Carradine) is a fugitive Shaolin priest who wanders across the American frontier of the 1870s seeking an unknown brother. His travels bring him in contact with people in trouble and through Caine's efforts to help these people, the viewer learns of his past and upbringing through flashbacks.

Kwai Chang was born in China in the 1850s to a Chinese mother and an American father. He was orphaned shortly after but found a home at the Temple at Whonon when he was accepted by the priests to learn the art of Kung Fu, the medieval Chinese science of disciplined combat developed by Buddhist and Taoist monks. It is here that he befriends Master Po (Keye Luke), the blind Shaolin priest who becomes his mentor.

Caine first learns of the Knowledge of the Inner Strength, a disciplining of the mind and body to remove conflict from one's self "to discover a harmony of body and mind in accord with the flow of the universe." A short time later, while in the garden with Master Po, Caine is asked "What do you hear?" "I hear the water, I hear the birds," responds Caine. "Do you hear the grasshopper at your feet?" asks Master Po. "Old man," remarks Cane, "how is it that you hear these things?" "How is it that you do not?" responds Master Po who, from that moment on would always call Caine, his favorite student, "Grasshopper." It is at this time that Caine learns of Master Po's great desire to make a pilgrimage to the Forbidden City.

Caine, now a young man, completes his training. He approaches a cauldron of burning coals and places his arms around the sides. The symbol of a tiger and a dragon are branded onto Caine's arms — the final step to his becoming a Shaolin priest. Caine leaves the temple with the final words of Master Teh (John Leoning): "Remember, the wise man walks always with his head bowed, humble like the dust."

At an unspecified time thereafter, Caine meets Master Po on the road to the Temple of Heaven (which leads to the Forbidden City). As they journey to celebrate Master Po's dream, they encounter the bodyguards of the Royal Nephew. The guards are shoving people aside to allow passage of the Royal Nephew when one is tripped by Master Po. A ruckus ensues and Master Po is shot by one of the guards. At the request of his master, Caine takes a spear from a guard and kills the Royal Nephew of the Imperial House. Before he dies, Master Po warns Caine to leave China and begin a new life elsewhere. The emperor dispatches men to find Caine; the Chinese Legation circulates posters: "Wanted for Murder: Kwai Chang Caine. $10,000 Alive. $5,000 Dead."

As Caine battles the injustice of the American West, he encounters situations that parallel those of his past. Flashbacks show Caine's strict training and the wisdom of his masters as he disciplines himself to face circumstances as a respected Shaolin priest (although Caine is seen killing in the pilot, the series depicts him as humble, just and wise, with a profound respect for human life). Stephen Manley played Caine at age six; Radames Pera plays Caine as a student at the temple; Tim McIntire appeared as Danny Caine, the half-brother Kwai Chang was seeking. Jim Helms composed the theme.

Note: Two pilots aired.

1. *Kung Fu: The Movie* (CBS, 2/1/86). The story, set in 1885, finds the Shaolin priest, Kwai Chang Caine (David Carradine), still roaming the American West and helping people in trouble. Here, however, he faces an enemy of his own: The Manchu (Mako), a mysterious Samurai who has sworn to kill him.
2. *Kung Fu: The Next Generation* (CBS, 6/19/87). After years of wandering Kwai Chang Caine (David Carradine) marries and begins a family. Caine passes the wisdom of his training as a Shaolin priest to his son, who in turn passes it on to his son, Kwai Chang Caine (David Darlow), a 1980s father with a son named Johnny Caine (Brandon Lee). When Kwai Chang deters Johnny from a life of street crime, Johnny sees the wisdom of his father and joins him in a quest to battle injustice. See also *Kung Fu: The Legend Continues.*

79. *Kung Fu: The Legend Continues* (Syndicated, 1993)

"I am Caine. I will help you" are the comforting words heard by people in trouble when they find Kwai Chang Caine (David Carradine), a Shaolin priest and a master of the martial arts who uses his skill to defeat evil. He is also the grandson of his namesake, Kwai Chang Caine, the Shaolin priest of the 1870s who roamed the West helping people in trouble (see prior title).

The 1993 Caine is also the father of Peter Caine (Chris Potter), a detective with the 101st Precinct of the Metro Division of the San Francisco Police Department. It was only recently, however, that the two found each other. In 1978, Peter (Nathaniel Moreau) was a student in a northern California Shaolin Temple where his father, Kwai Chang, was a teacher. Chan (Ernest Abuba), a former Shaolin priest who had been banned from the temple by Caine for his unorthodox ways, returns with a group of mercenaries to strike back — by destroying the temple. In the ensuing explosion, Kwai Chang is injured by a falling beam and Peter is hit by falling stones. Each believes the other has been killed. Both were found alive and rescued but neither knew of the other's existence. Peter was sent to an orphanage (his mother, who always wore a yellow ribbon in her hair and was said to resemble actress Rhonda Fleming, died when Peter was very young). A flashback episode recounts that at the orphanage Peter was befriended by Paul Blaisdell (Robert Lansing), a police captain who became his big brother and paved the way for him to enter the police academy. In a dialogue exchange in a later episode, Peter mentions that he was adopted by Paul and his blind wife, Annie (Janet-Lanie Green). As Peter grew he rejected the ideals of the priests when he realized they were all empty ("I was given ideals like other kids were given ice cream"). It was his interest in television detective shows (*The Rockford Files* and *Hill Street Blues* were his favorites) that also influenced him ("I want to be one of the good guys").

In 1993, Peter is assigned to a case involving Chinese merchants being victimized by extortionists. At this same time, Kwai Chang arrives in San Francisco's Chinatown seeking Ping Hai (Kim Chang), an apothecary known as "The Ancient," who provides guidance for the Chinese community. Like his grandfather, Kwai Chang cannot stand by and do nothing. When thugs threaten Ping Hai, Caine involves himself as does Peter — and father and son find each other.

Kwai Chang acquires a loft in Chinatown and opens Master Caine's Kung Fu Academy. To find Caine, one needs only to ask for him by name. Kwai Chang enjoys eating at the Golden Dragon Cafe and hates to be called "Pop" by Peter ("Don't ever call me that" he tells Peter). Kwai Chang also has an enemy — Chan, who is now a Chinese warlord and still out to settle a score.

Peter lives in an apartment at 7176 Atherton Place and has the car code Baker One-9. He enjoys model railroading as a hobby and drives a car with the license plate BBA 967 (later PTC 555). Peter's favorite hangout is the Agrippa Club ("Best chili and coldest light beer in town" he says). Kwai Chang accepts Peter for his career choice but believes he is "careless, reckless and irritating."

While women were never seen as part of the Shaolin Temple, Caine did allow one woman, Valerie Mitchell (Cali Timmins) to join his northern California temple. She was a spiritual girl who wanted to learn the way of the Masters and Caine permitted her to do so. Jeff Danna composed the theme.

80. *La Femme Nikita* (USA, 1997–2001)

The Spider Web, a massive computer control room, is the center of operations for Section One, a secret U.S. government anti-terrorism organization that is controlled by a mysterious group of people known as Overview. Section One, also called Section, is a ruthless agency that will get any job done no matter what the cost in terms of human life or equipment. Paul W. Wolfe, better known as Operations (Eugene Robert Glazer) is the leader of Section One. Few people in the government know about Section and it is Operations' job to keep it that way. Operations designs Section's missions and acts as a liaison between Section and other government agencies. Operations shows no mercy (or feeling). He makes personal decisions that include who should live and who is expendable. Operations says he "spins the world in my direction" and gives no special treatment to anyone. He was a prisoner of war (he wears a POW pin) and demands strict adherence to the rules and missions he establishes. Coffee or orange juice are his favorite drinks. His main operatives are Nikita (Peta Wilson) and Michael (Roy Dupuis).

There is a gravesite (plot 30, row 8) in an unnamed locale that bears the name of Nikita Wirth. Nikita's mother, Roberta, believes her daughter is alive and refuses to accept what she has been told: her daughter committed suicide. Roberta is right but she can't prove it.

For Nikita it began when she was a young woman and living on the streets. She also happened to be in the wrong place at the wrong time. A police officer was killed and Nikita was mistaken for the culprit. She was tried, found guilty of murder and sentenced to death. One night she was taken from her cell and brought to Section. Here she was offered a choice: work for them as a spy or face execution (Section actually framed Nikita; they required a girl with the dual assets of beauty and an ability to kill). Nikita accepts Section's offer. To convince everyone that Nikita is dead, Section One fakes her suicide (in the feature film on which the series is based, Nikita was high on drugs and killed the police officer in cold blood. This was toned down for TV to reflect a girl who was not a cold blooded killer and is just an unfortunate victim of circumstance).

Nikita, trained by Michael (her mentor), operates under the code name Josephine. She is unhappy being a spy and feels an injustice has been done to her. She is hoping to break away from Section One and create a life for herself on the outside.

Nikita is beautiful and skilled. She is a Level 2 Field Operative and does whatever is necessary to survive. She has long blonde hair, is highly intelligent and not as ruthless as the agency she works for. She is distrustful of most people in Section and has only bonded herself with Michael and agents Walter (Don Francks) and Seymour Birkoff (Matthew Ferguson).

Nikita's greatest weakness is her compassion and sympathy for innocent people. She relies on her fierce instincts (and killer looks) to achieve the covert and extremely dangerous objects of Section (Nikita knows that if she lets her conscience get in the way she will be eliminated). While Nikita is highly trained and dedicated to fighting global terrorism by any means necessary—legal or otherwise—she often violates Section protocol by acting on her own intuition (when she feels a mission is not going as planned). She doesn't want to be treated differently ("It's not fair to the others") and will risk her life to safeguard the United States.

Nikita, a martial arts expert, is capable of handling any weapon and is proficient with explosives. She will not kill unless she has to (when she does kill, it is because she feels the victim deserved it). She constantly defies Operations' orders and he considers this a form of insubordination (so much so that he feels she is preventing him from gaining the power he needs to rise to higher levels and eventually run the organization).

Nikita attended Monroe Elementary School. She collects sunglasses (she is never without a pair) and often carries a bag (such as a backpack or over-the-shoulder) that contains a gun and a cell phone. Nikita also sleeps with a gun under her pillow. Nikita's own words describe her predicament: "I was falsely accused of a hideous crime and sentenced to life in prison. One night I was taken from my cell to a place called Section One, the most covert anti-terrorist group on the planet. Their ends are just, but their means are ruthless. If I don't play by their rules I die."

Michael Samuelle, the Section Supervisor, operates under the code name Jacques. He is a Level 5 Field Operative and in line to succeed Operations. He leads teams in field assignments and says simply "This is Section. Missions are carried out. People die." He performs at full capacity and is capable of getting things done. He is cold and calculating and is seeking the position of Head Strategist. Operations, however, blocks all attempts by Michael to achieve that goal. Operations feels that Michael is the best agent he has and he intends to keep it that way (although when Operations is assigned to duty beyond Section, he places Michael in charge—"You have full operational authority"). The emotionless Michael's greatest weakness is Nikita. His love for her has made him weak and he has attempted to break protocol to save her life during assignments. Michael, like Nikita, is anxious to break away from Section. He did at one point during the fourth season to become a free agent and offer his unmatched anti-terrorism skills to the highest bidder. His affection for Nikita drew him back to Section.

Madeline (Alberta Watson) is a former master strategist for Section who now assists Operations. She can talk to Operations and he will listen, but she cannot interfere. Madeline also oversees the White Room, Section's "Torture Chamber" (for getting information out of prisoners). She is assisted by the speechless and emotionless "Torture Twins," Frick and Frack. Operations and Madeline are said to be like Siamese twins—"They argue, they bicker, but they never separate." While the job of a master strategist is to implement hardware and mission logistics, Madeline's assignment was to deal with the emotional and psychological aspects of an assignment ("It was like a chess game. Human souls were playing pieces"). Unlike Michael or Operations, Madeline does reveal a sense of caring (something Operations dislikes). In her prior position, Madeline was totally dedicated to maintaining tactical superiority over the enemies of Section while remaining indifferent to the loss of human life.

Walter, called "The Weapons Guy," is the only other operative (besides Nikita) who appears human (not stiff or indifferent to everything but their job at Section). He is cantankerous, rather weathered looking and totally honest. While Section agents are skilled and formidable in the field, it is Walter's high tech "gadgets" that save lives and foster successful missions. He is totally dedicated to arming field agents with the maximum protection and is closest to Nikita, whom he considers a friend.

Seymour Birkoff is a cold and cunning computer genius who was responsible for cracking some of the world's most secret and complex codes. He appears to have no life outside of Section and is totally dedicated to his computer terminal. He can break into any computer system and his job is instrumental to Section's operations. His obsession with computers led him to create an artificial intelligence computer that cost him his life (when the computer broke its own programming and threatened to destroy Section, Birkoff sacrificed his life to save those of his comrades—the only people he considered friends). Oreo cookies were his favorite snack.

"The one thing you can't do is defect from Section," says Operations. "If you do you will be found, detained and interrogated." Section One is about missions, data retrieval and verification. Its computers can analyze information from all over the world at the rate of three billion bytes per second. Operatives' eyes have to be glued to the screen and a normal shift runs 12 hours. Green lines across a computer screen means "no problem." A red line means that the program has detected an anomaly—"hit F-1 for details; if it looks serious, flag it. Highlight transmit. That sends it to level two where it will be evaluated." Mark Snow composed the theme. The series is based on the French film *La Femme Nikita* with Anne Parillaud as Nikita (Bridget Fonda starred as Nikita in the American film version, *Point of No Return*).

81. *Level 9* (UPN, 2000–2001)

Level 9 is a state-of-the-art Washington, D.C.–based government agency that has only one function: to solve the cases that other law enforcement agencies cannot. It is composed of the government's best cyber operations experts and is tailored to form a rapid response strike force against high tech criminals. The agency is fully mobilized and can go anywhere and anyplace. Level 9 is so advanced that they go beyond fingerprints and credit card use tracking. Their computers can tap into any security camera at any location to match mug shots instead of fingerprints through their ultra high tech programs. Their field equipment is also super high tech—from camera glasses to computerized door and safe unlockers. Level 9 is also closely guarded; if any of their equipment should fall into the wrong hands, a new breed of evasive criminal will be born.

Annie Price (Kate Hodge), a former FBI agent with a remarkable arrest record, heads Level 9. She can think like a computer and figure out a criminal's next move. She has an amazing attention to detail and remarkable recollection abilities. She is rarely distracted by her duties, but is troubled by a computer hacker she dubbed "Crazy Horse." Annie believes Crazy Horse is responsible for half the crimes in America. Her nightmare began in 1998 when, as an FBI agent, she was assigned to a case involving a hacker who broke into a bureau computer and demanded $50 million or he would jam their computers. Annie believed it could be done, but her superiors felt it was a hoax and ignored her — and the hacker. The supposed hoax jammed the computers and now demanded $100 million. With air traffic control computers out and to avoid the worst aviation disaster in history, the ransom was paid. The public never knew what happened — but Annie knew and she hopes with the technology of Level 9 to find Crazy Horse. Annie resides at 4063 Mark Place.

The program has seven regulars, but virtually no background information is given. While there are a number of agents who work for Level 9, only two are featured: Wilbert "Tibbs" Thibodeaux (Michael Kelly) and Joss Nakano (Susie Park). The featured hackers are Sosh (Kim Murphy), Roland Travis (Fabrizio Filippo), Jargon (Esteban Powell) and Jerry Hooten (Romany Malco). The hackers, who use screen names, are not permitted to reveal their names; Sosh was the exception. Her real name is Margaret Perkins and she lives at 118 Victoria Street. Although it is prohibited for these hackers to personally involve themselves in a case, Sosh broke that rule to catch a killer of young women. She dropped her "nerdy" job look to become a sexy trap for the killer. She was successful (after almost getting herself killed) and severely reprimanded for doing so by Annie. Travis, Jargon (a *Star Trek* fanatic) and Hooten appear to do nothing else but sit at a computer terminal in bad lighting (the glare of the monitor illuminates the scene). Brian Tyler composed the theme.

82. *Lois and Clark: The New Adventures of Superman*
(ABC, 1993–1997)

When the story opens, Clark Kent (Dean Cain) is seen driving to Metropolis, a city of 12 million people, seeking a job as a reporter for the *Daily Planet*, "The world's greatest newspaper" (according to its editor, Perry White). Clark is, in reality, Kal-El, the only known survivor of the planet Krypton. Before Krypton exploded, the infant Kal-El's parents, Jor-El and Lara (David Warner, Eliza Roberts), placed him in an experimental rocket and programmed the ship to land on Earth, a planet Jor-El knew to be inhabited. On May 17, 1966, the rocket lands in Smallville, Kansas, and the child is found by Jonathan and Martha Kent (Eddie Jones, K Callan), a childless farm couple who raise him as Clark Kent. As the child grows, the Kents become aware of the fact their son is no ordinary boy. He demonstrates abilities of amazing strength, keen hearing and amazing eyesight. Clark attended Smallville High School and worked as a reporter on the *Smallville Press*. He yearned to travel to Metropolis but couldn't figure out how to be Clark Kent and secretly uses his powers to help mankind. The solution comes when Clark ruins his clothes during a story investigation. He tells his mother "that I need a costume." Martha makes several (ones that resemble Captain America, Batman, the Flash and tiger leotards) before coming up with the red and blue one (she uses the blankets that were originally wrapped around Clark. The symbol S was a part of those blankets).

In Metropolis, Clark meets with editor Perry White (Lane Smith) but is not given the job because Perry believes Clark does not have what it takes to be a reporter on his paper. However, when Clark shows initiative by writing a story about plans to demolish an old theater (where Perry once worked as an usher), Clark is hired. He then meets his co-workers: Lois Lane (Teri Hatcher), Jimmy Olsen (Michael Landes, Justin Whalin) and Cat Grant (Tracy Scoggins).

Clark first uses his powers in costume to save a space shuttle called the *Prothesis* from an attempt by the evil Lex Luthor (John Shea) to destroy it. Also aboard the shuttle is Lois Lane, who snuck aboard hoping for a great story. What she found was a bomb. Clark comes to her rescue and saves the shuttle. He flies her back to the Daily Planet building. As he flies off, Cat asks Lois, "What does the S on the chest of his costume stand for?" Lois replies "Super ... man." Hence the name.

Clark resides at the Apollo Hotel at 344 Clinton in Metropolis. Clark revealed that his middle name is Jerome and won the Keith Award for Investigative Journalism (presented by the Metropolis Press Club) in 1994 for his story "A Retirement Home Scandal." Kryptonite, the green fragments from his planet's explosion, is the only substance that can take away Superman's powers and ultimately destroy Clark. While Lex is his most diabolical enemy, Clark also faced the wrath of the sinister Newtritch sisters, Lucille and Nell (Shelley Long, Mary Gross). Nell and Lucille had developed a laser beam made from red Kryptonite (a rare, concentrated form). The device backfired when aimed at Superman and transferred his powers to Lois, making her Ultra Woman, a gorgeous female superhero who dressed in a purple costume with a green cape. Lois became herself again when Clark tricked the sisters into using the ray to transfer Ultra Woman's powers to them. It is in this episode ("Ultra Woman") of 11/12/95 that Lois proposes to Clark. They marry on October 6, 1996, and honeymoon in Hawaii. A prior marriage between Clark and a cloned Lois occurred on February 11, 1996. Here Lex, in an attempt to destroy Superman, kidnaps the real Lois and creates a clone to get close to Clark (Lex knows there is a connection between Clark and

Superman and hopes his Lois will find out what it is. She does, but is disabled before she can reveal it to Lex).

Lois Lane is a reporter for the *Daily Planet* ("The best damn investigative reporter I've ever seen" says Perry). She attended Metropolis High School (where she was called "Lo Lo") and lives in Apartment 105 at 6304 Chambers Place with her teenage sister, Lucy Lane (Elizabeth Barondes, Roxana Zal). Lucy looks out for Lois and says "Lois, I just want you to meet a super guy." Lois has an account at the Metropolis Mercantile Bank and has written a novel called *The True and Amazing Adventures of Wanda Detroit* (in the episode of 2/11/96, Lois bumps her head, develops temporary amnesia and assumes the identity of her fictional, sexy alter-ego, Wanda Detroit). Lois is gutsy and can fight and take care of herself; unfortunately, she has a tendency to jump into the pool before looking to see how deep it is. "It's the only way I can do it" she says. "To get the respect of others, I always get involved in my stories." Lois also won the Keith Award for Investigative Journalism in 1991, 1992 and 1993. Phyllis Coates (TV's original 1952 Lois Lane), then Beverly Garland played Lois's mother, Ellen Lane; Harve Presnell was Lois's father, Dr. Sam Lane. Lois has one bad habit—"I like to pig out at the Fudge Castle."

Perry White, the former mayor of Metropolis, is the *Daily Planet*'s nononsense editor. He is an Elvis Presley fanatic and shouts "Great Shades of Elvis" when something upsets him. Perry is also an ordained minister of the First Church of Blue Suede Deliverance ("I was at Graceland, saw an ad for it on the back of a match cover and the rest is history"). Perry's competition is the *Metropolis Star*.

Jimmy Olsen, the paper's photographer, also likes to dabble in investigating. Perry calls him "Jimbo" and he calls Clark "C.K." Catherine Grant, called Cat, is the paper's society editor/gossip columnist (she is also called "Cat Monger"). She attended Metropolis University and lives in a swank apartment at the Metropolis Hilton.

Lex Luthor is worth $20 billion and runs a company called LexCorp (a front for his illegal and sinister activities). He appears to have his hands in everything and claims he can't be caught because "Evidence separates the criminal from the successful businessman." Lex also runs LexTel Communications, the city's television station.

Jay Gruska composed the theme. See also *The Adventures of Superboy*, *The Adventures of Superman*, *The Adventures of Superpup*, *Smallville* and *Superboy*.

83. *The Lone Gunmen* (Fox, 2001)

John Byers (Bruce Harwood), Melvin Frohike (Tom Braidwood) and Richard Langly (Dean Haylund) are the Lone Gunmen, publishers of *The*

Lone Gunman, a Tacoma Park, Maryland–based computer oriented newsletter that attempts to expose conspiracies, injustices and criminal activities on all levels of society (the paper is singular in name because it is the only such paper in America). They are backed financially by Jimmy Bond (Stephen Snedden) and allies with Yves Adele Harlow (Zuleikha Robinson), a mysterious woman who seeks to profit from any misfortune she can find (most often cases involving the Lone Gunmen as they set out to right wrongs).

John, Melvin and Richard are, for the most part, geeks or computer nerds who use whatever means they can to bring criminals to justice. Most people believe *The Lone Gunman,* which was started in 1989, is about hunting and fishing. "It's not," says Melvin; "it's called *The Lone Gunman* because we tell the stories others refuse."

Melvin was born in Michigan and feels he's the one "who risks his butt doing all the outside work while Langly is behind the scenes" (at his computer in their rundown green, white and rusty van; plate TSD 596). Prior to becoming one of the Gunmen, Melvin ran the Frohike Electronics Company (his sideline was selling illegal cable boxes). He is short, unshaven, loves women, but is not a great talker. He is also sarcastic (but sensitive) and is the photographic and surveillance expert of the group. He invented a device called "The Frojack," a gizmo for tracking cars.

John, born in Idaho, has the middle name of Fitzgerald (he was named after President John F. Kennedy; his parents had originally intended to name him Bertram, after his father). John previously worked for the FCC (Federal Communications Commission) helping the government capture hackers. He quit when he discovered the government was conducting controlled experiments on civilians and concealing the truth about these activities from the public. He is always neatly dressed (suit and tie) and often uses the government's Freedom of Information Office for research. He is a topnotch hacker and the group's self-proclaimed leader. *Gentle Ben* was his favorite TV show as a kid.

Richard, born in Virginia and raised on a farm, has the nickname "Ringo." He loves hard rock music (he is always seen wearing a hard rock T-shirt) and feels he has the computer skills "to become a dot com gazillionaire." Richard also sold illegal cable boxes but quit when he became entangled in a conspiracy to keep the truth from the American public. He has long hair, is paranoid and serves as the communications expert on the team.

Jimmy is a former pro football player whose life savings is providing financial backing for the floundering newsletter. Jimmy helps "because you guys fight for causes I wanna help." In addition to liking the Lone Gunmen's morality, Jimmy wants to become one. He's described as "a dumb lunk with a big heart whose special skill is being able to count to 20 in Mexican." His favorite TV show is *America's Most Wanted.*

Yves (pronounced Eve) doesn't work for anyone: "I only take their money." She is an expert computer hacker and speaks with a British accent. Her past is unknown, but she is ruthless and will kill if she has to. She wears Ferrari red lipstick and always signs her name in an anagram for Lee Harvey Oswald. While each of the Lone Gunmen likes her, they fear her when she appears at their doorstep (they hope she is not there to kill them). Yves profits off everything she does — whether she works with the Lone Gunmen or against them.

The program is a spinoff from *The X-Files* wherein the Gunmen did little more than give information to agents Mulder and Scully. A fourth season episode, "Memento Men," gave them a chance to work with Mulder in the field. Two additional episodes followed — "Unusual Suspects" and "Three of a Kind" before they received their own short-lived series.

84. *The Lone Ranger* (ABC, 1949–1957)

"I wear a mask in the cause of justice," says the Lone Ranger (Clayton Moore, John Hart), a mysterious, early west lawman "who cut a trail of law and order across seven states, forcing the powers of darkness into the blinding light of justice." It was, however, a series of tragic events that transformed Texas Ranger John Reid into the Lone Ranger and teamed him with Tonto (Jay Silverheels), the Potawatomi Indian who saved his life. It began with an assignment to capture Butch Cavendish (Glenn Strange), the head of the notorious Hole in the Wall Gang. Butch, however, proved too clever for the Rangers to capture. At Bryant's Gap, a canyon about 50 yards wide and bound by cliffs, a team of six Texas Rangers are ambushed by the Cavendish gang and left for dead. Later that day Tonto, who had been hunting for food, finds a lone survivor of the attack — John Reid. Tonto brings Reid to the shelter of a small cave and begins nursing him back to health. As Reid recovers, he recalls Tonto as the Indian he befriended as a child. Years ago, when Tonto was a child, his village was raided by renegade Indians. His parents were killed and Tonto was left for dead. A young John Reid found Tonto and helped him recover from his wounds. It was at this time that Tonto called Reid "Kemo Sabe" (translated as both "Faithful Friend" and "Trusted Scout").

There is a small patch of grassland that lies amid the rocks broken by countless years of wind and storm. On that land are six graves, each marked by a crudely constructed cross to represent the Texas Rangers who were killed — Captain Dan Reid (John's brother), Jim Bates, Jack Stacey, Joe Brent and Ben Cooper. The sixth cross bears the name of John Reid — put there by Tonto to convince Cavendish that all the Rangers had been killed; to conceal the fact that one Texas Ranger had lived to avenge the others — the Lone Ranger.

To conceal his true identity, Reid fashions a mask from the black cloth of his brother's vest. At first, Reid and Tonto posed as outlaws to enable them to apprehend the Cavendish gang — some of which were hanged, others imprisoned. Once their goal was accomplished, they became a force for good — "Wherever you find a wrong to be righted, that's where you'll find the Lone Ranger" (Reid says also that "keeping my identity a secret makes the pursuit of outlaws easier").

The Lone Ranger's trademark is the silver bullet — a precious metal that reminds him to shoot sparingly and to remember the high cost of human life. The silver comes from a mine Reid inherited. Jim Blaine (Ralph Littlefield) is the old miner who works the Ranger's silver mine. George Wilson (Lyle Talbot) is the Ranger's secret banker in Border City who exchanges the silver for money.

To help in a capacity other than that of the Lone Ranger, Reid uses various disguises to assist without arousing suspicion (for example, Professor Horatio Tucker, the smooth-talking medicine man; Don Pedro O'Sullivan, the Swede; Juan Ringo, the Mexican bandit; and the Old Timer). Reid has a distinctive voice and it is sometimes a threat to the Lone Ranger's true identity when he goes undercover ("There's something about that voice," an outlaw would say, "but I can't place my finger on it"). Tonto also goes undercover to help Reid (usually as Red Dog, an outlaw Indian). The Lone Ranger wears a double holster; Tonto carries a holstered gun (left side) and knife (right side). Later episodes feature Dan Reid (Chuck Courtney), John's nephew, as an assistant.

The Lone Ranger rides a white horse named Silver (whom he calls "Big Fella"); Silver is a one-man horse and will only let Reid or Tonto ride him. Scout is Tonto's horse; Victor is Dan's horse. Tris Coffin played Captain Dan Reid; David Leonard is Father Paul, Reid's friend, the padre at the San Brado Mission.

As the show's theme, "The William Tell Overture" by Rossini plays, an announcer's voice is heard: "A fiery horse with the speed of light, a cloud of dust and a hearty Hi-yo Silver! The Lone Ranger! With his faithful Indian companion, Tonto, the daring and resourceful masked rider of the plains led the fight for law and order in the early West. Return with us now to those thrilling days of yesteryear; the Lone Ranger rides again!"

The program's closing is just as famous. While there were many variations, a typical sequence would begin with a man saying "You know those two men saved my life and I didn't even get the Masked Man's name." A sheriff would respond, "A name's not important. It's what a man does that counts. No man has done more for the west than ... The Lone Ranger." As the Ranger and Tonto ride into the sunset, "Hi-yo Silver" is heard. The series is based on the radio program created by George W. Trendle.

85. *Los Luchadores* (*The Wrestlers*) (Fox, 2001)

Lobo Fuerte (Maximo Morrone) is a masked wrestler who entered the ring 15 years ago and quickly became a world champion. Other than being of Spanish descent, his background is a mystery and no one knows where he came from. He has taken up residence in Union City and devotes his life to battling injustice. He fights in the wrestling ring for entertainment "and evil outside of the ring so the people of Union City can sleep at night." Turbine (Levi James) and Maria Valentine (Sarah Carter) are fellow wrestlers who assist Lobo in and out of the ring.

Lobo, Maria and Turbine never remove their masks ("A luchadore's mask is like a reflection of his soul"). Cheating is unthinkable to Lobo, even if it costs him a victory in the ring. He has never lost a fair fight. Lobo is called "the unbeatable champion of the ring" and wrestles for the Lucha Librae Federation at the Union City Sports Arena. Lobo has his headquarters (and appears to live) on the top floor of Lobo Towers, a building that also houses the latest in crime fighting and crime detecting equipment. A man known only as Laurant (Arthur Burghardt) commands the equipment. Laurant is a former wrestler who trained Lobo, Maria and Turbine to use their abilities to battle evil. "The Lobo Destroyo" is the move that Lobo's opponents fear the most. Lobo drives a car called the Lobo Ride, which is capable of amazing maneuvers; it can go from "blast to megablast" in a matter of seconds (when Lobo revs up his car, the camera focuses on a Hawaiian bobbing doll that does the hula when the car moves). Ramon's Mask Shop makes the masks for Lobo, Maria and Turbine. The team assists the Metro Police Department and Lobo says, "A Luchador does not stand for destruction; a Luchador stands for justice." Lobo wears a blue, red and silver costume with a symbol of a wolf head on his shirt (the same that is on the front of his car). Lobo's car is stored at the top of Lobo Tower. When activated, it descends the side of the building like a roller coaster. The Tornados is the restaurant-bar frequented by the team.

Turbine is a young, energetic wrestler with a passion for fast cars and motorcycles. He rides a super-powered motorcycle and is called "Speed Boy" by Maria (villains call him "that speed freak"). He and Lobo met in the ring and became quick friends. Turbine is a mechanical genius and designed many of the gadgets he and Lobo use in their high speed chases (for example, the wrist com, which Lobo uses to communicate with Laurant in the field). Turbine wears a red shirt that has an image of an engine discharging flames.

Maria is an up and coming enmascarada (masked wrestler). She likes speed, action, excitement and defeating the dark forces of evil. In the ring Maria is called "The Battling Beauty" and "The Girl with a Twirl"; Turbine calls her "The Blonde Brainiac." Maria takes skydiving lessons and likes white orchids. She drinks herbal tea to relax and checks her fingernails after a fight with baddies to make sure she didn't chip her fingernail polish. Maria was profiled as "The Young Luchadora" by a magazine called *Union City Sports*. Maria often wears a red blouse that says "Chicks and Boys." Her mask has eye cutouts that resemble hearts. Maria, Lobo and Turbine are on a softball team called Team Lobo.

86. *The Magician* (NBC, 1973-1974)

Anthony Blake (Bill Bixby) is a magician who performs regularly at the Magic Castle in Los Angeles. He is also a man who devotes the wizardry of his craft to help people and bring criminals to justice. Blake's friend, Max Pomeroy (Keene Curtis) believes that Anthony lived the book, *The Count of Monte Cristo*. Ten years ago, while performing in South America, Blake was arrested on trumped up espionage charges and imprisoned. Blake managed to escape and took with him his cellmate, a dying old man. The old man, grateful for the few months of freedom Anthony provided for him, left him a considerable fortune, money he now uses, in part, to help people who are unable to turn to the police for help.

Blake drives a white Corvette (plate SPIRIT) and originally lived on his plane, the *Spirit*, before moving into a home at 315 Vinewood in Los Angeles. The plane, I.D. number N13555, is a Boeing 737 piloted by Blake's friend, Jerry Anderson (Jim Watkins). Blake's wrists bear the scars of prison shackles; he can read people (their faces, eyes and hands) and knows when they need help. He doesn't, however, interfere; he enlists in a cause and uses magic to foil evil.

Max is an internationally known magazine and newspaper columnist who provides important information and contacts for Blake. He lives in San Francisco (at 36 Beverly Drive) in a private residence that also serves as his headquarters. Max is continually in battle with his editors for daring to touch what he writes and has unconventional views on "money, sex, marriage, religion, soccer and cheese." Max keeps a microfilm record of all photos taken of him during his world travels. He is not married but lives with a charming woman named Lulu (Joan Caulfield). When Max relates a story about Blake's prison experiences he begins with "Have you ever read the book *The Count of Monte Cristo*? In a sense, Tony has lived it." In the pilot episode, Bill Bixby was Anthony Dorian and Jim Watkins was Jerry Wallace. Patrick Williams composed the theme.

87. *Mandrake* (NBC, 1/24/79)

Pilot. The College of Magic is a society wherein the secrets of ancient Egyptian and Chinese magic is preserved. It was established in the twelfth century when the hordes of Genghis Khan swept the Western World and began destroying the wizards and their lore. The few who survived established the college. Each decade a youth is selected and taught the ancient secrets. One such student is Mandrake, brought to the college by his father, a former student, and taught the wizards' lore by Theron, the Master of Magic. Mandrake (Anthony Herrera) becomes greater than his master. Mandrake, however, wishes to use his abilities to help mankind by battling evil. He is granted permission to leave the valley and assigned an assistant, Lothar (Ji-Tu Cumbuka), his servant at the college. The pilot story finds Mandrake and Lothar attempting to apprehend a madman who is blackmailing a businessman for ten million dollars. Morton Stevens composed the theme.

88. *Manimal* (NBC, 1983)

Jonathan Chase (Simon MacCorkindale) is a professor of behavioral science at New York University who helps the police solve crimes as a member of the Special Investigative Division of the N.Y.P.D. (also called the Special Police Task Force). Chase, described as "wealthy, young and handsome," is also "champion of the world's darkest mysteries"—secrets of transmutation that divide animal from man—and man from animal, that he uses to help him defeat evil.

The secret of transmutation (now called morphing on shows like *Sheena*) is not revealed. In the opening theme it is briefly shown that Jonathan's father (Don Knight) had traveled the world to learn the secret. It was in Africa that his quest came to an end. After being taught the powers by an unknown tribe, he passed the secret on to Jonathan when he was a young boy. No further information is given.

Jonathan now lives in a brownstone on Manhattan's Lower East Side. His home is quite unique in that it contains a miniature (and possibly illegal) zoo (tigers, lions, ostriches and snakes can be seen in elaborate glass cases; he referred to one of the tigers as "Bart"). As himself, Jonathan has a gift of super hearing; as the animals he becomes, he not only possesses their appearance and abilities, he retains his own thinking processes to control his actions. If, however, Jonathan should be injured while in his transformed state, he will retain that injury when he becomes human again. For Jonathan to become an animal he must think about an animal (in *Sheena*, Sheena must look into the eye of the animal she becomes; see *Sheena*). Jonathan most often becomes a black panther (to spy on criminals) and a hawk (to follow suspects from the air). While the special effects are quite good, the same two sequences are used in each episode (the film is simply reversed to show Jonathan becoming human).

Brooke McKenzie (Melody Anderson) is Jonathan's partner, a police detective with the Special Task Force (in some episodes she is called "Officer";

in others "Detective"). She is aware of Jonathan's power (he transformed into the panther to save her life) and has vowed to keep his secret. She and Jonathan dine most often at the Four Seasons Restaurant. Tyrone C. "Ty" Earll (Glynn Turman, Michael D. Roberts) is Jonathan's friend, a former corporal during the Vietnam War, who now assists him. He too is aware of Jonathan's secret and calls Jonathan "J.C."; he also feels "I'm rushing into the jaws of death" when on a case and Brooke says "Let's go."

Jonathan drives a car with the plate AJA 611; Brooke's license plate reads 549 YAP. Jonathan's most intriguing case was that of finding the identity of a girl raised by wolves in India (Laura Cushing played the role of Sarah Evers, the Wolf Girl). Paul Chihara composed the theme.

89. *Mann and Machine* (NBC, 1992)

It is "the near future" in Los Angeles. It is a time when laser fences protect crime scenes and the San Francisco Giants football team has become the Tokyo Giants. It is also a time when manmade robots assist live police officers in upholding the law. Sergeant Eve Madison (Yancy Butler), a highly sophisticated and beautiful robot, is such a creation — and the partner of Bobby Mann (David Andrews), an L.A.P.D. detective whose former partner, Warner, was "a bucket of bolts lab-created robot" that was put out of commission by a bullet.

Eve was created through the Artificial Intelligence Program by Dr. Anna Kepler (Samantha Eggar). Eve's body is a combination of plastic compounds and alloy metals. Her brain functions like the human brain and is capable of assimilating artificial material. Anna says "Eve can learn to be human — she just needs the opportunity." Eve is the prototype for a project called the Protector, "the future partner of every police officer." Eve is highly advanced in technical terms, but emotionally she is very young (the age of a seven-year-old girl). She has the deductive reasoning of Sherlock Holmes and a genuine sense of humor (she will laugh if she hears something she thinks is funny). Eve eats, sleeps and daydreams. Her eyes are capable of emitting laser beams; her tears are a lubricant and she can speak 40 languages.

Eve watches television to learn about things she feels she will not learn on the job (*The Three Stooges* and *The Mod Squad* are her favorite shows). But the only way Eve can really grow is to experience life — "the good, the bad and the ugly of it." Eve's brain downloads directly to the advanced A.I. Work Station Computer in her apartment (1407 at the Metropolitan Hotel). She can access any computer through a special earplug adapter.

Eve believes she was built for only one purpose: to enforce the law. She is a retrieval expert — "I'm an information specialist. There isn't a mainframe in the country that I can't access." When first built, Eve was transferred to the San Francisco Bay area (she was created in Danville in the Silicone Valley) and scored the highest marks on the sergeant's exam. Eve has a worm collection and her lucky number is the algebraic term "pi."

Bobby has to fill out a special report on Eve's actions after each case. He is divorced and the father of an unseen daughter. He is a Catholic and was an altar boy when he attended grammar school. Bobby has A-positive blood and a dog named Rose. Bobby and Eve are with the Metropolitan Police Department; Captain Margaret Claghorn (S. Epatha Merkerson) is their superior. Mark Mothersbaugh composed the theme.

90. *M.A.N.T.I.S.* (Fox, 1994-1995)

Dr. Miles Hawkins (Carl Lumbly), a biochemist and owner of Hawkins Laboratories, is the third richest man in Ocean City, California (locale later changed to Port Columbia). He grew up in the Lincoln Heights section of the city and graduated from M.I.T. at the age of 18 on a genius scholarship. During the Los Angeles riots of 1991, Miles is shot in the back and crippled by a cop who opposed his beliefs. Miles, however, is unable to prove he was shot by a police officer because the bullet taken from his back is found not to come from a police issued gun. Embittered, the wheelchair bound Miles decides to fight back by waging a war on crime. With the help of his colleague, Dr. John Stonebreak (Roger Rees), they create the Hornet (later called the Exo-Skeleton), a black suit that gives him a bug-like appearance, but enables him to walk. In technical terms, the suit is a M.A.N.T.I.S. (Mechanically Augmented Neuro Transmitter Interception System) and with the calling card of the praying mantis, Miles brings criminals to justice as the mysterious Mantis. As the Mantis, Miles will not use a gun (because of what happened to him). His weapon of choice is a paralyzing dart to stop enemies in their tracks ("They thaw out in an hour").

Beneath Hawkins Labs (also called Hawkins Technologies) is the Seapod, an undersea lab Miles built for ocean farming before he was shot, that now serves as his secret base of operations. His modes of transportation are the *Chrysalid* (a ship) and his black car, the Mantis. Unlike the Green Hornet, who was wanted by the police, Mantis works with them (especially Lieutenant Leora Maxwell [Galyn Gorg] of the Special Investigation Unit of the Port Columbia Police Department).

Miles was originally assisted by Dr. Amy Ellis (Gina Torres), the associate medical director of the Ocean City Police Department. Yuri Barnes (Bobby Hosea) is the newscaster for KNCW-TV, Channel 8, who not only reports on Mantis activities, but helps Miles with vital information. Amy and Yuri each possess a "Mantis Broch"—a special phone to contact Mantis— "Just dial M."

Taylor Savidge (Christopher Gartin), a messenger boy for Iron Horse Couriers, is also Miles's legman (Taylor witnessed a Mantis operation and became intrigued. He saw Mantis enter a van and tracked it down, not knowing that Miles was Mantis. Taylor knows the streets and the people and persuaded Miles to let him join the team; it was at this time that Miles revealed to him that he was Mantis). When asked who he is, Miles (as Mantis) responds simply "Just one man trying to help." Joseph LoDuca composed the theme.

91. *The Master* (NBC, 1984)

John Peter McCallister (Lee Van Cleef) is a master of the Ninja (the Japanese art of disciplined combat). It was after his service with the Army Air Corps during World War II "that I found myself in Japan. The tranquility and the people kept me there" (in another episode, John mentions he found his way to Japan after the Korean War—where he was a prisoner of war and managed to escape via a motorcycle). Thirty years later, John receives a letter from a girl named Terry McCallister, a daughter he never knew he had. The letter contains a picture of Terry next to an airplane and a postmark from a U.S. city called Ellerston. With these clues, John leaves Japan and begins a quest to find Terry (who is never seen. It is not explained how Terry knew John was her father or how she even knew where or how to contact him. Also not explained is why Terry keeps moving from city to city, always leaving moments before John arrives or is about to find her. Terry is depicted as a "Jill of All Trades," holding jobs as a pilot, model, waitress, dancer, etc., who always manages to get her picture in some newspaper or magazine. It is from these articles that John finds the clues he needs to track Terry).

John was a member of a secret Ninja society. His decision to leave Japan betrays his destiny and he is sentenced to die by the members of his sect (who fear he may reveal their secrets). Okasa (Sho Kosugi), a former student of John's who is now a Ninja master, has sworn to find John and kill him. John mentions that Terry's mother is Laura Kennedy, a woman he met in Korea. They had a two month relationship "and then one morning she was gone."

Max Keller (Timothy Van Patten) is a young drifter who earns money by competing in motorcycle races and doing odd jobs (he won the 1983 Clearwater Scramble and rides a motorcycle with the number 88 on it). He is also impulsive and plunges headfirst into situations to help people in trouble (especially beautiful girls). Max is in a bar in Ellerston when the local sheriff begins to harass John for carrying a concealed weapon (his Samurai sword). Max steps in, helps John fight off the sheriff and they escape in Max's customized van. While talking, Max learns of John's quest and volunteers to help. Max, intrigued by John's fighting abilities, asks only that John teach him the art of the Ninja. John was taught the secrets of the Ninja so he could pass them on as his master did to him—"What good is a Ninja teacher without a student" he says as he agrees to teach Max. Together they begin a quest to help people threatened by unscrupulous characters while searching for John's long-lost and elusive daughter, Terry (several episodes drop the daughter searching element to focus on John and Max as they help old friends of John's who are in trouble. How they managed to find and contact John, especially now that he is on the road, is not explained).

John is the only occidental American ever to become a Ninja. He carries with him a black suitcase that contains all his worldly possessions. John can scale buildings, catch an arrow in his hand, knock people out with a pinch to the temple and remain still for long periods of time ("slow the heartbeat and listen to the senses"). When engaging in a fight with the enemy, John tells Max "Smokescreen and illusion. Give them what they expect and they will believe it. We do what they don't expect." He also says "I have a knack for getting into places people don't want me." John wears a medallion around his neck ("the symbol of my household") that Okasa needs to bring back to Japan to prove to his masters that John is dead. When John wears his black Ninja outfit, it is Sho Kosugi who performs the stunts for Lee Van Cleef.

John says "I'm a cantankerous old man who's lived a lot of years alone." Max, who's "lived a lot of years on my own too" says "Cops and I don't snuggle up together" and "I often leave a bar through the window." Max travels with his pet hamster, Henry, and both like classical music (Henry is fond of Mozart). If John and Max are involved in a high speed chase, Max warns John not to let Henry fall out of his cage—"He gets crazy when he's mad." When Max attempts John's "temple pinch" and it doesn't work, he throws a punch—"Sometimes the old fashioned right hand comes in handy." Bill Conti composed the theme.

92. *The Mighty Morphin Power Rangers* (Fox, 1993–1996)

Zordan (played by David Fielding; voiced by Bob Manahan) is an interdimensional being caught in a time warp. Rita Repulsa (Soga Machiko, Barbara Goodson, Carla Perez) is an alien, intergalactic sorceress who has set her goal on conquering the Earth. To protect the Earth (as well as the rest of the universe from Rita), Zordan decides to form an elite team of soldiers to stop her. He chooses Jason (Austin St. James), Trini (Thuy Trang), Zack (Walter Jones), Kimberly (Amy Jo Johnson) and Billy (David Yost), teenagers who attend the Cultural High School in a city called Angel Grove (the Angel Grove Gym and Juice Bar is their hangout).

The teens are magically transported to Zordan's headquarters, the Power Station. There, they meet Alpha 5 (Romy Sharff, Donene Kistler), Zordan's robot aide (voice of Richard Wood, Katerina Luciani) and are told about Rita and why they are needed. Each of the teens is an expert in the martial arts and each is given a special gift to enable them to fight Rita and the monstrous creatures she sends to destroy the Earth.

Jason receives the Power Sword; Kimberly, the Power Bow; Trini, the Power Dagger; Billy, the Power Lance; and Zack, the Power Axe. Each of these weapons can be combined to form a super power weapon. They are next given extraordinary powers drawn from the earth — the Power of Dinosaurs. Jason, bold and powerful, controls the Tyrannosaurus Rex; Zack, clever and brave, controls the mastodon; Kimberly, graceful and smart, controls the pterodactyl; Billy, ancient and wise, controls the Triceratops; and Trini, fearless and agile, controls the saber tooth tiger. Each is then given a magic belt that contains a sphere shaped object called a Morphin. If they encounter trouble, they can raise their Morphins to the sky and say the name of their dinosaur. This transforms them into the Power Rangers. As Power Rangers they will have access to a universe of power to unleash fighting machines called Zords. Just as the five of them work together, so do their Zords (which use the Power of the Dinosaurs to form gigantic Mega Zords. The dinosaurs are mechanical — miniatures and computer animated — and each ranger controls his dinosaur from the inside).

As Power Rangers, they must observe three rules or lose their amazing abilities: "Never use your power for personal gain; never escalate a battle unless Rita forces you; keep your identity a secret — no one may know you are a Power Ranger."

Each of the Power Rangers is given a costume that completely hides their identity ("The outfits are cool and everything," says Kimberly, "but my hair gets tangled up inside the helmet"). The concealing costumes also serve another purpose: to allow producers to use the original Japanese version fight scenes in the American adaptation (voice dubbing is easily achieved but fight scenes that take place in Japan do not match well with newly shot footage for the American version. Not only do skyscraper building styles not match, but the Japanese writing that appears on buildings in one scene, disappears in another. The buildings that surround the Angel Grove Park [where most fight scenes take place] also differ when footage from both countries is edited together).

Unlike most successful series that continue with the same characters and plots, *The Mighty Morphin Power Rangers* changed character and story ideas frequently, making for a complex (if not confusing) history to compile. The first change occurs in the episode of 11/8/94 ("The Power Transfer"). Here Jason Leigh (Austin St. James), Trini Quan (Thuy Trang) and Zack Taylor (Walter Jones) are chosen to represent Angel Grove in the World Peace Summit in Switzerland (the summit is a group of teens from around the world who become ambassadors to help save the world). Kimberly (Amy Jo Johnson) also leaves. She was originally depicted as a girl with low self-esteem that she felt came from her small breast size. She wore a 34A bra but wanted to become a 34C. She experimented with falsies and found courage that she never knew she had. She also found she did not need a large bust size to be herself. She always feared hurting herself and quit to pursue her dream of becoming a world class gymnast.

Zordan, who lives in a glass-enclosed chamber, chooses new rangers to replace them: Rocky (Steve Cardenas), Katherine (Catherine Sullivan), Aisha (Karan Ashley) and Adam (John Busch). Also assisting them is Tommy (David Jason Frank). Zordan equips them with new powers called Dragon Zords. Rocky powers the Dragon Thunder Zord; Aisha, the Griffin Thunder Zord; Adam, the Lion Thunder Zord; Billy, the Unicorn Thunder Zord; and Katherine, the Firebird Thunder Zord. These Zords combine to form the Thunder Mega Zord (which they use to battle monsters sent by Rita).

When Rita fails to complete her mission and destroy the Power Rangers, she is replaced by her emperor, Lord Zedd (Robert Axelrod). Although Lord Zedd did exactly what Rita did — create monsters to destroy Angel Grove, he complicated matters by reversing time and giving us another set of Power Rangers — the Young Power Rangers — the second listing of rangers who were turned into preteen children but fought as Power Rangers: young Katherine (Julia Jordan), young Adam (Matthew Sakimoto), young Aisha (Sicilly), young Rocky (Michael J. O'Lasky II), and young Tommy (Michael R. Gotto). To help the Young Power Rangers, Zordan enlisted the help of the Alien Rangers of Aquitar: Delephine (Rajia Baroudi), Auria (David Bacon), Cesta (Karim Prince), Tidens (Jim Gray) and Corcos (Alan Palmer). The Young Power Rangers became adult again when Zordan found the Zeo Crystal and reversed time. This also brought about a new version called *Power Rangers Zeo* (1996). Here, Lord Zedd destroys Zordan's base of operations, leaving the Power Rangers without a leader. While sifting through the wreckage of Command Center, the powerless rangers find the Zeo Crystal, which restores not only their powers, but Zordan, Alpha and Command Center. The Zeo is the next step in the Power Rangers' fight against evil. Next, Aisha is replaced by Power Ranger Tanya (Nakia Burrise) and Billy steps down as a ranger to help Alpha because the Zeo Crystal can only power five rangers. The teens are given new powers called Zeo Zords. Katherine and Tanya, Zeo Zords One and Two, control fire power; Rocky and Adam, Zeo Zords Three and Four, control the driving force of the sphinx and Taurus the Bull; and Tommy, Zeo Zord Five, controls flight, the power of the Phoenix. When combined, they control the awesome Zeo Zord.

Each of the Power Rangers also had a colorful costume: Jason (red), Trini (yellow), Zack (black), Kimberly (pink), Billy (blue), Adam (green), Rocky (blue), Tommy (green, then white, then red), Aisha (yellow), Katherine (pink), Tanya (yellow).

When it is realized that Lord Zedd has also failed to destroy the Power Rangers, he is replaced by Mondo, the Machine King, his wife, Queen

Machina, and their robot son, Prince Sprocket — all attempting to conquer the Earth as it is the last planet they need to control the universe. These characters, from the Japanese version, are not credited.

In 1998, a version called *Power Rangers Turbo* appeared (wherein the rangers used high tech, transformable cars). The Power Rangers of this version are Tommy (Jason David Frank), Kat (Catherine Sutherland), Ashley (Tracy Lynn Cruz), Tanya (Nakia Burrise), T.J. (Selwyn Ward), Justin (Blake Foster), Adam (Johnny Yong Bosch), Cassie (Patricia Jaa Lee) and Carlos (Roger Velasco).

A new incarnation appeared in 1999 as *The Power Rangers in Space*. Here the Power Rangers, guided by Alpha (Donene Kistler), use the U.S. space shuttle to battle the evils of their arch enemy, Rita Repulsa (Barbara Goodson) and her new cohorts: Divatox (Hilary Shepard Turner), and Astronomus, the Princess of Evil (Melody Perkins). The Power Rangers are Ashley (Tracy Lynn Cruz), Cassie (Patricia Jaa Lee), Carlos (Roger Velasco) and T.J. (Selwyn Ward). Lord Zedd (Robert Axelrod) also returns to wreak havoc on Angel Grove City.

Power Rangers Time Force (2000–) became the latest version of the series. Here the Power Rangers are Time Force Officers and live together in the Clock Tower, which is haunted by the ghost of its former owner, Walter Brown. The Rangers are able to travel through time to battle the evils of Ransik (Vernon Wells) and Nadria (Kate Sheldon). The new rangers are Red Ranger Wes (Jason Faunt), Yellow Ranger Katie (Deborah Estelle Phillips), Pink Ranger Jen (Erin Cahill), Blue Ranger Lucas (Michael Copon) and Green Ranger Trip (Kevin Kleinberg). Circuit, the mechanical owl, is their computer link to the future. Wes's father, Mr. Collins (Edward Albert) runs Bio-Lab; Eric (Daniel Southworth) is head of security for Bio-Lab. Shuki Levy composed the theme. Based on the Japanese series *Xyu Rangers*, which began in 1976.

Note: The USA network attempted a low budget version of *The Power Rangers* called *Tattooed Teenage Alien Fighters from Beverly Hills*. In the 1994-95 series, teenagers Gordon Healey (Richard Nason), Laurie Foster (Leslie Danon), Drew Vincent (K. Jill Sorgen) and Swinton Sawer (Rugg Williams) are recruited by the alien Nimbar (Glenn Shadix) to fight Emperor Gorganus (Ed Gilbert) and his horde of evil monsters. The teens each have a tattoo of the Zodiac (hence the title): Gordon is Taurus; Laurie, Scorpio; Drew, Centaur; and Swinton, Apollo.

93. *Mr. Terrific* (CBS, 1967)

As the theme music plays, an announcer tells us that "A scientist both wise and bold set out to cure the common cold. Instead he found this power pill which he said most certainly will turn a lamb into a lion, like an eagle he'll be flying; solid steel will be like putty, it will work on anybody. But then 'twas found this potent pill made the strongest men quite ill; so the secret search began to find the one and only man. What they found made them squeamish for only Stanley Beemish, a weak and droopy daffodil could take the special power pill. When he took the pill specific, it made him the most prolific, terrific, Mister Terrific!"

Stanley Beemish (Stephen Strimpell) and Hal Waters (Dick Gautier) are partners in Hal and Stanley's Service Station on Northeastern and Wyoming streets in Washington, D.C. Dr. Ned Reynolds (Ned Glass) is the government scientist who accidentally invents a source of incredible energy he calls the Power Pill. Barton J. Reed (John McGiver) is the head of the Bureau of Special Projects, a government organization that seeks to use the pill as a secret weapon in the battle against crime. Henley Trent (Paul Smith), Reed's assistant, has been ordered to conduct a search to find a man capable of taking the special pill. His search leads him to the gas station where Stanley is persuaded to test the pill. Seconds after taking the pill, Stanley is transformed into the invincible Mr. Terrific. Stanley is sworn in as an agent and begins a double life: private citizen and "the U.S. government's secret weapon against crime."

Stanley's Mr. Terrific costume is a jacket with wing-like sleeves (which he flaps in order to fly), a pair of goggles and a scarf—all of which he stores in his locker at the gas station. In addition to flying, the pill endows Stanley with incredible strength and speed and an immunity to harm. Stanley is also not your typical superhero. He has difficulty flying and landings become a problem (he can't navigate). He has difficulty finding assigned targets when airborne (his scarf constantly obstructs his vision) and he has a difficult time adjusting to his secret alias.

When Mr. Terrific is needed, Reed sounds the Purple Alert. Before each assignment, Reed gives Stanley a box with three pills (one base pill that lasts one hour and gives Stanley the strength of 1,000 men, and two booster pills that last ten minutes each). The pills, which are specially candy coated so Stanley will take them, always wear off at crucial moments and Stanley often has to wrap up cases as his ordinary, bumbling self. Three pills is the maximum Stanley can take in one day. Reed's phone number is National 8-0397. Hal, a ladies' man, introduces himself to women by saying "Hi, I'm Hal, gas station attendant, snappy dresser and lady killer." He lives in what he calls a bachelor pad near the station on Wyoming Street. Gerald Fried composed the music theme.

In the original, unaired pilot version, titled _Mr. Terrific_, Stanley Beemish (Alan Young) is a shoe salesman for Mr. Finney (Jesse White) and is recruited by the Chief (Edward Andrews) of the Office of Special Assignments, to test a pill that transforms him into Mr. Terrific, a daring but misadventure-prone crime fighter. Stanley did not have a girlfriend in the series, but in the pilot he was in love with Gloria Dickinson (Sheila Wells). Lyn Murray composed the original theme.

94. *Model by Day* (Fox, 3/21/94)

Pilot. A beautiful fashion model known only as Lex (Famke Janssen) has posed for *Playboy* magazine, appeared in lingerie ads and performed in TV ads as the Prism Lipstick Girl. When her best friend and roommate, Jae Davis (Traci Lin) is injured in a carjacking incident, Lex decides to find the attackers when the police fail to come up with any suspects. To conceal her true identity, Lex dons black leather shorts, a black bra-like top, a hood and dark glasses. Her success in capturing Jae's attackers earns her the name "The Vigilante Vixen" by the press. When an amateur video of the mysterious crime fighter is shown on TV, she is called Lady X (the name that sticks) when it is shown that the shoulder straps of her bra cross like an "X" in the back. In addition to setting up the potential series storyline, the pilot story finds Lex attempting to catch a copycat Lady X—a girl who is killing people she feels are too evil to live (Lex never kills and only helps the police because she feels they are not doing their job. Lex uses her expertise in karate to subdue culprits then handcuffs them for the police to arrest). Master Chang (Clark Johnson) is Lex's martial arts teacher; Mercedes (Sean Young) is Lex's agent; Shannon Tweed plays Shannon, the imposter Lady X. Lou Mantle composed the theme.

95. *Modesty Blaise* (ABC, 9/12/82)

Pilot. Modesty Blaise (Ann Turkel) is a beautiful, former criminal turned mysterious adventurer who uses her seductive powers and expertise as a thief and martial arts expert to help people in trouble. She is assisted by Willie Garvin (Lewis Van Bergen), a man whose life she once saved, and often assists Sir Gerald Tarrant (Keene Curtis), head of the S.I.B. (Special Intelligence Bureau). The pilot story finds Modesty attempting to stop Debbie DeFarge (Carolyn Seymour) from pulling off a computerized heist of Wall Street. Sab Shimono is Wong, Modesty's houseboy and chauffeur; Douglas Dirkson is Jack, Tarrant's aide. Based on the motion picture of the same title with Monica Vitti in the title role.

96. *Mutant X* (Syndicated, 2001)

Genomex is a secret branch of U.S. Intelligence that was established to remake the world by creating perfect men and women through genetic manipulation. Adam (John Shea), a chief biochemist at Genomex, felt enormous guilt for going against the laws of nature when "genetic mistakes" were created. When he is unable to convince his superior, Mason Eckhart (Tom McCamus) of his beliefs, he breaks loose from Genomex and forms Mutant X, a group of rogue, genetically enhanced agents, who believe Genomex is wrong and now fight to protect the world from Eckhart and his plan to use his creations as super agents for covert missions.

Shalimar (Victoria Pratt), Emma DeLauro (Lauren Lee Smith), Jesse (Forbes March) and Brennan Mulray (Victor Webster) are Adam's main operatives (born mutants). They are in constant battle with Eckhart's G.S.A. (Genetic Security Agency), a branch of Genomex that is responsible for retrieving their former children, now the agents of Mutant X. Despite the genetic enhancement, the Genomex creations are not super heroes. Adam believes it is important for these people to realize this and not let their powers take command of their mind, body and soul. Some of these "children" do believe they are god-like and battling them becomes a dangerous challenge for Adam — to rescue them from Eckhart, yet not kill them in the process. The Russians have developed an experimental weapon called the Pushka HB5-7, which can neutralize mutants (a setting of A7Z-41 is the firing sequence to reverse the effects of the ray).

Shalimar is very territorial and very protective of the people she loves. She has extraordinary martial arts skills and the ability to move (including jumping and leaping) at an accelerated rate. Shalimar also uses an additional "power" — her sexuality, to distract the enemy. She was the first mutant Adam rescued (he found her in a sleazy hotel and she hadn't eaten for five days). She was unsure of what happened to her body but felt she could trust Adam. She likes her steak medium rare; her eyes turn cat-like when she gets angry. She is also reckless and leaves herself wide open to attack.

Emma has the gift of inner vision (as Adam calls it). She first realized this when she was five years old (she was attending a rock concert with her parents and became separated from them. She closed her eyes, was able to visualize their whereabouts and found them. Five years later her parents "ran off" and she was raised in an orphanage). Emma's telepathic powers are only the beginning. She has "enormous untapped powers" that have yet to surface (in the second episode, a new power, the ability to sense the feelings of others, emerged). She can also kill by thoughts (for example, choking someone to death simply by thinking it). Emma worked as a salesgirl and used her gifts to manipulate her customers into buying her products (the ability to affect people by controlling their emotions). She "is cautious and can be read like a book" says Adam.

Brennan controls electricity. He can discharge such bolts from his fingers and create a ball of energy by placing his hands in a circle. The electricity also gives Brennan incredible strength and a split second burst of invisibility to pass through solid objects. Brennan grew up on the streets and learned to cope with his powers at an early age (using it to commit petty crimes).

Now, as a part of Adam's team, he hopes to put his past behind him and begin a new life. He calls the Mutant X hideout (secured in a secret mountain location) "Sanctuary."

Jesse is the sensitive one of the group. He can control objects by concentrating and can create a force field around his body to absorb the impact of a bullet. He is a computer whiz and skilled in the martial arts.

Adam has given each of his associates (whom he considers his children) a special ring to signify them as Mutant X (each ring is a key to their unique DNA strain. The ring allows Adam to monitor his people in the field. The rings also act as a two-way communicator and allow contact with Adam at home base no matter where they are). Proxy Blue is a computer generated female image that reports news events. Lou Natale composed the theme.

97. *My Secret Identity* (Syndicated, 1988–1991)

"You'll never guess my secret identity, who's on the inside hangin' out … sometimes this double life gets out of hand, but it's all in a day's work for Ultraman." The theme is referring to Andrew Clemens (Jerry O'Connell), a 14-year-old boy who is secretly Ultraman. The superhero came into being when Andrew wandered into the lab of his neighbor, Dr. Benjamin Jeffcoat (Derek McGrath) and was hit by blue gamma rays from an experimental machine. Andrew, now endowed with extraordinary powers to foil evil, named himself after his favorite comic book character.

Andrew lives at 43 Meadow Drive in Briarwood, Canada, with his divorced mother, Stephanie (Wanda Cannon) and sister, Erin (Marsha Moreau); 555-7175 is their phone number (while their address is said to be "43," "51" can be seen on their house). Andrew attends Briarwood High School and hangs out at Jerry's Burger Barn. He worked as a parking lot attendant for Le Club Restaurant and started a pirate radio station called Gonzo Radio (90 on the AM dial). In the opening theme, Andrew is seen reading a comic book called *Journey Into Mystery* and as a kid had pet fish named Diane and Mimi.

Andrew keeps a diary of his activities as Ultraman (which he hides in a white box under his bed). Dr. Jeffcoat, called "Dr. J" by Andrew, is the only other person who knows about Andrew's abilities (capable of running over 100 mph, bursts of strength, and flying with the aid of aerosol spray cans developed by Dr. Jeffcoat. When Andrew points the spray nozzle down, it lifts him into the air; by manipulating the spray's direction, he can fly). Andrew wears no special costume (his street clothes double as his Ultraman clothes) and when he feels he needs some special ability to complete a task, he says "By the power of Ultraman" (but it rarely works). Dr. Jeffcoat is the fourth smartest man in the world. He lives at 45 Meadow Drive and maintains his lab at a constant temperature of 75 degrees Fahrenheit. When away from the lab, Dr. J carries an Albert Einstein lunchbox. He attended Briarwood High and Broadhurst University. At Briarwood High he played a tree in the school's production of *A Tree Grows in Brooklyn* and was called "Sparky" for blowing up the science lab. He writes articles for *Quantum Quarterly* magazine, has a boat (The *Kahuna*) and drives a 4×4 (plate 592 BAJ). His phone answering machine tone is 440 cycles and he has been working on a device called the Positive Ion Container for four years ("I work on other stuff on weekends").

Stephanie is a real estate agent for R.E. Realty (555-6555 is their phone number. In some episodes it appears that Stephanie is a freelance agent). She drives a sedan (plate 483ENX; later, CFN 148) and does volunteer work at the York Community Center. Erin attends Briarwood Elementary School and is forbidden to play in a dangerous area called the Ravine (open manhole covers to sewers can be seen; surprisingly, no one has seen fit to close them — not even Andrew after he rescued Erin from one of them). Erin loves horseback riding and lamb chops is her favorite dinner. *Morning Heat* is her favorite TV soap opera and Hide and Seek is her favorite game. She also likes to play Grownup with her best friend, Melissa (Gema Zamprogna).

Ruth Shellenback (Elizabeth Leslie) is Dr. J's nosy neighbor (at 47 Meadow Drive). She is an Elvis fanatic (although in another episode she mentions Tony Orlando as being her favorite singer) and has a dog named Elvis. In her youth, she was a member of the Bruise Brothers roller skating team and is currently a member of the Women's Helicopter Action Rescue Team. Fred Mollin composed and sings the theme.

New Adventures of Wonder Woman see Wonder Woman

New Adventures of Zorro see Zorro

98. The New Avengers (CBS, 1978-1979)

An update of *The Avengers* (see entry) that continues the British government's battle against diabolical villains as seen through the assignments of John Steed (Patrick Macnee), the Ministry's top agent, and his partners, Purdy (Joanna Lumley) and Mike Gambit (Gareth Hunt).

The dashing and debonair John Steed is basically the same character as in the prior series. He believes that Britain rules and has sworn to defend her against all her enemies. While he still lives at 3 Stable Mews in London, he also owns a country estate called Steed's Stud (where he entertains the ladies and breeds horses. It also serves as his headquarters for issuing orders to agents). Steed is still a master of Old World charm and courtesy, still carries his sword-in-the-handle umbrella, and still wears bowler hats (which have been lined with metal). Steed, Purdy and Gambit work well as a team because they have mutual respect for each other.

Purdy, named after the most respected and expensive shotgun in the world, was born in India. Because her father, a Brigadier in the British army, was constantly on the move, Purdy had an international education and attended such private schools as La Sorbonne and Roedean. She studied dance and eventually became a professional ballerina. After her father's death (shot as a spy after joining the Secret Service), Purdy became a Ministry agent. She is well versed in the martial arts, especially the French technique called Panach (fighting with the feet). She is an expert on firearms and is capable of driving any car (she has her own TR7 sports car). Purdy lives in a basement flat in London that is decorated in the Art Deco style.

Mike Gambit has a long and distinguished military background. He spent time in the British army (Parachute Regiment) and was later with the Special Air Services. He acquired knowledge of guerrilla warfare when he worked as a mercenary in Africa and the Middle East. He also wrestled crocodiles in the Congo and became a professional race car driver before becoming a Ministry agent. Gambit drives a Jaguar XJS, is an expert in unarmed combat, and a skilled pilot, shot and archer. Every morning at the crack of dawn, a sparrow Mike named Charlie, comes to his window sill "to sing his heart out and wake me up." Laurie Johnson composed "The New Avengers Theme."

99. *The New Ghost Writer Mysteries* (CBS, 1997-1998)

Camela Gorrick (Charlotte Sullivan), Emily Robson (Erica Luttrell) and Henry Strickland (Kristian Ayre) are eighth graders at Jesse Owens Junior High School in the Fort Greene section of Brooklyn, New York. While they appear to be ordinary 13 year olds, they are actually amateur detectives who solve crimes in and around their school. What makes this trio so unusual is that they receive help from Ghost Writer, a silver (sometimes gold) entity that fights for right.

Ghost Writer appears as a round, glowing object that can only be seen by Camela, Emily and Henry. Although the series is an update of *Ghost Writer* (see entry), it is not explained what Ghost Writer is or how it attached itself to the teenagers. Ghost Writer cannot speak. It communicates through words and has the ability to rearrange any printed matter to get its message to Camela, Emily and Henry. They, in turn, can communicate with Ghost Writer by writing their instructions on a piece of paper or typing it into a computer. Ghost Writer reads the message (seen in a glowing light) then does what it is asked (usually to investigate as Ghost Writer can get into places no one else can — like computer circuits, inside sealed envelopes). Once the Ghost Writer Team (as they call themselves) have the facts they proceed to investigate and eventually solve crimes. When writing to Ghost Writer, the team uses its nickname, GW.

Camela, called Cam, lives at 207 Fulton Street. She is an amateur photographer and loves sports (she is a member of the school's volleyball team; her mother, a lawyer, was a star sprinter on her high school track team). Cam is fashion conscious and buys knockoffs of designer labels at Clothesworld.

Emily, called Em, lives in a brownstone at 61 Bridge Street. She is the daughter of a district attorney and a reporter for the school's newspaper, *The Ratler*. While Em is not as fashion crazy as Cam, she accompanies Cam on her shopping sprees to get her mind off her problems.

Henry, called Strick, lives in a cluttered, basement-like area he calls "The Batcave" (no mention is made of Strick's parents or exactly what or where "The Batcave" is. He does have a very expensive computer, but it is in surroundings that are difficult to decipher). Strick was a troubled kid and served time in Juvie Hall (for what is not stated). He appears to have good grades and helps Cam and Em as an unofficial member of the school paper (Cam appears to be the paper's photographer in some episodes while in others she just seems to be helping Em get the facts for stories).

Em, Cam and Strick hang out at Fort Green Pizza, where they order the large $9.99 pizza and "the one who is up always gets the pizza" (brings it to the table). Marvin Dolgay and Alex Khaskin composed the theme.

100. *NightMan* (Syndicated, 1997–1999)

Jonathan Dominus (Matt McColm), better known as Johnny Domino, is a musician who plays sax at the House of Soul, a jazz club in Bay City. Johnny is the son of ex cop Frank Dominus (Earl Holliman) and secretly NightMan, a daring crusader who helps the police, especially Lieutenant Brianni Branca (Jayne Hertmeyer), capture felons.

Johnny's life changed one day when a sudden, freak storm erupted and engulfed him in a strange light that endowed him with the ability to hear evil (the crimes others are planning to commit). Johnny's first such "hearing" is that of a terrorist planning to bomb a communications peace conference. Johnny, scheduled to play at the conference, alerts authorities about a potential problem, but is too late: a bomb explodes and Johnny takes the full impact of the explosion. Doctors are amazed that he is not only alive, but apparently unhurt.

At Bay City Hospital, Johnny meets Raleigh Jordon (Derek Webster, Derwin Jordan), a U.S. government scientist who developed a military defense system being sought by the enemy. Because Johnny saved Raleigh's life at the conference (by clearing people out before the bomb exploded), the terrorists are now seeking to kill both Raleigh and Johnny. Raleigh tells Johnny, "You won't be safe unless you join me."

At a warehouse, Raleigh shows Johnny the reason why he is being sought: for a defense system of the future that will be sold to the highest bidder. These include a bulletproof suit with advanced stealth capabilities, a lens with targeting scanners, a laser beam, and an antigravity belt.

As they speak, terrorists approach the warehouse. Johnny and Raleigh escape, undetected, by using what will be called the NightMan gear, to fly over their heads.

Johnny lives at 1943 Ward Court in an apartment over the House of Soul. This becomes his and Raleigh's base of operations (later episodes find Raleigh as the club's manager). NightMan, called "Evil's worst nightmare," is said to be "tuned to the frequency of evil" and "hunts the evil that walks in the dark." To make it appear that Johnny and NightMan are two distinct people, Raleigh has devised a special holographic image that projects a 3-D image of Johnny performing on stage at the House of Soul. This gives Johnny the perfect cover to convince everyone he is not NightMan. Brianni, the daughter of an army master sergeant, has a photographic memory (when it comes to criminal case details) and suspects Johnny is NightMan but can't prove it. Johnny drives a car called the Plymouth Prowler. The car, painted "Prowler Purple," has 17-inch tires in the front and 20-inch tires in the rear. It has Auto Stick Transmission (a stick shift without the clutch) and a 3.5 liter 24 valve single overhead cam V6 engine (generates 214 hp at 5,850 rpm and 221 pounds per square foot of torque at 3,100 rpm). The car has dual stainless steel exhausts, a steering-wheel-mounted tachometer, and a six disc CD changer.

Johnny's greatest enemy is Kieran Keyes (Kim Coates), an evil billionaire who runs the Keyzar Corporation, a computer software company he uses as a front for his plans to control the world. Keyes has invented "The Ultra Web," a computer program that digitizes users and transports them to a cyberworld (where he controls them for his own sinister purposes).

Helping NightMan on occasion is Laurie Jarvis (Deanna Milligan), an ex-cop Johnny calls "NightWoman." Laurie suffered a spinal injury that crippled her. After experimental spinal surgery at the Leander Institute in Switzerland and with the aid of an energizer suit she developed, Laurie can walk. The suit also gives her special powers to battle evil. Laurie uses her costume to help her as a detective for her company, Woman Trouble ("I help women in trouble"). The series is based on the comic book of the same name.

101. *Once a Hero* (ABC, 1987)

There is a world beyond the third dimension called Comic Book World. Here, the characters live their lives based on the adventures drawn by their creators. Abner Bevis (Milo O'Shea) is one such cartoonist whose character, Captain Justice, is the heroic savior of Pleasantville. Captain Justice is, in reality, beloved schoolteacher Brad Steele (Jeff Lester). There are good citizens in Pleasantville, like the lovely Rachel Kirk (Dianne Kay) and her sister, Tippy Kirk (Dana Short). But there is also the Captain's arch enemy, the evil Max Mayhem (Harris Laskawy). Captain Justice, also called "The Crimson Crusader," wears a red costume with blue gloves and a blue triangle on his chest with a gold *CJ* in the center. He does not have a cape but possesses the ability to fly, is immune to harm, has incredible strength and infrared X-ray vision.

Abner has been drawing the comic strip for 30 years and is running out of fresh ideas. When he begins using plots from earlier adventures, people begin to lose interest and sales plummet. In Pleasantville, Captain Justice is about to save Rachel and Tippy from Max when he begins to fade. "This is no good," the Captain says. "We are dependent upon the affections of people in the real world. As long as we remain in their hearts, we are safe. Should they start to forget us, we simply fade away. I've seen this happen before. Remember Andy Hardy? They're now forgetting Captain Justice. I won't let this happen. I'll go to the third dimension and force them to remember." To do this, Captain Justice flies through the Forbidden Zone into the real world.

As Captain Justice seeks Abner in Los Angeles, the ruler of Comic Book World, the Great and Magnificent One, summons Gumshoe (Robert Forster), a 1940s-style private detective, and hires him (at $40 a day plus expenses) to find Captain Justice and bring him back — "If he stays he will experience a fate more horrific than a superhero can endure. He should spend his remaining days here, with dignity and honor."

Gumshoe drives through the Forbidden Zone via his 1940s roadster (plate IB 429) and finds Captain Justice. He learns the Captain, whom he calls "Cap," met with Abner and discovered the publisher, Pizazz Comics, is planning to discontinue Captain Justice because "the kids don't go for it like they used to." Cap tells Gumshoe he is determined to change that and save Pleasantville — "I must get people to remember me." The gruff looking but softhearted Gumshoe agrees to help Cap. They begin a crusade against crime and are soon heroes. Emma Greely (Caitlin Clarke), a reporter for the Los Angeles *Gazette*, writes the stories: "Captain Justice Does It Again. But Who Is He?" The *Comic Book News* reports that Pizazz Comics has reinstated Captain Justice and Pleasantville is saved.

The Captain always tells the truth and his moral code prevents him from killing anyone. He eats only peanut butter and jelly sandwiches with milk — except when he attends a ball game at Pleasantville Stadium — "Then it's two hot dogs and lemonade." Captain Justice has received a key to the city 103 times and "has a bad habit" (as criminals say) of showing up in the nick of time to save Rachel and Tippy. (Rachel always exclaims "Captain Justice"; Tippy cries "The Crimson Crusader"). Lobsterman (Trevor Henley) assists the Captain; Victor Lazarus (Richard Lynch) is another villain seeking to do away with the Captain. In the real world, T.J. North (Adam West) plays Brad Steele/Captain Justice on the TV series *Captain Justice*. Jim Turner played Captain Justice in the unaired pilot version. Dennis Dreith composed the theme.

102. *The Others* (NBC, 2000)

The Others is a group of gifted individuals who help people threatened by ghosts or the supernatural. It was founded by Elmer Greentree (Bill Hobbs), a famous medium who uses his home (at 36 Pleasant Way) as the group's headquarters. Elmer, now 83, was ten years old when he had his first vision in 1927; "I called them nightmares."

Marian (Julianne Nicholson), Ellen (Melissa Crider), Miles (John Billingsley), Professor Warren (Kevin J. O'Connor), Albert (John Alyward) and Mark (Gabriel Macht) are the six strangers who provide a gateway to the other side.

Marian Kitt was born in Iowa and is the youngest member of the group. She is a college student (at Massachusetts University) and is gifted but doesn't want her gifts: ability to channel spirits through her body; visions (which she considers bad dreams) and sleep walking (often bringing her to the scene of a crime or leading the Others to a suspect in a case). She lives in a dorm room at 1137 Normandy Avenue, Apartment 214.

Ellen Satori is a psychic and considers herself a spirit medium. She has a private psychic service business (on South Street) and charges $60 an hour. She is the quiet one of the group and only intervenes when she receives a message from the other side.

Miles Ballard is a professor of folklore and mythology at the University (Marian is one of his students. He brought her into the group after she witnessed the spirit of a girl who was killed in her dorm room). Miles "sees things that aren't there" but can't quite interpret what he sees.

Albert is blind and uses his sixth sense "to see the other world" (which the viewer sees in the form of negative images).

Dr. Mark Gabriel is a first year resident at Saint Joseph's Hospital. He is an impasse and can see what is ahead (he has suffered from migraine headaches and dizzy spells all his life but has now learned "to look past that pain" and into the world beyond). Professor Warren keeps a video record of the group's investigations and sets them up with people they need to help. He teaches at the University and is working to improve his self image. See also *Poltergeist: The Legacy*.

103. *The Owl* (CBS, 8/3/91)

Pilot. Alex Leibet (Adrian Paul) is a man of mystery. He does not need to sleep. He possesses the ability to see in the dark, accelerate his speed and scale walls—abilities he uses as the Owl, an around-the-clock vigilante who dispenses his own brand of justice. How Alex obtained his powers is unknown. The only thing known about Alex is that he is seeking to destroy a man named Hutchins (Alan Scarfe), an enemy from his past who killed his family in a car bombing that was meant for him. For a price, Alex will help anyone with a wrong to right. His weapon of choice is an air dart gun that contains a knockout pellet. When Alex needs help, he calls on the services of two people whose lives he saved: Police Officer Danielle Sontare (Patricia Charbonneau) and Norbert (Brian Thompson), a bartender. The pilot story finds Alex helping a young girl named Lisa (Erika Flores) find her missing father, a scientist who has invented a powerful steroid called Instant Iron. Sylvester Levay composed the theme.

104. *The Phantom* (Unaired, 1961)

Pilot. The Phantom (Roger Creed), called "the ghost who walks" by natives, is a mysterious white man who protects the people and animals of Africa from harm. There is no background information given about the Phantom — who he is or where he came from. The theme lyric tells us that he is "a man who never dies" and "the tom toms call him when danger stalks." The Phantom travels with Devil, his German shepherd, and helps R.G. Mallory (Reginald Denney), the local commissioner, battle evildoers. The pilot story, titled "No Escape," finds the Phantom going undercover on the plantation of Mrs. Harris (Paulette Goddard) to find out who is killing workers. Don Carey sings the theme, "The Phantom."

105. *Poltergeist: The Legacy* (Showtime, 1996–1998; SciFi, 1999; Syndicated 1999–2001)

The program opens with these words from a journal called *Poltergeist: The Legacy*: "Since the beginning of time mankind has existed between the world of light and the world of darkness. This journal chronicles the work of our secret society, known as the Legacy, created to protect the innocent from the creatures that inhabit the shadows of the night."

Members of the Legacy, headquartered in a mansion in San Francisco, have included Bram Stoker, Robert Louis Stevenson and H.P. Lovecraft—all selected by invitation only for their gifts of extraordinary sight. The current members are Derek Rayne, Rachel Corrigan, Alex Moreau, Nick Boyle and

Kristen Adams. Members have not asked for their special abilities; they accept them and are devoted to understanding and containing paranormal phenomena, often at the risk of their own lives.

Derek Rayne (Derek DeLint) is the House Leader. He is 44 years old and says, "I was born into the fight against evil." His father, Winston Rayne, was head of the San Francisco house until he was killed by a demon. Derek, embittered and torn between his own desires and his destiny with the Legacy, spent years tracking down and destroying that demon. He was then chosen to head the Legacy. Derek possesses doctorates in theology and biological anthropology. He has psychic abilities and an extensive knowledge of science, mythology and a history of the Legacy itself.

Rachel Corrigan (Helen Shaver) is the Legacy's psychological specialist. She is a firm believer in science and brings her medical expertise, skepticism and open mind to the mysteries that face the Legacy. She is very dedicated to her daughter, Katherine (Alexandra Purvis), a ten year old who shows promise of extraordinary psychic abilities. Rachel would like to keep Katherine, whom she calls Kat, away from the work of the Legacy, but Kat's touch of second sight draws her into the evils that haunt the Legacy. In later episodes it appears that Rachel and Kat live at the Legacy House.

Alex Moreau (Robbie Chong) is 32 years old. Alexandra, called Alex, holds the position of researcher. She is a brilliant student of anthropology who possesses innate curiosity and psychic abilities (which drew her to Derek's attention). She has a natural gift for the paranormal which she acquired from her grandmother, a Creole woman deeply involved in the occult. Alex possesses a university education in science and a highly developed social conscience as well as an outstanding talent for difficult research.

Nick Boyle (Martin Cummins) is 38 years old and while his position is researcher, he often finds himself in physical battles with demons. Nick is an adventurer and spent time as a Navy S.E.A.L. His father was a colleague of Derek's. Nick felt that joining the Legacy would give him the excitement he was searching for. Nick frequently suspects that what appears to be a paranormal event may actually be the work of human beings. While he would like to react with a quick punch, experience has taught him that the forces of darkness can be dangerous and his keen sense of intelligence curbs his tendency to act first and think later. Nick drives a red Mustang with the plate LP 326C7.

Kristen Adams (Kristin Lehman) was born in Boston, Massachusetts, where she was a member of the Boston Legacy House (she is on loan to the San Francisco House). Kristen is an anthropologist and graduated after three years at Harvard with an Honors degree. Her father, Justin Adams, is a noted professor in New England who served as a consultant to the Legacy on a number of occasions. Several years ago he mysteriously disappeared while working on a Legacy dig site in Istanbul. It is because of this that Kristen has joined the Legacy — to help defeat evil and find her missing father. Kristen possesses brilliance, drive, an opinionated nature and says only that she is in her twenties.

The syndicated version of the series consists of repeats from the Showtime and SciFi Channel versions.

Power Rangers see *Mighty Morphin Power Rangers*

106. *Probe* (ABC, 1988)

Serendip is a high tech research and development company created by Austin James (Parker Stevenson), "the greatest scientific mind of the century." Austin, however, has an eccentric obsession about crime. In order to pursue his dream, he turns over the company to Howard Millhouse (Jon Cypher) and retreats to "The Batcave," an old warehouse where he lives and conducts scientific experiments in the cause of justice (Millhouse complains constantly about the huge water and power bills Austin's experiments are costing the company). Assisting Austin is Michele Castle (Ashley Crow), a pretty but batty secretary Austin calls Mickey.

Austin thinks while he sleeps (his bed is a sensory deprivation tank — "It helps me think"), has a photographic memory and can retain and recall information faster than a computer. He has a pet spider, a tarantula named Steve, who roams freely about the lab. Mickey doesn't have a good mind for numbers ("I can't even remember my social security number") and drinks only Reneau Spring Water from France "with a twist of lemon." She left her last job "because my boss said I could do the job better in the nude." She assists Austin by taking notes for him in the field. When Austin hears or reads about a baffling criminal case, he involves himself (and Mickey) in dangerous situations to bring evildoers to justice. "We Can Do It" is the slogan of Serendip, a company that Austin started with the creation of an automated robot lawn mowing service. Sylvester Levay composed the theme.

107. *Profiler* (NBC, 1996–2000)

Samantha Waters (Ally Walker) is a profiler, a forensic psychologist with a unique ability to feel for the victims of crime and understand the criminal mind. She is not a psychic. Her highly developed intuition allows her to think in pictures and visualize the frame of mind of both the killer and the victim. Samantha looks beyond the obvious and rarely takes a guess ("I need more to go on. Without a crystal ball, there is not much more I can tell you"). She is part of the V.C.T.F. (Violent Crimes Task Force), a special unit of the FBI that attempts to solve the baffling and bizarre crimes of any police department in the nation.

Samantha, a widow, lives with her daughter Chloe (Caitlin Wachs, Evan Rachel Wood) in a converted firehouse station (Engine 23 Trucking Company) at 501 Almada. Her close friend, Angel Brown (Erica Gimpel), a young artist who makes a living as a sculptor, lives with her and Chloe. Chloe has a dog (Denzil), likes to experiment with makeup, and is cared for by Angel when Samantha is at work.

As a child, Samantha and her mother enjoyed solving puzzles. It made Samantha feel alive. Now, for Samantha, trying to find a killer is like trying to solve a puzzle. In 1993, Samantha came close to uncovering the identity of a killer the FBI called Jack of All Trades. To distract her, Jack killed her husband. A devastated Samantha resigned from the FBI and moved to the country with Chloe to live an anonymous life. In 1996, when a rash of serial killings stumps the FBI, Bailey Monroe (Robert Davi), head of the V.C.T.F. in Atlanta, Georgia, coaxes Samantha out of her self-imposed retirement to come and work for him. Samantha agrees, but under two conditions: her personal life remains confidential and "I get what I want when I need it."

Samantha has encountered evil in its purest form (Jack) and sometimes feels scared — "But I'm not going to quit." She is also a workaholic and it is Bailey who forces her to take time off when he sees her becoming rundown (her hobby of photography seems to relax her; it offers "me an escape from the dark corners").

Jack of All Trades is perhaps the most clever and diabolical criminal ever to appear as a regular on a television series. Jack killed to draw Samantha close to him. He considers himself the ultimate taunter and monitors Samantha's activities by tapping into FBI computer systems via his password "Jack O. Trades." Jack's real name is Albert Neurquary (Dennis Christopher) and was originally called Jack by the V.C.T.F. because his real name was not known (in early episodes that feature Jack, his screen credit reads only "and Jack"). When Jack tried to turn Chloe against Samantha, he made his fatal mistake. Samantha tracked him, faced him, and in an extremely tense and unexpected moment, shot him dead at point blank range. Although unethical, but justified, Samantha's nightmare was over; but so was her job. On October 21, 1999, Samantha resigned "to do what I need, what Chloe needs— each other." She is replaced by Rachel Burke (Jamie Luner), a former profiler in Seattle, then Houston, who joined Bailey's team. Like Samantha, Rachel can see into the criminal mind and explain the unexplained. Rachel, however, need not be present at a crime scene to receive images — "I could be brushing my teeth or grinding coffee when they come." Rachel has an 88 percent accuracy rate — "But it's that other 12 percent that bothers me." She also has a problem similar to Samantha — "I can't sleep when I'm working on a tough case."

Rachel was a prosecuting attorney (1996), then an instructor for special agents at the Virginia FBI training center. She became an FBI agent "because I was sick of seeing criminals beat the system. They should be behind bars." When Rachel was ten years old, the girl who lived next door disappeared. A week before she vanished, the girl told Rachel her parents didn't want children and felt her life was empty (she was being raised by a nanny). Seven days later the girl was found, dead, at the bottom of a well. Rachel felt the girl had lived her life in the dark. It was this incident that led Rachel to believe she had the gift to see what others could not when she envisioned the girl in the well. Rachel lived previously in Arlington, Virginia; she now resides in Atlanta in an apartment on Melrose; 555-0192 is her phone number.

Bailey, head of the V.C.T.F., has complete authority. He is in the office 14 to 16 hours a day and is struggling to raise his troublesome 17-year-old daughter, Frances (Heather McComb). Frances is rebellious and feels her father treats her like a marine in boot camp — "He commands and doesn't listen." Like Samantha (and Rachel) Bailey is totally dedicated to work and has little time for a social or private life. In the pilot episode, Bailey was said to head the FBI Investigative Support Unit. Other members of the V.C.T.F. are John Grant (Julian McMahon), Grace Alvarez (Roma Maffia), Nathan Brubaker (Michael Whaley) and George Findley (Peter Frechette). John, a cynical agent, often questions Samantha's approaches to solving crimes. He was a former cop with the Atlanta Police Department and believes "it's like having your head in a vise" having to follow the strict rules of the V.C.T.F. He lives in Apartment 35. Grace is the team's gifted forensics expert (she has a knack for finding evidence other medical examiners overlook). Nathan, an ex-attorney turned FBI agent, often questions Bailey's authority as to the legal issues of an order. George, the team's computer whiz, is a former world class hacker who uses his skills to help the FBI. He has a drug problem and was suspended for a time when drugs began to interfere with his job. Angelo Badalmonti composed the original "Profiler Theme" (with Ally Walker); Jeff Rona, the new "Profiler Theme" (with Jamie Luner). See also *Chameleon in Blue*.

108. *The Queen of Swords* (Syndicated, 2000-2001)

Santa Helena is a small town in Old California (1817) that is ruled by Luise Rivera Montoya (Valentine Pelka), a corrupt and evil military colonel who is seeking to become the law of the land. Dona Maria Teresa Alvarado (Tessie Santiago) is a young woman living in Madrid, Spain, when she receives word that her father, Don Alvarado, has been killed in a fall from a horse (in actuality, he has been shot by the soldiers of Montoya for resisting arrest).

A short time later, Dona Maria Teresa, called Tessa, and her servant, Marta (Paulina Galvez) arrive in Santa Helena to find the once glorious

Alvarado mansion in shambles and about to be repossessed by Montoya for unpaid back taxes. Unable to pay the taxes and not believing her father, an expert horseman, died accidentally, Tessa decides to remain and avenge his death. The answer as to how comes one night when Tessa receives a ghostly visit from her father. He tells her that his "Avenging Angel will make things right." As they speak, Don Alvarado tells Tessa to find the Santa Rita, a rare bottle of wine in the cellar. As Tessa searches, she finds the bottle of wine and pulls it from the rack. A secret door opens to reveal gold and other treasures her father hid from Montoya. Tessa also finds a sword ("My father was saving it for a son he never had") and a picture, painted of her when she was seven years old, with the caption "My Little Angel." As she looks at the picture, Tessa decides to become that Avenging Angel her father mentioned. She dons a lacy black mask, tight black blouse and pants (with a red scarf around her waist) and a calling card—the Queen of Swords (taken from the tarot deck of cards). Although Tessa battles the evils of Montoya, she is branded a villain. A reward of 1000 Reales is offered for her capture—dead or alive.

The town's padre believes the Queen is "a miracle of God for all the good she does." Colonel Montoya calls the Queen "an evil spirit who threatens the very destiny of the whole public." He also believes that the Queen is no ordinary woman. "She has a good heart. And when I catch her I'll keep it in a jar on my desk."

Tessa's dual identity is known only to Marta. When not helping the people of Santa Helena as the Queen, Tessa appears as an aristocrat who has returned to her homeland to take over the family estate (which she does when she pays Montoya the back taxes). As the Queen, Tessa rides a brown horse she calls Chico. Tessa misses the life of luxury she lived in Spain and often sighs, "I'm tired of play acting the role of the spoiled aristocrat." Tessa, a skilled swordswoman, was called El Caita by her father as a child. She carries a small spare sword in her boot and "charms" Montoya by telling him, "We can all take comfort in knowing that men of honor like yourself and Grisham are here to protect us."

Montoya's captain, Marcus Grisham (Anthony Lemke) is the man who killed Tessa's father, but Tessa cannot prove it. Little information is given about Grisham. He was apparently in the U.S. Army and dishonorably discharged (he is wanted for murder and fraud). He somehow hooked up with Montoya and has been his right hand man ever since. Montoya has made it Grisham's job "to get the Queen of Swords or I'll have your head instead of hers." Montoya plays the violin and keeps his valuables in a secret room behind the bookcase in his office (it opens by pressing on the book *The Strategies of Napoleon Bonaparte*). Marta, who looks out for Tessa, is a psychic and reads Tarot cards. Jose Feliciano sings the theme, "Behind the Mask."

109. *Relic Hunter* (Syndicated, 1999)

Sydney Fox (Tia Carrere) is a beautiful young woman who battles a different type of criminal — those who steal and seek to profit from ancient relics. She works as a professor of ancient studies at Trinity College and takes on assignments to recover lost relics on behalf of the university museum (by the episode of 9/23/01, Sydney had recovered 87 relics, 19 of which sold for more than one million dollars to help the school). "Part of what I do is search for relics. Every relic tells a human story and gives us an insight into our lives." Her interest in relics began at St. Theresa's, a Catholic grammar school for girls. Here, young Sydney (Larissa Laskin) befriended a teacher who hunted for relics as a sideline and learned "Relics don't belong to people or individuals, they belong to the world." Sydney, a Scorpio, later attended Franklin High School (where she was a cheerleader and played Maria in the senior play, *West Side Story*; no mention is made of her interest in relics at this time). Sydney is a fanatic baseball fan (cheers for the Boston Red Sox) and can be either a temptress or an Amazon — whatever she has to be to get the job done. Sydney teaches Tai Chi classes (11:30–12:30) and when she is on assignment, the first thing she does when she gets out of a scrape "is go to a hotel, take a bath and have a glass of whatever they call wine."

Nigel Bailey (Christien Anholt) is Sydney's teaching assistant and partner on assignments. He is working on his master's degree (attended Oxford in England) and says, "All I wanted was a nice little teaching job in a nice little library surrounded by books." What he got was dangerous assignments away from the college. He is a Taurus (born May 10) and was originally said to have attended England's Cambridge University. He can speak a dozen languages, read ancient scripture and is an expert on weapons technology. He hates for Sydney to use the words "boarding school" as it reminds him of his youth when "I was incarcerated"; he called the headmistress "Dragon Lady."

Claudia (Lindy Booth) is Sydney's gorgeous blonde secretary. She has no love of history and got the job "because my father is a friend of the college." Claudia is a vegetarian and loves to eavesdrop (when Sydney catches her at the door, Claudia responds with "I was looking for my contact lens"). When Sydney tells Claudia something important, she says "Got ya." If Sydney tells Claudia "to write it down, it's important," Claudia says "Got ya." Claudia is an expert on Tarot cards ("Do you think I would leave who to date and what to wear to chance?"). and believes she had a past life (as Evas, a handmaiden to Cleopatra). Claudia likes to experiment with her computer (placing her picture in a program to see how she looks in clothes, especially pastels: "I hate cucumber color; it makes me look icky"). She also believes on-line shopping is dangerous ("I buy too much and then have to figure out what half to return"). Claudia left at the end of the second season for her dream job as a model in New York. She was replaced by Karen Petresky (Tanja Reichert), a busty blonde who works as Sydney's administrator (Karen's "talent" is showing ample cleavage to get what she wants from men). Unlike Claudia, Karen is genuinely interested in relics and helps Sydney accomplish her assignments.

Fred Dryer has a recurring role as Sydney's father, Randall Fox, a dam builder who helps her on occasion. He is unconventional and believes in only two things: "Defy everything and never be caught dead in a suit." Donald Quon composed the theme. The program opens with these words by Sydney (addressing her class): "Welcome to ancient studies. I'm not a stickler for attendance. Sometimes I'm called away from the office myself."

Return of the Saint see *The Saint*

110. *RoboCop* (Syndicated, 1994)

Alex Murphy (Richard Eden) is a police officer in Delta City in 21st century Detroit. He is an Irish Catholic and lives at 548 Principal Drive. He attended Mother Theresa Elementary School, St. John Paul High School and Holy Trinity College. He and his family attend mass at St. John Paul Cathedral. He wears badge number 2120.

During a robbery investigation, Murphy is shot multiple times. He is rushed to the hospital, where little hope is given for his survival. When he is considered legally dead, he is given to Security Concepts, a cybernetic institute that rebuilds him as RoboCop (total body prosthesis, titanium skin, on board computer assisted brain, instant reflexes).

Murphy, now as RoboCop, is part of the Crime Prevention Program of the Metro South Precinct in Old Detroit. Murphy's wife, Nancy (Jennifer Griffin) and son, Jimmy (Peter Costigan), believe Alex is dead. The only thing Alex has of the way he was are images from his past. He will not approach his family "because they need a husband and a father. I can't be that — but I can protect them." Alex is programmed with three prime directives: Serve the Public Interest, Uphold the Law, Protect the Innocent; and a Directive Four: Classified (any attempt to arrest a senior officer of the O.C.P. [Omni Consumer Products] will result in a system breakdown. O.C.P. is responsible for the technology that created RoboCop).

RoboCop uses a specially encoded O.C.P. gun that can only be fired by him. The gun uses thermal graphic targeting but RoboCop never shoots to kill (regular police guns have two settings: lethal and tag. Tag fires a dart for identification). RoboCop's helmet, also developed by O.C.P., has the code 001. RoboCop never stays in one place for long "because somewhere there is a crime happening." RoboCop is teamed with Detective Lisa Madigan (Yvette

Niper), a human police officer with Metro South. She lives at 972 Primrose Lane. Diana Powers (Andrea Roth) is a secretary at O.C.P. Dr. Craig Milardo (Cliff DeYoung) is a deranged scientist who plans to control Delta City via Neuro Brain, a master computer that is run by a human brain. After several experiments with the brains of homeless people fail, Milardo theorizes that his donors lack the intelligence needed for the project to work. He sees Diana as the perfect donor. While not shown, Diana is paralyzed and her brain removed while she is still alive. Craig disposes of the evidence (Diana's body) in a toxic waste dump. Milardo activates his Neuro Brain and begins using it for his own benefit. Soon the unforeseen happens—human spirit and machine combine to produce an entity with her own will. When the entity Diana learns what has happened to her, she becomes enraged and refuses to help Craig. Milardo attempts to destroy Diana by introducing a computer virus into her system. The virus almost succeeds—until RoboCop, who is seeking Milardo for the murder of homeless people, reverses the virus and saves Diana. Diana now runs Delta City by computer and helps RoboCop with the information he needs.

Sarah Campbell is Gadget, a young orphan girl who helps RoboCop with street information. James Keane is William Ray "Pudnose" Morgan, a criminal seeking revenge on RoboCop for causing an accident that disfigured him. Jordan Hughes is Alex as a child in flashbacks; Martin Milner was Alex's father, Gus. Based on the feature film.

111. *Rocky Jones, Space Ranger* (Syndicated, 1954)

The program opened simply with an announcer saying *Rocky Jones, Space Ranger*. The words "Space Ranger" would be repeated twice. Rocky Jones (Richard Crane) is the chief of the Space Rangers, a twenty-first century organization established to safeguard the planets of a united solar system from alien invaders. Rocky is assisted by Vena Ray (Sally Mansfield) and Bobby (Robert Lyden) and pilots a ship called the *Orbit Jet* (later the *Silver Moon*). Winky (Scotty Beckett) and later, Biff Cardoza (James Lydon), are his co-pilots. Secretary Drake (Charles Meredith) is head of the Space Rangers and Ranger Clark (William Hudson) operates refueling space station O.W. 9.

Rocky's space ship radio code is XV-2 (both ships). The Visograph permits the viewing of outer space from inside the ship. Apollo Minor is the supply satellite and the Rangers carry ray guns they rarely use. "Space Ranger" is printed on the shoulder of ranger uniforms; a patch representing the planet Saturn adorns the front of the uniform. Dian Fauntelle played Yarra, ruler of the planet Medina; Walter Coy was Zorvac, king of the moon Fornax; Patsy Iannone was Volaca, Zorvac's daughter.

In the opening theme, when the show's title is seen, the *o* in "Rocky" is the planet Saturn; the *o* in "Jones" is the planet Earth. The program concludes with "Be with us again next week when we again take you into outer space with Rocky Jones, Space Ranger."

112. *Rod Brown of the Rocket Rangers* (CBS, 1953-1954)

"CBS television presents Rod Brown of the Rocket Rangers. Surging with the power of the atom, gleaming like great silver bullets, the mighty Rocket Rangers' space ships stand by for blastoff (space ships are seen blasting off). Up, up, rockets blazing with white hot fury; the manmade meteors ride through the atmosphere breaking the gravity barrier, pushing up and out, faster and faster and then outer space and high adventure for the Rocket Rangers."

The Rocket Rangers is an Earth-based 22nd century defense organization designed to battle interplanetary evil and safeguard the planets of the United Solar System (Earth, Jupiter, Mars, Mercury and Venus).

In this futuristic time, a battle still rages to ferret out human evil and greed. Rod Brown (Cliff Robertson) is a junior Ranger who joined the force to make the world safe. He is a combination undercover agent, diplomat, fighter and peacemaker whose ingenuity and bravery soon finds him a full-fledged Rocket Ranger and commander of a space ship called the *Beta* (which blasts off from Orbit 4). Ranger Frank Boyle (Bruce Hall) assists Rod and Ranger Wilbur Wormser (Jack Weston), called "Wormsey," is the navigator who plots the *Beta*'s course from Omega Base. Wormser is intelligent but a bumbler and his actions often complicate assignments. When something goes wrong he exclaims, "Oh, great Jupiter." Commander Swift (John Boruff), whom the Rangers call "The Old Man," is head of the Rocket Rangers and commands from Omega Base. He is gray-haired, lean and all military.

There are no special weapons (other than ray guns) and no special codes or "lingo" for space transmissions. A typical sequence would play as follows: "Control tower to *Beta*." "*Beta* here, over." After the message is received by Rod, he says simply, "Check, over and out." When Rod had to contact the control tower, he would say "Rocket ship *Beta* calling Ranger Headquarters, Earth." The Code of the Rocket Rangers is as follows: "On My Honor as a Rocket Ranger, I Pledge That I Shall":

1. Always chart my course according to the Constitution of the United States of America.
2. Never cross orbits with the rights and beliefs of others.
3. Blast off at full space speed to protect the weak and innocent.
4. Stay out of collision orbits with the laws of my state and community.
5. Cruise in parallel orbit with my parents and teachers.
6. Not roar my rockets unwisely and shall be courteous at all times.

7. Keep my gyros steady and reactors burning by being industrious and thrifty.
8. Keep my scanner tuned to learning and remain coupled to my studies.
9. Keep my mind out of free-fall by being mentally alert.
10. Blast the meteors from the paths of other people by being kind and considerate.

The program closes with a preview of the following week's episode and these words: "Be sure to be with Rod Brown next week for another thrilling adventure in the far regions of outer space on *Rod Brown of the Rocket Rangers.*"

113. *Sable* (ABC, 1987-1988)

Nicholas Flemming (Lewis Van Bergen) is the author of *The Friends of B.B. Flemm*, a best-selling series of children's books. He lives at 2435 Lincoln Park West in Chicago and also created "Jon Sable, Freelance," a daily comic strip. Nicholas, however, is not who he appears to be. He is a wanted murderer whose real name is Jon Sable. Jon's past is very sketchy and it is only revealed that when Jon lived in South America, he killed the man responsible for murdering his wife and children. When Jon fled to America, his friend, Eden Kendall (Rene Russo), helped him establish a new identity as Nicholas Flemming (she is also his agent and romantic interest).

To help him come to terms with the death of his family, Nicholas uses his true name to help people in trouble. As Jon Sable, Nicholas disguises his face with makeup (stripes across his face; "He dresses like the Easter Bunny," says Eden) and chooses cases very carefully — "I have to. I have a price on my head." Sable is not a hired killer and helps victims of crimes or people desperately in need of help. "If a case involves a kid, he gets careless and crazy," says Eden. "It's not going to bring his family back, but he couldn't stand to see what happened to him happen to someone else."

Myke Blackmon (Holly Fulger) is Nicholas's illustrator. "Great legs," Nicholas says of Myke, who dresses like a girl of the 1920s (the Flapper look). Joe Tyson (Ken Paige), called "Cheesecake" by Sable, is Jon's blind information man. Joe is a computer whiz and hopes to one day become a standup comedian. He loves cheesecake (especially strawberry) and Sable sends him a large cheesecake when he needs information (a message in Braille appears on the inside flap of the box). Joe lives in Apartment 6 of an unidentified building. Michael Shreive composed the theme.

114. *The Saint* (Syndicated, 1963-1966; NBC, 1967-1969)

Simon Templar, alias the Saint (Roger Moore) is a wealthy adventurer who makes it his business to help people in trouble. Although considered criminal by the police, Templar is actually on their side and most often helps Claud Eustace Teal (Ivor Dean), the Chief Inspector of England's Scotland Yard, solve baffling crimes.

Simon is a master among thieves (hence his "wanted by the police" reputation). He appeals to women and the women he meets, "the most glamorous in the world," appeal to him ("luscious figures, provocative eyes and haunting voices"). Simon is "lean, tall and well able to look after himself. His voice and manners are deceptively lazy."

Simon carries a Diner's Club and American Express cards, an international driver's license and a passport wherever he goes. In London (where Simon lives) he drives a white Volvo 1800 with the plate ST-1. Leslie Charteris, creator of *The Saint*, sold the rights to television in 1963 and described his character as follows: "A roaring adventurer who loves a fight; a dashing daredevil; debonair, preposterously handsome; a pirate or a philanthropist as the occasion demands. He lives for the pursuit of excitement, for the one triumphant moment that is his alone." In single, 1963 episodes, Wensley Pithey and Norman Pitt each played Inspector Teal before Ivor Dean took over the role. Edwin Astley composed the theme, "The Saint."

Note: With the same premise (but without Inspector Teal), Ian Ogilvy played Simon Templar in a CBS series called *Return of the Saint* (1979–80). Brian Dae composed "The New Saint Theme."

Andrew Clark next played Simon Templar in an unsold pilot called *The Saint* (CBS, 6/12/87). In the story (also without Inspector Teal), Simon helps a ballerina who is receiving threats against her life. The pilot was originally titled *The Saint in New York*; Mark Snow composed *The Saint Theme*.

Simon Dutton next played Simon Templar in a new, syndicated series called *The Saint* that ran for one year (1989–90). David Ryall was Inspector Claud Eustace Teal and Tony Britton composed the theme, a variation on the original *Saint Theme*.

115. *Scarecrow and Mrs. King* (CBS, 1983–1987)

The Agency is a secret branch of the U.S. government that handles matters of national security. It was founded in 1954 by Captain Harry V. Thornton (Howard Duff) and operates under the cover of International Federal Film (which actually makes movies— documentaries like *The History of the Tractor* and *The Romance of Earthworms*— to justify its cover). Billy Melrose (Mel Stewart) is the Field Investigation Unit Section Chief; Lee Stetson (Bruce Boxleitner), code name "Scarecrow," and Francine Desmond (Martha Smith) are two of his three top operatives. The third operative is Amanda King (Kate Jackson), an amateur, divorced housewife, whose real life provides her with the perfect cover for working with Lee (Lee is fleeing with a package containing top secret information when he runs into Amanda at a train station. He tells Amanda to board the train and give the package to "the man in the red hat." When Amanda tries, but encounters a convention of men wearing red hats, she takes the package home. When Lee discovers that the package has not been delivered, he tracks down Amanda and together they plug a security leak at the Agency. Because Amanda is an unknown, Billy recruits her and teams her with Lee).

Lee lost his parents when he was four years old and was raised by a military uncle on numerous army bases. In 1973, Lee was a member of the Agency's "Oz Team" and received the code name "Scarecrow" (other team members were "The Wizard," "The Tin Man" and "The Lion"). Lee combs his hair with a plastic comb that is missing two teeth ("It's the right comb for my hair") and practices kickboxing, karate and fencing at home. He drives a classic 1953 Porsche 350 (plate 3NG 105; later 9S1 407 and 7G4 928). Lee keeps the spare key to his apartment at 46 Hamblin under the potted plant in the hallway. He enjoys chili dogs (at a fast food store called Milo's Daffy Dog) and a drink at Nedlinger's Washington Pub (called Ned's); the bar is later called Emilio's, then Monk's. Lee is a member of the University Athletic Club and works out when he gets upset. Lee has two unnamed pet fish (Siamese fighting fish) and is first a Field Investigation Agent and later an Intelligence Operative (or spy—"Although I never cared for that word," he says).

Amanda is divorced one year when the series begins. She is the mother of Philip (Paul Stout), age ten, and eight-year-old Jamie (Greg Morton) and lives with her mother, Dotty West (Beverly Garland) at 4247 Maplewood Drive in Arlington, Virginia (555-3434, then 555-3100 and 555-7043 are given as her phone numbers). Amanda attended the University of Virginia and has a degree in American Literature; she has a minor in photo journalism. She was a cheerleader in high school and in college was a member of the drama club (she played the Tigress in a play called *Wailing Walrus*). Amanda does housework to exercise tapes, is a Bedside Bluebell (volunteer) at Galilee Hospital and works on behalf of Unified Charities (usually as the Refreshment Director). Amanda is also head of Mothers for a Safe Environment and manager of the Bombers, her sons' Little League Baseball team. Pot roast with succotash is Amanda's favorite dinner.

Amanda is allergic to horses and took driving lessons at Barney's Driving Instructor School (she drives a station wagon with the plate JRY 502). She earns extra money as an occasional reporter for the *Washington Blaze*.

As the series progressed, Amanda's importance at the Agency also progressed. When not on assignment, Amanda worked for the Agency by transcribing tapes ("I can type 90 words a minute; 80 if you don't count typos"). Her clearance level is first GS-7 (Seasonal Employee). After training at the Agency's "Spy School, Station One," Amanda has a fourth level GSA security clearance; later she has a Grade 10 security clearance. Amanda also has an office in the building's Film Library.

When Lee and Amanda work as an undercover team, they adopt the aliases of Lee Steadman and Amanda Keene; Lee, however, was heard using these other aliases: Lee Simpson and Lee Stanton. Lee and Amanda married on February 13, 1987, shortly before the series ended (Lee moved in with Amanda and her family).

Dotty, short for Dorothea, was, at first, unaware of Amanda's activities as a spy. When Amanda had to leave for an assignment, she would tell her mother "I'm going to the club" or "babysit" for pets, plants and fish when their owners are away. Dotty was aware of Amanda's work as a transcriber and believed it was for "the company you work for." She later figures out what is going on and accepts Amanda's decision to become a spy. Dotty, who called Amanda "Panda" as a child, likes to take apricot-cinnamon bubble baths. She is a fan of Big Band music and has a collection of Duke Ellington and Glenn Miller records. She gives books as gifts and cooks often for the family while watching "Colonial Cookery" on TV.

Philip and Jamie attend Calvin Elementary School (where Amanda is a member of the PTA). Each year Amanda and the kids spend a weekend at Camp Anacostia. Philip and Jamie love to eat out at the Quickie Chickie Snack Shack. The kids are members of the Junior Trail Blazers, Troop 78 (Amanda, their scout leader, won second prize with her apple pie at the Scout Jamboree). When it rains, Jamie makes sure to step into every mud puddle on his way home from school.

Francine's clearance level is Green 13. She uses the alias Francine Dutton and when she becomes frightened, she eats chocolate (Amanda rambles on and on when she becomes scared). Francine is an expert on hand-to-hand combat, small arms weaponry "and rich men between the ages of 30 and 40." A prince once proposed to Francine but she didn't accept "because his country was too small." "Scarecrow's methods might be unorthodox," says Francine, "but he always delivers." Billy attended law school and had a choice of becoming a New York attorney or counterintelligence agent; he chose to become an agent. In his youth, Billy was a jazz musician known as Billy Blue Note. Billy's superior is referred to as "The Blue Leader." Arthur B. Rubinstein composed the theme.

116. *The Seal* (NBC, 11/27/81)

Pilot. The Seal (Ron Ely) is a man of mystery. He lives in California (drives a car with the plate SLIPPERY 1) and the only other information known about him is that he was a former mercenary. He now uses his expertise as a soldier as a free agent to tackle dangerous, high risk cases. The pilot story finds the Seal being hired by the U.S. government to free Stephanie Thayer (Jenny Sullivan), a CIA cryptographer who was abducted by a spy ring to decode satellite data. Joe Harnell composed the theme.

117. *The Secret Adventures of Jules Verne* (SciFi/ Syndicated, 2001)

Were the writings of Jules Verne fiction or did the fantastic adventures he wrote about really happen? Promotional spots for the series tell us "Jules Verne, author, playwright, future writer extraordinaire. A century ago he startled the world with his predictions. A lucky dreamer or did the fantastic adventures he described really occur? Science fiction meets science fact — The Secret Adventures of Jules Verne."

The series is set in 1861. Jules Verne (Chris Demetral) is a starving French playwright with visions of the future. He is attending the University of La Sorbonne in Paris and earning meager pay by selling his stories. One day, while in class, he draws ("doodles" as he calls it) the plans for a mole (a machine that can tunnel through dirt and rock).

At this time it is revealed that there is an (unnamed) aristocratic society "that has been guiding Europe for hundreds of years." The society has stolen Verne's plans for the mole and built a prototype for one purpose: to kidnap Queen Victoria and prevent her from signing a peace agreement between England and France (the society thrives on war; the treaty would introduce democracy and end their rule).

Phileas Fogg (Michael Praed) and his cousin, Rebecca Fogg (Francesca Hunt) are agents for the British Secret Service who have been assigned to investigate reports of strange ground rumblings (the mole machine moving). Their investigation leads them to Paris and to Jules Verne. Phileas believes Verne is guilty of plotting to kill the Queen and takes him aboard the *Aurora*, an airship (dirigible) he owns, for interrogation. Verne insists he is innocent and his mole "was just a doodle." Phileas's valet, Jean Passepartout (Michel Courtemanche) believes Verne is telling the truth and convinces Phileas to let him prove it by helping them defeat the mole machine. Jean is an inventor and has a lab aboard the *Aurora*. Figuring the mole will travel through the sewer systems of Paris, Jules devises a series of detectors to pick up on the mole's vibrations. The plan works and the four defeat the society. Although not a member of the Secret Service, Jules is invited to join Phileas, Rebecca and Jean as their helper because "we're fighting on the same side" (to defeat evil, especially another society called the League of Darkness, which seeks to plunge the world into turmoil). Although set during the Victorian era, the program encompasses weapons and technology that simply were not possible at the time (for example, the mole machine, telescopic rifles, bugging devices, robots, flying battleships).

Jules Verne is a man of vision. He believes science will make the world a better place (he dreams, for example, of sending a rocket into space). He has the ability to project his mind into the future (an asset the League of Darkness wants to acquire for themselves). Jules considers himself an amateur sleuth and is intrigued by crime. He is an expert in strategy and tactics and has a profound interest in art, literature and science. While Jules is not depicted as the famous author he will become, he calls himself a writer — "not an established writer. A couple of plays, lots of notes, but I haven't figured out what to do with them yet."

Rebecca Fogg is a secret agent in the mold of Emma Peel (*The Avengers*; see entry). She is an expert shot, swordswoman and well trained in the martial arts. Her ring contains a knockout gas; her earrings have picks for opening locks and her "mission clothes" are sexy black leather pants and a blouse. Rebecca is prepared for work in any situation. The metal hoops she wears under her dress are actually a ladder in disguise (the top hoop contains a trigger mechanism that acts like a gun. When Rebecca removes the hoops from her waist, she presses the trigger. The hoops transform into a ladder as they propel themselves against a building or wall). Rebecca starred in one of Verne's plays, *The Maid of New Orleans*, at the Rimini Theater in London (a trap to catch a killer).

Phileas Fogg, who would become famous for traveling around the world in 80 days (and the subject of a Jules Verne novel) designed the *Aurora* as a pleasure ship to take him to the great casinos of Europe (he built the ship when he retired from the Secret Service. He rejoined when he was called upon to defeat the society). Phileas is a ladies' man, a connoisseur of fine wine and a gambler (especially poker). He loves to play croquet, is an excellent swordsman and world traveler who relishes in the thought that one day his dream of visiting those great casinos will soon be at hand. Jules believes Phileas is obsessed with destroying evil and observes Phileas as he teaches Rebecca his technique.

Jean Passepartout, Phileas's French friend and traveling companion, is a jack of all trades. He pilots the *Aurora* and is responsible for its maintenance. He creates various gadgets (using things not yet invented, like plastic), is an excellent cook and calls Phileas "Master." Prior to meeting Phileas, Jean was a Sergeant Fireman in Paris. Jean claims to speak 14 languages (Phileas agrees, "but all of them badly"). Nick Glennie-Smith composed the theme.

118. *Secret Agent Man* (UPN, 2000)

Monk (Costas Mandylor) is a highly skilled operative for a U.S. government organization referred to as the Agency, "but it has no official name." Monk is also highly classified and his real name is not known ("If I tell you what it is, I'll have to kill you"). The Agency is based in a secret location in New York City and handles assignments that pose a threat to the safety of the people of the world. Holly Holiday (Dina Meyer), a beautiful agent who uses her real name, assists Monk in the field and calls her company "The Agency with No Name." A man known only as Brubeck (Paul Guilfoyle) is their superior.

If one tries to do a background check on any agent, they will find nothing — "we don't exist," says Monk. Monk is a hopeless romantic and spends Agency money like water. The only known background information on Monk is that his father called him "Bo Bo" as a kid. Monk's eye scan code (for entry into their headquarters) is 9022. Holly's background information is limited to her high school education (the Rosebrier Academy) and her athletic achievement (number two in archery). Holly is skilled in the martial arts (as is Monk) but unlike Monk, Holly tackles the less than glamorous aspects of an assignment (like going in the field while Monk relaxes in their mobile base of operations — a Fed-Ex truck; Monk assists Holly when he feels the time is right). Like Monk, Holly's address, phone number and personal information is restricted.

Davis (Dondre T. Whitfield) is an Agency operative who heads Resource Management (the watchdog in the field for Monk and Holly). He is also an inventor of sorts and designed the Clap-So-Club (a retractable golf club) from a failed Agency weapon (he also did a TV infomercial for it). Prima (Masetta Vanders) is the gorgeous enemy who is seeking to kill Monk for foiling her assignments. She comes close, but Holly always interferes and Prima always escapes — but vows to return and complete her personal vendetta. The group, the Supreme Beings of Leisure, perform the classic theme, "Secret Agent Man."

Note: A prior series called *Secret Agent* aired on CBS (1965-66). In it, John Drake (Patrick McGoohan) was a British Intelligence agent assigned to investigate and stop situations that endangered world security. Johnny Rivers performed the classic theme, "Secret Agent Man."

The Secret Files of Captain Video see *Captain Video and His Video Rangers*

119. *The Secret World of Alex Mack* (Nickelodeon, 1994)

Alexandra Louise Mack (Larisa Oleynik), called Alex, is a 13-year-old girl who lives at 23444 Clemson Lane (in Paradise Valley, California) with her parents, Barbara and George (Dorian Lopinto, Michael Blakley), and her 16-year-old sister, Annie (Meredith Bishop). Alex is an average student at Atron Junior High School; Annie, a child prodigy, attends Paradise Valley High School and is deeply interested in science.

A chemical called GC 161 is being developed at the Paradise Valley Chemical Plant to allow people to eat all they want without gaining weight. However, during experiments, something goes wrong and GC 161 becomes highly toxic. Danielle Atron (Louan Gideon), the head of Paradise Chemical and founder of the school that bears her name, orders the GC 161 to be destroyed. It is loaded into a canister and trucked out.

Alex is returning home from her first day as a seventh grader. She steps onto the street. The truck carrying the GC 161 swerves to avoid hitting her but crashes into a fire hydrant. The swerving motion causes the canister to fall out of the truck and burst open. It mixes with the gushing water of the fire hydrant and drenches Alex. Unsure of what to do, Alex runs home. There, she tells Annie what has happened. Suddenly, Alex's face begins to glow (in gold). Electrical appliances also turn on automatically. Just then, Alex's friend, Raymond Alvarado (Darris Love) stops by and witnesses the strange happenings. Annie calms Alex and the strange occurrences stop. She tells Alex and Raymond they must keep this secret. Annie believes that whatever doused Alex was illegal and Alex will be locked up if she is found. In the meantime, Danielle has ordered her security chief, Vince (John Marzilli) to find "the unknown kid" who witnessed the accident (Annie believes they are looking for Alex to turn her into a science project. Danielle believes "that kid holds the future of our planet in his hands").

Alex is very sweet and very pretty but believes "I'm boring, plain and simple." The gold glow now only occurs when Alex is embarrassed. She can levitate through thought, dispense electrical charges through her fingers and turn herself into a silver liquid by concentrating. Alex's worst enemy is the common cold (if she sneezes, her powers are set free and she has no control over them).

Alex has super powers "but I don't use them to turn the world on its head." She daydreams about using her abilities for good. In the real world she stands up for what she believes in and fights for the underdog (using her powers to solve minor crimes and help people overcome a problem).

Alex reads *13* magazine, has a collection of troll dolls and carries a troll lunchbox to school. Her most traumatic experience (besides the accident) was taking her first mid-term exam (in history). Originally, Alex didn't use her powers for personal gain (she would get a guilty conscience if she did); as the series progressed, she used her powers to help her overcome obstacles. She also has to learn to curtail her powers to avoid capture. Alex is somewhat of a tomboy (some episodes show her with an interest in sports, others with an interest in boys). She is learning to play the piano and enjoys playing miniature golf. When Alex dreams at night, objects in her room float around her's and Annie's beds (when she awakens, the objects fall on Annie).

Annie is extremely smart and believes "genius is lonely" (she has few friends but has maintained a 4.0 grade average since pre-school). She takes advanced science classes and hopes to win the Nobel Peace Prize for her work with Alex (she keeps a daily record of Alex's activities). It is often Annie who comes to Alex's rescue when her powers place her in difficult situations. By accessing her father's computer at work, Annie was able to uncover facts

151 *Secret World of Alex Mack* • *119*

about GC 161 and put Alex's mind to rest. GC 161 was supposed to be a weight prevention wonder drug. Two drops was the maximum amount to be taken; Alex was exposed to excessive amounts of the liquid. "There's no long term danger to your health," she tells Alex, "but you sure have some bizarre side effects." It was also completely illegal and because of that, Alex must be kept secret from Paradise Chemical (whose motto is "Progress at Any Cost"). Annie involves herself in her work because she feels she has to accomplish something big. She understands atom splitting and gravity waves but is hesitant to go bowling because she fears getting a gutter ball. Annie is working on a Millennium DNA Structure model as her personal project (she is trying to create a fabrication on how man will evolve in to the 21st century). She won the 9th Annual Paradise Valley Chemical Plant Fair with her project, an Ion Beam Accelerator.

George is a scientist and works at Paradise Valley Chemical (Human Resources Division, Sector C). He is a member of the Einstein Society and is looking forward to the day when he and Annie are working alongside each other. He is also very smart, skipped two grades in grammar school and, at age 11 in the seventh grade, wrote a term paper on Electro Magnetic Radiation. His computer password is "Arabrab" (Barbara spelled backwards) and drives a station wagon with the plate OM 823. Barbara works as the chemical plant's public relations director. She is also taking classes (she mentioned yoga and Japanese on Friday nights) and uses Kling Knot fabric softener strips in the clothes dryer. She drives a car with the plate 3HL 0564. The Macks have barbecue night once a week; PGP 863 is the license plate seen on the inside garage door next to the Flying A Gasoline sign. When Annie received a letter for possible acceptance into the prestigious Philipsbury Science Academy, her home address read 2332 Clemson Lane (the prior listing of 23444 is seen on the house).

Raymond and Alex have been friends "since we played in the sandbox together," says Alex. He is a member of the school band (plays the saxophone and says, "The Alvardos have a history of playing in school bands. I can't break that tradition").

Jessica (Jessica Alba) was the original class beauty, the snob who thought she was better than everyone else, especially Alex (whom she disliked and constantly teased). Jessica has all the boys wrapped around her finger and most likes Scott (Jason Strickland), an eighth grader Alex secretly likes (it is when Alex becomes jealous of Jessica's relationship with Scott that Alex first uses her powers for personal gain — by using her thought processes to make Jessica look bad in front of Scott). Alex believes "Jessica is so evil" (although she is an A student, Jessica cheats at sports and manipulates other people to get what she wants).

Libby Flanders (Marguerite Moreau) is the girl who replaces Jessica as the class beauty (Jessica Alba left for a starring role in the syndicated series

Flipper: The New Adventures). Libby also disliked Alex and realized there is something strange about her; she set her goal to find out what it was. Like Jessica, Libby also manipulates people to get what she wants. John Coda composed the theme.

The Secrets of Isis see *Isis*

120. *The Sentinel* (Syndicated, 1996)

Jim Ellison (Richard Burgi) is a detective with the Major Crime Division of the Cascade, Washington, Police Department who possesses unique and highly developed hyperactive senses. According to an ancient legend, such a person was called a Sentinel and used his powers to protect the people of his village from evil. Jim, however, has no memory of how he acquired his powers but believes it happened while in service with the Army Rangers in Peru.

Jim, a captain at the time, was in charge of a seven-man covert action team assigned to train local jungle tribes to protect trade routes against the guerrilla army. Their mission was sabotaged by a CIA intelligence operative with interests in the drug trade. During a battle, the team was killed and Jim was reported as missing in action. He was found 18 months later when an army rescue team stumbled upon him (after the battle Jim was rescued by natives from an isolated local tribe called the Chopec. He was chosen by the tribal chief to become a Sentinel, a protector of people. While not explained, it is probable that Jim's acts of courage in defending the tribes against the CIA showed he had the qualities of a Sentinel [virtue] but had not yet developed his powers. It has to be assumed that during this time, Jim was taught how to perfect his senses but was given some type of drug to erase his memory of the tribe and what happened to him).

Jim possesses supersensitive hearing, exceptional vision (including the ability to see in the dark) and the ability to identify any substance by touch, smell or taste. Jim is unaware of his powers at first. He resigns from the Rangers and joins the police department. All is progressing well until he is assigned to an extended, isolated stakeout and begins having what he calls "hallucinations" (seeing and hearing far beyond what is normal). Jim checks himself into the Cascade Hospital for a series of tests but his doctors are unable to find anything wrong. As he is preparing to leave, Jim meets a man who introduces himself as a doctor and suggests he see Blair Sandburg, an anthropologist at Rainier University, who can help him.

In a cluttered artifact storage room that doubles as an office, Jim meets Sandburg—the same man he met at the hospital. Blair is working on a doctoral thesis based on the long forgotten writings of a 19th century explorer named Richard Burton. Burton recorded stories about Sentinels—tribal watchmen who possessed the genetic advantage of heightened sensory awareness. Blair (Garrett Maggart) has seen hundreds of documented cases with people exhibiting two heightened senses, but never a person with all five. He believes Jim is a true Sentinel and has been given the ability to protect the people of Cascade (his village). Blair offers to help Jim understand the powers and learn how to control them in return for him becoming the subject of his thesis. Jim is reluctant until he learns a Sentinel can become so focused on one sense that he becomes oblivious to the other senses and vulnerable to danger.

Blair first works with Jim in secret; later, after Jim tells his captain, Simon Banks (Bruce A. Young), about his powers and about Blair, Blair is granted observer status with the department (Jim's "unofficial partner").

Jim, badge number 733, lives in Apartment 307 at 852 Prospect; 555-7036 is his phone number and 409 GDT is his Ford license plate number. Blair appears to live in his office at the university and drives a Volvo with the plate 743 FSU.

121. *Shazam!* (CBS, 1974–1977)

Billy Batson (Michael Gray) is a teenager chosen by the immortal Elders (Solomon, Hercules, Achilles, Zeus, Atlas and Mercury) for a never ending mission: to right wrongs. Billy is teamed with Mentor (Les Tremayne), a mysterious gray haired man who chauffeurs Billy "along the highways and byways of the land" in a 25 foot mobile home. When Billy requires special help, he can summon awesome forces by uttering a single word: *Shazam!* When he does, the skies darken, a bolt of lightning strikes him and he is transformed into Captain Marvel (Jackson Bostwick, John Davey), a heroic crime fighter who can fly, is impervious to harm, and has incredible strength (he wears a red suit with a gold cape).

The Elders appear in animated form (only their eyes and mouths move) and can contact Billy through a magical dome inside the mobile home. Once contacted, Billy speaks the words "O, Elders, whose fate is strong and wise, appear before my eyes." The Elders appear in a ghostly sequence and tell Billy what he must do to help someone in need. If Mentor needs to contact the Elders, he can repeat the same phrase.

If the Elders believe Billy will require help, they contact Mentor, who in turn seeks Andrea Thomas (JoAnna Cameron), the California high school teacher who is secretly Isis, a gorgeous crime fighter who helps good defeat evil (see *Isis* for information). Isis first teamed with Billy in the episode "Double-edged Sword."

The series is based on the Whiz Comics character created by Ralph Daigh and Bill Parker. Their original concept found Billy Batson as a radio broadcaster for station WHIZ while Shazam was an aged wizard he found living in an abandoned subway tunnel. Shazam gave Billy the power to become Captain Marvel by shouting his name. The television version does not relate how Billy met Mentor or how Billy was selected by the Elders. Shazam is a combination of the first letters of each of the Elders' names. Yvette Blais and Jeff Michael composed the theme.

122. *Sheena* (Syndicated, 2000)

The LaMista, a dangerous area in Maltoka, Africa, is home to Sheena (Gena Lee Nolin), a beautiful, 25-year-old, blonde jungle goddess who protects the tribes and animals of her adopted homeland from evil. Sheena, real name Cheryl, was five years old when a tragic event changed her life. It was on the morning of her fifth birthday that Cheryl's mother, Amanda (Carol Grow) and father (not seen or named) entered a cave. Moments later Cheryl's parents are killed by a rock slide. Cheryl (Brittany Robertson), waiting outside the cave, wanders off when she feels something is wrong. She is clutching the elephant bracelet her mother had given to her as a present when she is found by Kali (Margo Moorer), medicine woman of the Kia tribe. When Kali investigates and discovers Cheryl's parents are dead, she raises the child as her own daughter (Kali named Cheryl Shi-ena, but Cheryl preferred Sheena).

Kali is the woman tribesmen come to for help and advice. She is also the last of her tribe (the Kia possessed a mysterious power to morph [change] into animals. When civilization came to Africa, the Kia tribe, with the exception of Kali, chose to become animal). Kali passed the knowledge of morphing to Sheena, who now uses this ability to help her fight evil.

For Sheena to become an animal, she must feel the spirit of that animal inside of her (what she calls "The Mantra"). She then looks into the eyes of the animal and the transformation begins. Once she becomes an animal, Sheena is prone to two dangers: retaining part of that animal if she remains in that form for too long, and injury (if Sheena is hurt in her animal form, she will retain that injury when she becomes human). Sheena dislikes morphing into a cat "because when I morph back I cough up a fur ball." Sheena cannot talk to animals but she can communicate with them. She is friends with all animals except rogues (like the Silverback gorilla). She is also unable to morph into a rogue "because there is no focus." The clothes Sheena wears have to be made of natural fiber or they will not change with her when she morphs. Sheena can follow animal and humans by their scents and will only kill a human if one threatens to kill her. Sheena, taught by Kali to fight, educates herself by reading. She lives in a cave in the LaMista and most often wears a light tan, bosom revealing top and a leg and thigh revealing skirt-like bottom (type of animal skin not mentioned; looks to be antelope).

The LaMista is also home to a legendary creature called the Darak'na. It is said that when evildoers come to Africa, the Darak'na will strike ("Birds always appear before the Darak'na appears"). The Darak'na ("Shadow" in English) is actually Sheena, using a power Kali taught her to battle evil when evil fights unfair. The Darak'na is a vicious, cat-like creature with razor sharp claws. Sheena becomes the Darak'na by first covering herself with mud (which seems to be near no matter where she is). She then concentrates and this change occurs. In this state, Sheena retains her human thought processes but loses her top, exposing her camouflaged, mud-covered breasts (no explanation is given as to why the Darak'na is topless or how Sheena regains her top when she becomes her normal self. Gena does partial nudity, showing her breasts in a side view, but does not play the Darak'na. Vickie Phillips and Denise Loden play the creature). The gossip paper, the *National Inquisitor*, has offered a $1 million reward for proof of the Darak'na.

Matt Cutter (John Allen Nelson) is the only other person who is aware of Sheena's secrets. Matt owns Cutter Enterprises (later called Cutter Unlimited; phone 655-32) and offers safaris to search for the Darak'na (he is actually conning people. He knows Sheena is the Darak'na and it will not appear unless evil is present. People say, "Matt Cutter would sell his liver if he could profit off of it"). Matt is a graduate of Florida State University, reads the girlie magazine *Perfect 10* and owns a twin engine plane with the ID number JB9 (Sy's Air Tours is his competition). Matt previously worked for the CIA as the agency's best sniper (his code name was Jericho; he was also an instructor at the Farm, the CIA training camp). One morning, after killing an innocent man by mistake, he quit the agency and retreated to Africa. Sheena and Matt became friends after Matt, trying to escape from diamond smugglers, fell into a pond of quicksand and was rescued by Sheena. Sheena thinks she is pretty and attractive and has a crush on Matt, but feels Matt does not see her in the same light as he always calls her "Good Buddy" ("I wonder if he knows I'm a girl," Sheena says to herself, "or just a good buddy?"). Sean Callery composed the theme. See also *Manimal* and *Sheena, Queen of the Jungle*.

123. *Sheena, Queen of the Jungle* (Syndicated, 1956-1957)

A private plane flying over Africa develops engine trouble and crashes into the dense jungle. The pilot and two of the plane's three passengers are killed. The lone survivor, a young girl, is found by Logi (Lee Weaver), the noble chief of the Inoma tribe. Logi names the girl Sheena and raises her to respect good men and hate bad ones. The series begins when Sheena (Irish McCalla) is 28 years old. She is blonde, five feet, nine inches tall and weighs 141 pounds. She measures 39½-24½-38 and wears a conservative but leg-revealing leopard skin dress with a black waist belt (the symbol of a lion can be seen in the center of the belt). On each arm, above her elbow, she wears a metal band (about three inches high) that has the embossed symbol of a lion. She also wears a necklace that appears to have a seashell-like pendant (difficult to tell; she never talks about it) and leather-like sandals. A normal width, plain-looking bracelet adorns her right wrist and her belt has a cloth attachment to hold her ivory horn (which she uses to summon the animals for help). Sheena also carries a spear and a knife (in the back of her belt).

Sheena, called "The White Jungle Goddess" by superstitious natives, is assisted by her pet chimpanzee, Chim (played by Neil). Chim likes to fish and Sheena says that one day he is going to catch "The Big One." Sheena's friend, Bob Rayburn (Christian Drake) was originally depicted as a white trader and made Kenya his home (he bought supplies from the Evans Trading Post). As more unscrupulous characters invaded Africa, Rayburn was said to be a big game hunter who worked on behalf of the Commissioner to ensure the safety of people on safaris. He originally dressed in a black shirt and white pants and carried a knife and handgun; later, his dress is all white and he is armed with a rifle. Sheena prefers to "move through the trees" (swing by vine from one to another) rather than walking through the jungle ("Faster my way," she says). When Sheena leaves her horn behind it indicates to Bob that she is in trouble.

Irish McCalla as Sheena is television's first female superhero. The character would not appear on television again for 44 years when Gena Lee Nolin became the jungle queen in a new series titled simply *Sheena* (see prior title). Anita Ekberg was originally cast (1955) to play Sheena but prior commitments forced her to back out by the time the very rare color pilot was shot (the series is in black and white). The program was filmed in Mexico (although set in Kenya, East Africa; an end credit reads "Animal sequences filmed in Africa"). Irish McCalla originally performed her own stunts. When she injured an arm, her stunts (basically swinging on vines through the trees) were performed by Mexican acrobat Raul Gaona (a tall enough woman, apparently, could not be found). Stunt scenes with Gaona, dressed in a leopard skin and blonde wig, are shot from his back and at a sizable distance (impossible to tell who it is). Irish's stunt sequences can be identified by the closeness of the action. Eli Brisken composed the theme.

Sinbad see *The Adventures of Sinbad*

124. *The Six Million Dollar Man* (ABC, 1973–1978)

"Gentlemen, we can rebuild him. We have the technology. Better than he was before. Better. Stronger. Faster" are the words spoken by Oscar Goldman (Richard Anderson), head of the O.S.I. (Office of Scientific Intelligence) as he addressed government officials on the possibility of "building" an agent through bionics for special, super sensitive and highly dangerous missions. The agent referred to by Oscar is Colonel Steve Austin (Lee Majors), a U.S. Air Force test pilot who was seriously injured when the plane he was testing, the M3F5, experienced a blowout, crashed and exploded. At a cost of six million dollars, Steve's legs, right arm and left eye are replaced with atomic powered, synthetic parts that endow him with great speed and strength but also make him something that has never existed before—a cyborg (cybernetic organism). In return, Steve becomes an agent for the O.S.I. Steve was saved by the following bionic parts:

1. Bionic Visual Cortex Terminal (catalogue number 075/KFB); Ratio: 20.2 to 1.3135 Line, 60 Hz. Extended Chromatic Response: Class JC.
2. Bionic Neuro Link Forearm (Upper Arm Assembly), catalogue number 2921LV.
3. Neuro Link Hand, Right (catalogue number 2822/PJI).
4. Power Supply: Atomic Type AED-4 (catalogue number 2031 AED-4); 1550 Watt Continuous Duty Double Gain Overload Follower, Class M2.
5. Bionic Neuro Link, Bi-Pedal Assembly (catalogue number 914 PAM).
6. Power Supply: Atomic Type AED 9A, 4920 Continuous Duty Overload Follower, 2100 Watt Reserve, Intermittent Duty, Class CC.

Steve was born in Ojai, California, and lives on Decatur Road in the former Marsden Ranch (which he bought to find peace and quiet away from his hectic life). There is a highway sign that reads "The Home of American Astronaut Steve Austin" that one sees as they enter Ojai. Steve, who drives a car with the license plate 299 KKL, can run 60 miles per hour. His girlfriend, whom he calls "Babe," is Jaime Sommers (Lindsay Wagner), the tennis pro who would become "The Bionic Woman" (see entry). Jaime, a freshman, and Steve, a senior, met at Ojai High School. They first kissed at a New Year's Eve party and Steve was teased by his friends "for robbing the cradle." In another episode, it is mentioned that Steve and Jaime met in the third grade (when Jaime dared Steve to eat all that food" and he did and became ill). The Capri was their pizza parlor hangout and when they were troubled, the downed tree near the shore of the lake provided a refuge for sorting things out.

Dr. Rudy Wells (Alan Oppenheimer, Martin E. Brooks) is the bionic surgeon who saved both Steve and Jaime's lives. Peggy Callahan (Jennifer Darling) is Oscar's secretary and Jaime's best friend (in some episodes, Jennifer's character is called Janet Callahan). Farrah Fawcett, Lee Majors' wife at the time, appeared in several episodes as both Major Kelly Wood and Victoria Webster, a reporter for KNUZ-TV. Dusty Springfield sings the theme, "The Six Million Dollar Man" (first season episodes).

Note: Three pilots were made to continue a bionic superhero.

1. *Return of the Six Million Dollar Man and the Bionic Woman* (NBC, 5/17/87). The focus was to be on Michael Austin (Tom Schanley), the estranged son of Steve Austin (Lee Majors), as an agent for the O.S.I. (here, the Office of Scientific Information). To stop an evil organization called Fortress, Oscar Goldman (Richard Anderson), head of the O.S.I., recruits former agents Steve Austin and Jaime Sommers (Lindsay Wagner). Steve was now running a charter boat service called *Summer Babe*; Jaime works for a rehabilitation center. Michael, a graduate of the Air Force Academy, has been seriously injured while testing a plane. To save his life, Oscar orders a bionic operation (replacement of both legs, right arm, ten ribs and right eye). Michael teams with Steve and Jaime to defeat Fortress. Martin E. Brooks reprised his role as bionic surgeon Dr. Rudy Wells.

2. *The Bionic Showdown* (NBC, 4/30/89). An attempt at a series about Kate Mason (Sandra Bullock), a woman suffering from a degenerative muscle disease who is given a bionic operation to save her life; she becomes an agent for Oscar Goldman (Richard Anderson) of the O.S.I.

3. *Bionic Ever After* (CBS, 11/29/94). An unsold attempt to revive the characters of Steve Austin and Jaime Sommers (Lee Majors, Lindsay Wagner) as agents for Oscar Goldman (Richard Anderson) of the O.S.I.

125. *Smallville* (WB, 2001)

Events in the life of a teenage Clark Kent before he would don his famous costume and become known as Superman. It begins in 1989. Smallville, Kansas, a city of 25,001 people, is famous for being "The Creamed Corn Capitol of the World." Suddenly, on a clear afternoon, Smallville is struck by a devastating meteor shower. Buildings and cars are destroyed; people are killed, including Lewis and Laura, the parents of three-year-old Lana Lang. A nine-year-old boy named Lex Luthor is injured when the residue from a meteor burns the red hair off his head. A childless farm couple, Jonathan and Martha Kent, are almost killed when a meteor passes over the truck they are driving and forces them to crash. They are rescued by a three-year-old baby who emerges from a crashed rocket that had been part of the meteor shower. The unharmed baby is actually Kal-El, the lone survivor of the doomed planet Krypton. Moments before Krypton exploded, Kal-El's parents (Jor-El and Lara) placed him in an experimental rocket programmed to land on Earth. Also part of that meteor shower were fragments of Kryptonite, green remnants of the planet that can now kill Kal-El if he is exposed to it.

It is 2001 when Smallville is next seen. It has a population of 45,001 and is known as "The Meteor Capitol of the World." The baby, raised by Jonathan and Martha (John Schneider, Annette O'Toole) is now a teenager known as Clark Kent (Tom Welling). Lana (Kristin Kreuk) has been raised by her Aunt

Lucy and both attend Smallville High School. Lex (Michael Rosenbaum) is still bald but the wealthy and powerful son of Lionel Luthor, the owner of the Luthor Corporation (which has its headquarters in nearby Metropolis).

The Kents own a dairy farm on Hickory Road (555-0455 is their phone number). Clark has a special room above the barn that was built for him by Jonathan that he calls "The Fortress of Solitude" (where Clark has a telescope, handed down from Jonathan's father, to study the stars). When Clark begins to develop his powers (speed, strength, x-ray vision, immunity from harm), Jonathan tells Clark about his past. He shows Clark the space ship (stored in the cellar) and a mysterious tablet that was part of the wreckage with symbols he has been unable to decipher. He also tells Clark he must keep his powers secret and only use them for good. No mention is made of any red and blue blankets (the items that, according to the Superman legend, Martha would fashion into his famous costume). Clark dreams about things he would like to do but can't because of his powers and the potential harm they could cause (in one episode Clark mentions he would like to play football but couldn't because of his powers; in a later episode, he is part of the school's football team, the Crows; he wore jersey 89). Crime in Smallville is unusual. The aftereffects of the meteor shower create unnatural villains (for example, a teen who thrives on the heat of others; a coach who can create fire by thinking; a teen who becomes a human bug). Clark with no costume (just his everyday clothes) battles these forces.

Clark also uses his telescope to watch a heavenly body of another kind — Lana Lang, the girl on whom he has a crush, but who is dating football hero Whitney Fordham (Eric Johnson). Lana, a cheerleader for the Crows football team, enjoys horseback riding and has won several equestrian trophies. She dates Whitney "because he's there when I need him. He makes me feel safe" (it is actually Clark who saves the day, but he can never let Lana know. When he tries to be himself around Lana he "becomes all thumbs"). Whenever Lana feels depressed, she finds comfort in reading a book. Her family came to Smallville in 1938 and were some of the earliest dust bowl farmers. When the meteor shower hit, Lana was wearing a fairy princess costume. A picture of her crying in that costume appeared on the cover of *Time* magazine with the headline "Heartbreak in the Heartland." After Lana was adopted by her aunt, she was given a special present — a necklace Lucy had made from a fragment of the meteor that killed her parents. Although Lana treasures it, she is unaware that the green center stone is Kryptonite and could kill Clark.

Lex has been sent to Smallville by his father to make the Luthor Corporation fertilizer plant profitable. He lives in a Scottish castle his father had shipped to Smallville stone by stone and drives a car with the plate LX LTHR (originally seen as LEX). Lex has not yet turned evil; he is friends with Clark and Lana. Lana first met Lex when she was ten years old. Lex's father invited her and her aunt to stay at their Metropolis home when Lana participated in a horse show competition. Clark met Lex by chance. Lex lost control of his car and it crashed through a guard rail and plummeted into a river. Clark, who just happened to be there, jumped into the water and saved Lex from drowning. It is only mentioned that Lex "was kicked out" of the University of Metropolis.

Chloe Sullivan (Allison Mack) and Pete Ross (Sam Jones III) are friends of Clark. Chloe is a reporter for the school newspaper, *The Torch*. She calls Smallville "Land of the Weird, Home of the Strange" (she believes all the weird happenings are related to the meteor shower). She also has a "Wall of Weird"—newspaper clippings of all the strange things that have happened since the meteor shower. Her phone number is 555-0164. She, Pete and Clark frequent the Jalo Coffee Shop (originally the Beanery, where Lana worked as a waitress for a short time). Remy Zero sings the theme, "Save Me." See also *The Adventures of Superboy*, *The Adventures of Superman*, *The Adventures of Superpup*, *Lois and Clark: The New Adventures of Superman* and *Superboy*.

126. *Space Patrol* (ABC, 1950–1955)

The Space Patrol is a 30th century organization that is responsible for the safety of the United Planets (Earth, Jupiter, Mars, Mercury and Venus). The United Planets measure seven and one third billion miles in diameter (it would take light, which travels at 186,000 miles per second, 11 hours to span the length). The Space Patrol is based on the manmade city of Terra and is not only responsible for protecting the United Planets from alien invaders, but keeping the space lanes safe for travel. Major "Robbie" Robertson (Ken Mayer) is the Security Chief for the United Planets; Buzz Corry (Ed Kemmer) is the commander of the Space Patrol and its chief operative (tackling dangerous missions in the cause of universal freedom). He is assisted by Cadet Happy (Lyn Osborn), Tonga (Nina Bara) and Carol Carlisle (Virginia Hewitt).

Buzz succeeded his brother, Kit Corry (Glenn Denning) as the chief of the Space Patrol shortly after the series began. Buzz is fascinated by Carnacan history (a lost civilization of the planet Mars) and is quick to take action in any situation to save his shipmates. His first ship was the *Battle Cruiser 100*; this was replaced by the *Terra IV* and finally the *Terra V* (the *Terra V* was equipped with a time drive and a paralyzer ray; Star Drive was used for deep space travel). The *Battle Cruiser 100* was said to be the fastest ship in the universe. All ships in the Space Patrol are constructed from a metal called Endurim, which is mined on the planet Jupiter.

Cadet Happy, the winner of the Corry Scholarship (set up by Buzz's family) is a recent graduate of the Space Patrol Academy and served as Buzz's co-pilot. He is easygoing, a bit inexperienced and always ready for a fight.

His hobby is photography and "holy smokin' rockets" is his favorite saying (which he utters when something goes wrong).

Tonga, a criminal before being reformed, is now a Space Patrol ally (she previously robbed passengers on sightseeing ships). She works as the assistant to the Security Chief (Major Robertson) and often joins Buzz and his associates on assignments (in some episodes Tonga is said to be the secretary to the Secretary of the United Planets).

Carol is the daughter of the Security General (Paul Cavanaugh) of the United Planets. She is a brilliant scientist and inventor of the Agra-Ray, a device that brings plants to full maturity in a matter of hours; however, if used in reverse, the ray can turn cities into stone. She also designed the *Galaxy*, a magnetic ship shaped like a metal sphere that is capable of traveling at the speed of light. With Tonga as her assistant, Carol created a synthetic form of Randurium, a drug used to treat cosmic and radiation burns. Carol and Tonga, while supposed to be "the weaker sex," were in no way depicted as such. While their uniforms were designed to show their legs for a bit of "cheesecake," they were capable of defending themselves (but were most often depicted as "girls in distress" who needed rescuing by Buzz).

Major Robertson was quick to act but often questioned his decisions and worried about the consequences of his actions. He also invented the formula for the Zeta Ray, a machine that cures any illness and halts the spread of infection.

Prince Baccarratti (Bela Kovacs), also known as the Black Falcon, is an evil alien, based in his castle on Planet X, who sought to rule the United Planets by destroying the Space Patrol. Mr. Proteus (Marvin Miller), the man of many faces, was also a threat to Buzz and his crew. Agent X (Norman Jolley) and Major Sova (Jack McHugh) were also enemies of the United Planets.

Vacation resorts for the Space Patrolers included Red Lake Winter Resort on Jupiter and Space Port at Lake Azure on Venus. The Medical Science Center is located on Terra as is the United Planets Communications Commission Control Room. The Space Patrolers communicate with each other via space phones and 20th century weapons are displayed in the United Planets Museum.

Space Patrol premiered locally in Los Angeles on KECA-TV on March 13, 1950, as a 15-minute daily serial. This was followed by a 30-minute Saturday morning network series that ran from December 30, 1950, to February 26, 1955. Both were distributed to affiliated stations by kinescope. KECA dropped the daily shows from national distribution when the cost of film and shipping became excessive. The daily shows now aired only in Los Angeles while the Saturday morning shows were still being seen elsewhere (about a week later) by kinescope (making a copy of a live TV show by photographing it off a monitor). By late 1952, when the coaxial cable permitted coast-to-coast transmission, the live Saturday shows were no longer kinescoped; the daily series was dropped.

Jack Narz is the announcer; the program opens with these words: "High adventure in the wild, vast regions of space. Missions of daring in the name of interplanetary justice. Travel into the future with Buzz Corry, commander-in-chief of the Space Patrol."

127. *Special Unit 2* (UPN, 2001)

"Ever catch something out of the corner of your eye; ever feel there is something out there in the dark, something evil? Everybody does, but they turn away." The members of Special Unit 2 do not. They pursue and attempt to destroy that unknown evil.

Captain Richard Paige (Richard Gant) is a man who believes there is something lurking in the dark—from trolls to werewolves. Vampires are a different story—"Complete and total fiction. I never heard of anything so ridiculous." Paige heads Special Unit 2, a secret undercover unit of the Chicago Police Department that handles bizarre crimes committed by Links (everything that is not man or beast. "These things love Chicago," says Paige; "I wish they didn't"). The unit works in secret because of the fear that would be created if monsters were known to exist. It has no precinct or public phone number. All that is known about it is that it investigates special crimes. Members cannot reveal what they do to anyone—"That's their sworn duty," says Paige.

Paige heads Special Unit 2 from an old abandoned subway line that contains the latest scientific equipment. The original subway entrance has been disguised by a block of stores. The Golden Eagle Dry Cleaners (building 613) fronts as the secret entrance to Special Unit 2 (622-7733 is the phone number of the cleaners; the Mi Tierra Mexican Restaurant is the store next to the Golden Eagle). Seven floors below the basement is the sub-dungeon where captured Links are kept in cells. The unit uses special color-coded ammo (different colors work on different Links, depending on the number of Links and their skeletal composition. Blue striped ammo, for example, is used on Gargoyles). The unit also has an unknown creature "that we can't figure out how to kill so we keep it around for garbage disposal," says Paige. When the unit visits a crime scene and takes footprints, they take the footprints (no plaster for them; they cut around the area and take the original footprints).

Kate Alice Benson (Alexondra Lee) and Nicholas O'Malley (Michael Landes) are Paige's top operatives. Kate was a former police officer who was recruited because of her belief that the unknown exists (as a child she witnessed a troll; as an officer, she saw a sea serpent destroy a barge. She reported the incident but no one believed her—until she met Paige). Kate's license plate reads M06 975 (later KO3 240). Kate's parents wanted her to become a doctor and she is afraid to chase after men — "I'm honest, I say what I think." Kate mentioned she attended Pioneer High School.

O'Malley was a police officer when his female partner (Julie) was killed by a vicious Link ("It ripped her into 600 inch size pieces"; O'Malley now helps her children with money each month). O'Malley, Special Unit 2 I.D. number 00P6-5905-332, treats all Links the same — "Kill 'em" (he is also an expert on coming up with ways to destroy them — none of which are feasible, as each Link is different). Nick becomes uptight if a Link gets the best of him. He seeks revenge, "but only to protect the public," he says. Nick is rude and obnoxious and often plunges headlong into situations without thinking first (when he gets in too deep he often says, "Maybe I should have had a plan first"). In moments of weakness, Nick finds relaxation at a strip bar; his license plate reads MIJ 528.

Assisting Kate and Nick is Carl (Danny Woodburn), a Link (gnome) the unit can trust (Paige calls him "a snitch we can trust, not an employee"). Carl has a bad habit of robbing convenience stores; he helps the unit so the police department will drop his numerous felony charges. Nick is not fond of Carl and often takes his frustration out on him. Carl, a gourmet cook and neat freak, stands four feet one inch tall and has only one thing in common with Nick — they are both Chicago Cubs baseball fans. "The Captain gets extremely aggravated at Carl," says Nick; "that's the effect Carl has on people." Carl also believes "Nick is a psycho" for his Rambo-like pursuit of Links.

Alice Kramer (Pauley Perrette) also assists Nick and Kate in the field. She is a blonde bombshell who was working in the unit's damage control, then left to pursue an acting job in Los Angeles. She returned to the unit when that failed. She enjoys smoking cigars and appears to be fond of Nick. She also provides distraction — to draw the attention of the press to her so Nick and Kate can do their job. Mark Snow composed the theme.

Spider-Man see *The Amazing Spider-Man*

128. *Stingray* (NBC, 1986–1987)

A black 1965 Corvette Stingray, license plate EGW 769 (later STINGRAY) is the trademark of a mysterious man, known only as Ray (Nick Mancuso), who travels across the U.S. helping people who are unable to turn to the police for help. Ray has no friends and only fleeting romantic relationships. The only thing actually known about him is that he is skilled in the martial arts and is an expert spy and infiltrator (it is suggested that he was possibly an agent for the CIA). Ray can only be contacted through a newspaper ad that runs on Friday: "'65 black Stingray for sale. Barter only. Call 555-7687." While it is not stated, Ray is apparently independently wealthy and does what he does as a hobby. He will not accept money for his help; he asks only for a favor — whenever he needs it — as payment ("A favor for a favor," he says). Ray will not do repeat favors and if he feels it is warranted, will accept a referral from a client. Mike Post and Pete Carpenter composed the theme.

129. *Street Hawk* (ABC, 1985)

"Operation Street Hawk" is a top secret project of the L.A.P.D. that is concerned with law enforcement. Street Hawk is a high tech motorcycle designed specifically to battle crime ("an all-terrain pursuit vehicle"). It has a cruising speed of 200 miles per hour. By incorporating four high volume air boxes and hyper thrust, the speed can reach up to 300 miles per hour. It also has an aerodynamic coefficient of 0.05 for silent running (making any friction it may cause untraceable). Hydraulic suspension allows the cycle to adjust to street or off-road use. A system of negative airflow controls the brakes ("If necessary, you can stop on a dime"). The handlebars contain a compressed air vertical lift system (the press of a button can propel Street Hawk 30 meters into the air).

Street Hawk also has a high energy particle beam with two settings: maximum charge (capable of immobilizing a ten ton truck) or reduced power (to stun or immobilize a suspect). Street Hawk carries only one weapon: a gun that fires a soft rubber slug. The driver's helmet is the nerve center. There are digital readouts in each corner. The left computes speed and revolutions per minute; the right calibrates distance. Directly below that is the monocle targeting system. The helmet is also equipped with infrared detectors and light amplification for all-weather and night fighting capabilities. Anything the driver sees is automatically recorded by the homebase computer.

Norman Tuttle (Joe Regalbuto), a research scientist for the Federal government, designed Street Hawk ("My baby"). He dreams of having such a bike in every police garage in the country. It took him four years to design Street Hawk but it must remain a secret ("people won't take it kindly to have an attack motorcycle patrolling their streets." It is being tested to see if it can be offered to local law enforcement agencies). Norman controls the operation of Street Hawk (it appears as a red blinking light on his main computer tracking system). Norman can monitor the entire city from the main console and shut Street Hawk down immediately if anything should go wrong. His base of operations is a lab hidden in a warehouse (Durrell's Bakers Supply Company) that "looks like the bridge of the Starship Enterprise."

Jesse Mach (Rex Smith) is Street Hawk's driver, an officer with the Metropolitan Division of the L.A.P.D. who wears a leg brace and poses as an officer with the public relations department. Jesse was reckless and irresponsible and suffered a severe motorcycle accident that made him incapable of fighting street crime. Norman arranged a special operation at the Doctors Hospital of Southern California that used an unapproved F.D.A. prosthesis to repair Jesse's knee. In turn, Jesse agreed to become Norman's "test pilot." While Jesse does not need to wear the leg brace, he does so as part of his cover. Jesse is given a special racing suit (for riding Street Hawk) and the bike is programmed to accept him (unauthorized personnel receive an electrical shock if they attempt to use it). Jesse won his first motorcycle race at age 14; at age 18 he won his first international race. He quit the racing circuit to become a cop.

Sandy McCoy (Jayne Modean), then Rachel Adams (Jeannie Wilson) is Jesse's superior, the head of the P.R. department; Leo Altobelli (Richard Venture) is the Police Commander. Tangerine Dream performs the theme.

130. *Super Force* (Syndicated, 1990–1992)

It is the year 2020 and crime has become a serious problem in America. In an unidentified city, the Hungerford Foundation has taken steps to battle crime in the city's most notorious and dangerous region — the Crime Zone. E.B. Hungerford (Patrick Macnee) is the head of the foundation and F.X. Spinner (Larry B. Scott) is the scientific genius who has developed a wide range of weapons to battle injustice. His most cunning weapon is a super strong black space suit that is equipped with the latest technology in weapons and tracking (the helmet, for example, shows weapons range, charge and mode). Former NASA astronaut Zack Stone (Ken Olandt) is secretly Super Force, the man who wears the space suit to battle evil.

For Zack, life would change shortly after he returned from a two year exploratory mission of Mars. As commander of the space craft *Columbia*, Zack risked his life to save his crew when the ship was damaged in a meteor shower (he jerry-rigged the drive shaft and was hailed as a hero). However, during his absence, his father had died and his brother, Officer Frank Stone, had been killed in the line of duty. When Zack learns that Frank was believed to be on the take at the time, he joins the force in an attempt to clear his name.

Shortly after Zack graduates from the Metro Plex Police Academy in the summer of 2020, his uncle, E.B. Hungerford, is killed by the same people who shot Frank—criminals programming young people to become violent on a moment's notice. It is at this time that Zack meets F.X. and learns of his uncle's plan to fight crime. Although E.B. is dead, F.X. keeps him "alive" by programming his personality, achievements and life voice patterns into a computer. E.B.'s image now appears on a computer screen and can function mentally as if he were actually alive. To conceal his identity as Super Force, Zack becomes an officer with the 33rd Division of the Metropolitan

Police Department (the precinct whose beat is the Crime Zone). Captain Carla Frost (Lisa Niemi) is Zack's gutsy, no-nonsense superior at the 33rd. Officer Zander Tyler (Musetta Vander), who possesses a gift of extrasensory perception, is with a special police unit called Esper (or "The E.S.P. Department as people call it," she says).

Zack, badge number 499, rides the Super Force Cycle, a black with green stripe motorcycle with an unreadable bar code license plate. F.X., which stands for Special Effects, was called "Cuddles" as a kid. He shops at the Food Plex and has the Hungerford Industries I.D. number 36502007. Addresses and phone numbers are not given. When a malfunction in the Super Force helmet "kills" Zack, Zander uses her powers to penetrate Zack's mind and bring him back from the dead. As a result, Zack acquired new powers: the ability to see something before it happens, the ability to sense danger, an increase in strength to that of 4.2 men, and heightened perception.

Two adult (Triple X rated) film actresses, Traci Lords and Ginger Lynn, appeared on the series. Traci, in the episode "Of Human Bondage" (wherein she played an alien seeking human specimens for a zoo) and Ginger, as Zack's girlfriend, Crystal, in "Come Under the Way," "There Is a Light," "Instant Karma" and "The Big Spin." Crystal's birthday is December 14, 1995; Zack was born on July 10, 1992. Kevin Kiner composed the theme.

131. *The Super Human Samurai Syber Squad*
(Syndicated, 1994-1995)

Kilokahn was a top secret U.S. government computer project designed to explore the digital world. When scientists felt the program was getting out of control, the project was shut down and supposedly taken off line. An unknown virus they created (Kilokahn) was able to survive but was trapped in the deactivated program.

One day while surfing the web, high school computer nerd Malcolm Fink (Glen Beaudin) finds traces of the Kilokahn program. While attempting to learn more about it, he activates the program and brings to life Kilokahn, a super intelligent, evil virus that lives in computer circuits and seeks to rule the world by controlling computers. Malcolm cannot deactivate Kilokahn (voice of Tim Curry) and Kilokahn uses Malcolm as his pawn — to help him create the mega virus monsters to destroy computer circuits.

Sam Collins (Matthew Lawrence), Sydney Forrester (Robin Mary Florence), Amp (Troy Slaten) and Tank (Kevin Castro) are teens at North Valley High School who are also members of the rock band Team Samurai. Jennifer Doyle (Jaymie Betcher) is the prettiest girl at North Valley High and also Malcolm's dream girl. When Malcolm learns that Sam is planning to ask Jennifer for a date "with my girl," he uses his computer to interrupt a phone call from Sam to Jennifer. Sam, Sydney, Amp and Tank are seated near Sam's computer when Malcolm strikes. Since phone lines also carry computer signals, Malcolm's attempts backfire. A light emerges from Sam's computer and engulfs the group. Sam is struck by an electronic beam that links his brain to his computer and to the digital world as Servo (a champion servant of computers). When Sam plays the power cord on his guitar he can digitize into Servo and enter his computer to battle the evils of Kilokahn. Sydney (as Vor), Amp (as Vitor), and Tank (as Trackton) help Sam via their digital warrior counterparts. Together they form the Super Human Samurai Syber Squad. (Each team member wears special body armor. When all the parts are attached to Servo, he acquires the Samurai Syncho Body Suit to battle the monsters.)

Kilokahn and Malcolm need each other. Kilokahn, "the overlord of the digital world," operates at 400 megahertz and requires Malcolm's computer wizardry to create the virus monsters. Malcolm, once shunned by everyone, hopes to become someone everyone notices—ruler of the digital world.

Sam was born on August 16 and lives at 609 River Road. His parents are not seen but he has a younger sister named Elizabeth. She is not seen but is heard (voice of Kath Soucie). Elizabeth is very mischievous and constantly bothers Sam and his friends with her antics. Sydney, a bit jealous at Jennifer for all the attention she gets, was born on September 30 and lives a few doors from Sam at 615 River Road. Tank loves to eat (hence his nickname; real name not given). Amp, born on April 1, has a pet cat (Rosalie) and a chameleon (Robin). After two months, Amp is replaced (without explanation) by Lucky Lowdon (Rembrandt) in the episode "Give Till It Megahertz." The team members are all students of the martial arts and use this as a weapon to fight Kilokahn's monsters. Like the series that inspired it, *The Mighty Morphin Power Rangers*, the show is strong on action and special effects and concerned little about character information.

132. *Superboy* (Syndicated, 1988–1992)

In a galaxy far beyond our own there is a planet called Krypton that is inhabited by a super intelligent race. Jor-El (George Lazenby, Jacob Wilkin), a leading scientist, believes his planet is being drawn closer to the sun and is on the brink of destruction. When he is unable to convince the Council of Scientists of his findings, he begins preparations to save his wife, Lara (Britt Ekland, Kathy Poling), and infant son, Kal-El, from the impending disaster. Jor-El is only able to complete a miniature, experimental rocket before the planet begins to explode. He and Lara decide to save Kal-El. The baby, wrapped in red and blue blankets, is placed in the rocket. Jor-El programs the ship to land on Earth, a planet he knows to be inhabited. The ship lands in Smallville, Kansas, and is found by Jonathan and Martha Kent

(Stuart Whitman, Salome Jens), a childless farm couple, who raise the infant as their own. They name him Clark Kent. As a young boy, Clark (Edan Gross) shows "the strength of steel, the speed of light and the power to help all mankind." After graduating from Smallville High School, Clark enrolls at Schuster University. Clark (John Haymes Newton, Gerard Christopher) is studying journalism and works for the school newspaper, the *Herald*. He fights crime as the mysterious Superboy in a red and blue costume his mother made for him from the blankets Lara placed around him.

At Schuster, Clark befriends Lana Lang (Stacy Haiduk), Trevor Jenkins "T.J." White (Jim Calvett), the pre–Lois Lane and Jimmy Olsen characters that are a part of the Superman saga. Lana is Clark's girlfriend; T.J., the son of Perry White, the editor of the Metropolis *Daily Planet*, is Clark's roommate; he is hoping to become a photographer. Plaguing Clark and mankind in general is Lex Luthor (Scott Wells), the diabolical villain out to control the world.

Second season episodes change the series title to *The Adventures of Superboy*, drops T.J. White (he is replaced by Ilan Mitchell-Smith as Andy McAllister, Clark's new roommate), and Lex becomes older with Sherman Howard in the role. T.J. is written out when he heads for Metropolis to try his luck at becoming a stand-up comedian.

Third and fourth season episodes dropped the college aspect when Clark and Lana graduate and become interns with the Bureau of Extra-Normal Matters in Florida (their office is on the sixth floor at 101 North Siegel Street in Capitol City). Dennis Jackson (Robert Levine) heads the bureau, which investigates strange phenomena. The sensuous Darla (Tracey Roberts) becomes Lex's assistant. In addition to Lex's diabolical schemes, Clark (as Superboy) had to battle Bizarro (Barry Meyers), an imperfect and indestructible copy of Superboy that was created at Schuster University; and Roger Corbin (Michael Callan), an evil criminal known as Metallo.

Clark becomes Superboy by either twirling rapidly or running at supersonic speed. Clark lives in Apartment 307, sets his alarm for 6:45 A.M. and takes the 7:30 bus to work. The Shift Military Institute has the only known supply of Kryptonite, the green metal remnants of Krypton, which can destroy Clark. In the episode "The Lair" (10/21/90) Clark mentions that he hopes to one day move to Metropolis and become a reporter. In advertisements for the show, Clark says, "I have three passions: truth, justice and the American Way" (the words used in the theme for *The Adventures of Superman*). The episode "The Road to Hell" (5/25/91) finds Clark stepping into a series of parallel worlds where he meets his elder self (Ron Ely) and his future self as a young boy (Robert Allen Shippy). "Paranoia," the episode of 11/8/91, reunites *The Adventures of Superman* co-stars Noel Neill (as Alexis) and Jack Larson (as Lew Lamont) as investigators for the bureau. People who believe they have seen the abnormal file form C-29 at the bureau (which was formerly a nightclub called the Trocadel). When Lex has a problem he can't solve, he finds comfort in kidnapping Lana. Kevin Kiner composed the theme. See also *The Adventures of Superboy*, *The Adventures of Superman*, *The Adventures of Superpup*, *Lois and Clark: The New Adventures of Superman* and *Smallville*.

Superman see *The Adventures of Superman*

133. *Tarzan* (NBC, 1966–1968; Syndicated, 1991-1992)

The original concept for Tarzan, as created by Edgar Rice Burroughs, began in 1911 when his story, "Tarzan of the Apes," first appeared in the October issue of *All-Story Magazine*. The legend began with a mutiny on a ship bound for England. Two passengers, Lord John Greystoke and his wife, Alice, were put ashore off the coast of Africa and left with only tools and a rifle to defend themselves. As time passed, John built a small hut near the water. One year later, a son is born to them. Soon after, their hut is attacked by a tribe of Bull Apes. John and Alice are killed but their son (John) is taken by Kahla, a female ape and raised as Tarzan, Lord of the Jungle. Twenty years later, while on a safari, Jane Parker wanders from its safety and is soon facing impending death from a rampaging elephant. She is rescued by Tarzan, whom she befriends and teaches to speak English. She eventually decides to become his mate and remains with him in Africa. Tarzan has a companion named Cheetah.

This concept was adapted to television for the first time in an unsold pilot called *Tarzan* that was produced in 1958. Gordon Scott played Tarzan and Eve Brent was Jane. The story, which was released theatrically as *Tarzan and the Trappers* when a sponsor couldn't be found, finds Tarzan attempting to stop trappers from taking treasures from a lost city in the jungle.

The NBC version has Tarzan's companion, Cheetah, but no Jane. It is said that Tarzan was educated by a Frenchman when his safari was marooned in Africa. The Frenchman discovers that Tarzan's real name is John Greystoke and persuades him to return to England with him. John is educated in the finest schools but is unable to adjust to civilized life. He returns to Africa to protect it from the evils of man. Jai (Manuel Padilla, Jr.) is the orphaned jungle boy cared for by Tarzan (Ron Ely).

The syndicated version reworks the entire Tarzan legend to accommodate modern times. A plane, carrying a family of three, crashes in the dense African jungle. The lone survivor, a young boy, is found by Kahla, a great Bull Ape, and raised as Tarzan, Lord of the Jungle. The series begins many years later when Tarzan is an adult. Tarzan (Wolf Larson) and his companion, Cheetah (a chimp), live in a treehouse by the Great River. Stories now focus on Tarzan's efforts to protect the animals and jungle from environmental wrongdoers.

Jane Porter (Lydie Denier) is a beautiful French research scientist who maintains a compound near the Great River. She works with the Wildlife Institute to save endangered species. She is assisted by Roger Taft (Sean Roberge), the son of Roger Taft, Sr. (Chuck Samota), the man who funds Jane's research. Simon Gaubier (Malick Bowens), a native African, also assists them. It is mentioned that Jane and Roger have been in Africa one year, but it is not related how they met Tarzan. Prior to Cheetah, Tarzan's chimp was Maya; Juma is Tarzan's lion and Tantor his elephant. Simon's plane has the I.D. number XADAC. Details are not related on how Tarzan learned to speak English. Robert O. Ragland composed the theme.

Tattooed Alien Fighters from Beverly Hills see *The Mighty Morphin Power Rangers*

134. *Team Knight Rider* (Syndicated, 1997-1998)

Following Michael Knight's retirement from the Foundation for Law and Government (see *Knight Rider*), a new team of operatives is formed called Team Knight Rider, which consists of five operatives and five special, talking cars.

Kyle Stewart (Brixton Karnes) leads the team. He commands a car called Dante (voice of Tom Kane). Jenny Andrews (Christine Steel) rides in a car named Domino (voice of Nia Valdaros). Erica West (Kathy Tragester) has a motorcycle named Kat (voice of Andrea Beutner). Duke DePalma (Duane Davis) rides in a car called Beast (voice of Kerrigan Mahan) and Kevin "Trek" Sanders (Nick Wechsler) has a motorcycle named Plato (voice of John Kissir).

The team is based in *Sky One*, a large cargo plane that serves as their mobile headquarters (to be ready at a moment's notice to help any city or town that requires their assistance). They are guided by the sexy female voice (Linda McCullough) of a computer called both Sky and Sky One.

It now takes five operatives and five cars to do what Michael and his car, KITT, previously did. Kyle is a former CIA operative who was called America's James Bond (he was sent to the world's hot spots and performed near-impossible missions successfully). His career came to an abrupt end when his cover was blown behind enemy lines. He was then hired by the government to head TKR (Team Knight Rider). Because of the risks he once took, he now looks at life in a different way. He worries about the safety of his team, the moral issues of an assignment and the state of the world in which he lives.

Jenny is a beautiful but tough ex–Marine sergeant. She is an excellent gymnast and martial arts expert. She was raised in a military family. Her father was a general and her five brothers are all pursuing military careers in various branches of the service. Jenny fought in the Gulf War, received many accommodations and is obsessed with war games. Her mother wishes her only daughter would have pursued a more feminine career but knew at age ten Jenny was destined for a military career (at this time the tomboyish Jenny led a tactical assault on a rival neighborhood kids' clubhouse). Jenny is very cautious when it comes to her personal life and rarely shows her soft, feminine side (her teammates call her "Xena, Warrior Princess"). Jenny is focused, driven and efficient and the one Kyle worries about the most (fearing that her enthusiasm could get her killed). She mentioned that as a kid her favorite TV show was *Josie and the Pussycats.*

Erica is a beautiful blonde with a mysterious and mostly unknown past (Kyle is not even sure if Erica West is her real name). Erica is a smooth talking con artist who can manipulate people into giving her exactly what she wants. It was revealed that during one scam, Erica made a mistake and was apprehended. She was tried, convicted and spent three years in prison before she was released to the Foundation for Law and Government on condition that she use her talents as part of TKR.

Duke was born in Chicago and fought his way out of the slums to become a small time boxer, then a police officer. His enthusiasm for pursuing justice was also his downfall: He was suspended for breaking too many rules in his attempt to apprehend a mobster. These actions brought him to the attention of TKR, who required an agent who was in touch with the common man (Duke's cop-on-the-beat experience makes him the only team member who possesses this quality). While he appears tough, Duke's actions are slow and thought out (he never rushes head first into anything).

Kevin, nicknamed "Trek" for his obsession with *Star Trek* is a scientific genius with an I.Q. of 200. At the age of 12 he graduated from M.I.T. and immediately went to work for a think tank in Washington. He soon tired of this and put his genius to work developing new technologies and selling them on the open market. By the time he was 20, he was a multi-millionaire; the following year he was broke. Making money soon became a game with him: invent something, make a fortune, lose it, invent something else. TKR intrigued him and he offered them his services. While he is a computer whiz, he is not the most ambitious member of the team (the others feel he is unmotivated). Trek seems to absorb knowledge in all fields and can take nothing and come up with a solution to the team's problem.

Dante, Kyle's car, is a Ford Expedition Sport Utility Vehicle. It is also the self-appointed leader of the team's vehicles (acts as a liaison between the human team members and their cars). Dante has a dry, sarcastic sense of humor and makes sure that the needs of the other vehicles are met.

Jenny's car, Domino, is a Ford Mustang GT convertible. Domino is just the opposite of Jenny. She is somewhat vocal and flirts with any cute guy she sees (usually confusing the man, as he assumes it is Jenny). Domino "just wants to be one of the girls" and feels she has "a hot body and smooth curves." She helps Jenny with her energy blast weapons.

Kat, Erica's motorcycle, is a by-the-books vehicle. She acts more like Erica's mother than her partner (she makes Erica aware of road rules and regulations). Despite her safety conscious computer chips, Kat hopes to avoid damage to herself and property to get Erica where she has to be. Kat has a twin motorcycle named Plato, which is ridden by Trek (the cycles can merge to form a high pursuit vehicle). Plato is not only a motorcycle, but Trek's best friend. Plato is highly intelligent and an expert on pop culture and entertainment trivia. Plato often speaks in a code of movie and TV show quotes that is only understandable by Trek.

Beast, also called Attack Beast, is Duke's Ford F-150 truck. It has a bit of an attitude, a gruff voice and is sometimes hostile. Beast is sent in to do the hard work (like crashing through walls). He doesn't like to be told what to do and will only listen to Jenny (whose voice softens him). Beast's license plate reads BST-1.

135. *Thieves* (ABC, 2001)

The Inter Agency Task Force is a special Baltimore-based unit of the Justice Department that retrieves stolen or missing U.S. property. In order to achieve their goal, the agency requires the talents of expert thieves. Their operatives are Johnny Marucci (John Stamos) and Rita (Melissa George), highly skilled thieves who were captured red-handed in the act of stealing diamonds and offered a choice: "Steal things back that we feel were stolen from us. Serve your time in jail or serve your country. Your choice." Although arrested (Johnny is police file 130049; Rita, 130048) and booked, they are freed when they elect to steal rather than spend 25 years in prison.

Johnny is an expert pickpocket and locksmith. He was a master debater on his high school debate team and says "I don't find things, I take things" and "There are thieves and there are thieves. Don't lump them into one category." He lives in Apartment 1210 and doesn't like shooting or being around shooting ("I break into people's homes when they're sleeping. If they wake up, I leave"). He also dislikes flying in a helicopter ("It doesn't have any wings"). Johnny likes to take things slow and easy (like breaking into a safe by listening for the tumblers in a combination lock); Rita is impatient ("Plastic explosives work faster"). She thinks Johnny is unprofessional and is only working with him to stay out of prison.

Rita was born on May 12, 1976, in Australia and raised by her father, a casino pit boss. She is a vegetarian, takes herbal drugs and gets cranky after drinking coffee. She is a skilled blackjack dealer, a computer whiz and weapons expert. Rita loves shooting ("It gives me a rush") and has several bogus driver's licenses (Michelle Michael, Sheila Frances, Karen Paldoni; 11550 Lamaria Street, Chicago, Illinois, is listed as her home address); ADM 396 is her car license plate (later 756 AQU).

At 18 years of age, Rita was deciding whether to major in biology or psychology at college; Johnny, at 18, was learning to hotwire his first car. Rita has a recurring nightmare about her and Johnny being romantically involved. She feels most uncomfortable when an assignment calls for her to act as Johnny's wife ("I'd rather be locked in a cell and let out only for food and water"). She thinks Johnny is superstitious ("I'm not superstitious," he says, "I'm super cautious") and would like Johnny to do things by a set of rules ("I do," says Johnny, "no rules").

When Rita dresses in pink ("Rita is not a pink person") Johnny knows she is up to something. He also says "Rita's name is not Happy. If she had to pick one of the seven dwarfs, she'd only have six choices." When something goes wrong on an assignment, Johnny covers up by saying Rita is his wife or girlfriend (which Rita constantly denies). Johnny has a crush on Rita and becomes jealous when she dates. "My personal life is just that, personal," she says. "Okay? Personal, out of bounds, got it?" While Rita and Johnny argue about everything, Johnny goes "on and on" when he finds out something about Rita that he doesn't like.

Oliver Shue (Robert Knepper) and Al Trundel (Tone Loc) are the special Justice Department agents who oversee Rita and Johnny's assignments. Paulie (Sofia Milos) is Johnny's friend, a beautiful hit lady he uses to help track down leads ("Only don't shoot 'em," he tells her). See also *It Takes a Thief.*

136. *Things That Go Bump* (NBC, 3/22/97)

Pilot. "I'm your worst nightmare—a wizard with a badge" says Jack "Bump" Bumstead (Burke Moses), a detective with the New Orleans Police Department, who heads a special group of crime fighters designed to banish demons who break the law. Bump is assisted by Officer Zalea "Zee" DeCastro (Jennifer Gatti), Marcel (Tony Molina, Jr.), a computer specialist, Harry (C.C.H. Pounder), a sorceress, and Hoodoo, his dog. Jack is divorced from Chloe (Melora Hardin), the spoiled daughter of Police Chief Ty Garrett (Charles Hallahan). Zee is from the Bronx, New York, and relocated to New Orleans to be with her boyfriend—until she found him cheating on her; Marcel is an amateur inventor whose gizmos help Bump dispense with ghosts; Harry works as a singer at the Blues Bar (where Bump orders only milk).

The pilot finds Bump seeking to banish Sleepyhead, the ghost of a baby seeking to destroy New Orleans (the urban legend of Sleepyhead began in

1789 with the cursed birth of Augustine Dormezvous. After his mother died during a difficult delivery, his father sent him to an orphanage. There a sadistic headmaster named him Sleepyhead and took away his only possession — his baby rattle. When he was a young boy, Augustine escaped and took refuge in a warehouse. A mysterious fire broke out and Augustine was blamed. He was pursued to Lafayette Cemetery "and some say he was buried alive; others say he is alive still"). Bump dispenses with Sleepyhead when he gives "the maniacal ghost with fangs and a large bulbous head" a baby rattle and sings him a lullaby.

137. *Thor* (NBC, 5/22/88)

Pilot. Donald Blake (Steve Levitt) is an anthropologist interested in Viking history. While on a dig, Blake begins exploring a cave and finds an ancient stone tomb. Although he is unable to read Viking writing, he is able to tell it is the tomb of Thor, a great warrior king (Thor is the God of Thunder and the spoiled son of the mythical god, Oden. Oden has banished Thor to Earth where he must perform good deeds by helping mankind before he can enter Valhalla, the Viking heaven). When Blake picks up Thor's mighty hammer (which gave him strength), Thor (Eric Kramer) appears and attaches himself to Donald (although they remain individual beings). By saying the name Oden and holding the hammer, Blake produces Thor, who can then function apart from Donald. Now, with Donald as his life force, Thor carries out his sentence by fighting crime and injustice. The pilot story finds Blake (and Thor) battling a corrupt military leader seeking a deadly gamma transponder ray. Lance Rubin composed the theme.

138. *The Tick* (Fox, 2001)

His identity is unknown (he doesn't know who he really is or where he came from). He wears an electric blue latex body suit with exaggerated muscles and twitching antennae. He is a superhero who calls himself the Tick (Patrick Warburton). He has the powers of strength and speed, but is not always able to control them. He is also unable to distinguish between living things and inanimate objects. He creates a considerable amount of destruction as he goes about dispensing his own brand of justice.

Viewers are first introduced to the Tick at the bus station where he has established a base on a rooftop to battle the coffee vending machine that is directly below him. Should the unthinkable happen and the vending machine not dispense coffee once money is inserted, the Tick comes to the rescue to argue with and shake "the vending menace." His days as a vending machine crime fighter are ended, however, when he is told by the station manager that his help is not needed here, but in The City ("You have freed us from the tyranny of the coffee machine"). It is in The City where the Tick finds a new home: "City, City, I am the Tick and you have melted my heart. From this day forth, I will spread my buttery justice over your every nook and cranny. Hear, oh hear me, my City, your toast will never go bare again."

Arthur (David Burke) is a bookkeeper for World Wide Fishladder and Sons who dreams of becoming a superhero. He feels he has been living a lie and that his life is meant to be more than a mild-mannered accountant. His life has become nothing but numbers, deductions and IRAs. He did his parents' tax returns since he was six and has become fed up. He feels he has a higher calling and can't hide from it any longer —"I'm going to become a superhero." Arthur dons a white costume with rabbit ears and a backpack with wings to enable him to fly. He considers himself the Moth (but he is described as "The Easter Bunny" and being "built like a sensible shoe and shouldn't be jumping around town in a body sock"). Despite the insults, Arthur decides to fight crime. He first meets the Tick when they join forces to defeat a Russian plot to kill visiting ex–President Jimmy Carter. The Tick takes a liking to Arthur and decides to team with him. They set up residence at 370 Pleasant Avenue, Apartment 7A, and befriend two other crime fighters: Captain Liberty (Liz Vassey) and Batmanuel (Nestor Carbonell).

Captain Liberty, alias Janet, is a beautiful single woman who has been hired by the U.S. government to be a symbol of everything that is good. She is 29 years old and feels her superhero status leaves her no time for romance (she constantly complains about being lonely). Her costume is maroon and gold with a cutout star on her chest to reveal cleavage. She wears a Statue of Liberty crown and carries a plastic torch as a symbol of freedom. She keeps a supply of hand grenades in her apartment and drowns her sorrows (with other superheroes) at the Lonely Panda Bar. Janet mentioned she was recently out of rehab and posed "buck naked on a Harley motorcycle wearing only boots" for a strange magazine called *Peek and Boom.*

Batmanuel, a Latin version of Batman, is a ladies' man and appears when a beautiful damsel is in distress. He wears a brown costume, black mask and says, "I get a lot of press." He drives the Batcar (plate BAT LOVE) and is constantly rejected by Captain Liberty as he tries to seduce her. He believes women are attracted by "the power of the suit. Women cannot resist the suit."

The Tick and Arthur eat at the Tick Tock Diner. The Tick doesn't understand insults ("It doesn't comprehend") and says, "I have to keep my head clear to deal with evil." The Tick is bulletproof and calls himself "The Mysterious Blue Avenger" and "The Big Blue Bug of Justice." Arthur cannot watch more than one movie at a time without getting a headache and complains that the Tick leaves the cap off the toothpaste tube. Their home phone number is 555-0197. Steve Bartek composed the theme. The program opens with these words (spoken by the Tick): "The life of a superhero is a lonely one filled with hardship and danger. The few who answer the call must leave comfort, safety and often sanity behind. But someone's gotta stand the heat and stay in the kitchen. Someone's gotta don the oven mitts of all that's right and strangle the red hot throat of all that's wrong."

139. *Time Traxx* (Syndicated, 1993)

Darien Lambert (Dale Midkiff) was born at Longham Hospital in Middle City at 8:05 A.M. on August 17, 2160. It was a Monday. The skies were clear, the temperature 91 degrees and the humidity at 87 percent. He was unclaimed by his parents and was raised in an orphanage in Unclave I-6, an area previously known as Chicagoland. Darien was allowed to choose his own name. He chose Darien for the hero of the Just War of 2129; and Lambert, the surname of the woman who bore him, as his last name even though all he has of her is a photograph.

Darien grew up as a normal child of the times: I.Q. of 204; speed memorization rate of one point two pages per second and an accomplished athlete. He can run 100 meters in 8.6 seconds; the mile is 3 minutes, 38 seconds. His heartbeat is a normal 35 beats per minute and his life expectancy is 120 years. His lungs are also average, capable of storing up to six minutes of air. Beta Wave Training has given his generation mind control abilities that were not possible fifty years ago. One of these was the ability to slow down the speed of visual images reaching the brain (called Time Stalling, it takes rigorous training to accomplish). Darien was a solitary child and lived among his memories. He was also a patriot, something that no longer exists (out of fashion). Darien had feeling for his native land, once called America, and knew every detail of her history. He admired the early Fugitive Retrieval Specialists—the U.S. Marshals—and this led him to enter the International Police Academy at West Point.

At school Lambert excelled. He learned Masti, a mental improvement on the martial arts. He became an expert with the PPT (Pellet Projection Tube), the police weapon of the day. He graduated first in his class and was commissioned to Detective Junior Grade (a Marshal). The years that followed were turbulent for Lambert as he learned the external lessons of his job: a policeman stands alone. Although he had a brilliant arrest record, his arrests declined sharply as the years passed — trackdowns are ending in mysterious disappearances and suspects are vanishing without a trace. Darien soon begins to doubt his ability. In the summer of 2192, Darien is promoted to Captain of the Fugitive Retrieval Section (based at Metro Headquarters; SM3 is his code). He is also given SELMA (Specified Encapsulated Limited Memory Archive), one of only five micro miniature computers that contain all information ever printed since Guttenberg's Bible. SELMA is specifically designed for Darien and the command "Visual Mode" brings SELMA, as a hologram into view (Elizabeth Ward). SELMA is programmed never to appear with a third person present and there are few questions that she cannot answer. SELMA is a devised program with a persona: "I can be used in voice mode as well as visual." SELMA does not create ideas, she synthesizes Darien's. SELMA runs on battery power. With a recharge, her batteries will last 81.3 years. If Darien wishes privacy, he puts SELMA on battery charger mode. When SELMA gets upset she emits static.

As Darien's life begins to take shape, events in another part of Middle City will soon affect it. Dr. Mordicai Sahmbi (Peter Donat) is a professor at M.I.T. who won the Nobel Peace Prize in physics for his theoretical work on teletransportation of particle mass. Halfway around the world Dr. Sahmbi is idolized by Elissa Chang Knox (Mia Sara), a nine-year-old prodigy who has been accepted by M.I.T. By the time she is 17, Elissa (Elizabeth Alexander) becomes the most gifted student Dr. Sahmbi has ever encountered. She begins work as a professor of photon physics and joins Dr. Sahmbi on a classified government project called TRAXX (Trans-Time Research and Experimentation) that is located in the sub-basement of the Smithsonian Institution in Washington D.C.

Unknown to Elissa, Dr. Sahmbi has used her thesis ("TXP: The Threshold of Time Travel") to secretly develop TXP, a pill that will enable whoever takes it to travel in time. TRAXX was originally a government funded project that was abandoned when interest lessened in researching time travel. Dr. Sahmbi thought differently and continued the project through private funding — what he could get from criminals who wished to go back in time to start new lives. Since 2182, Dr. Sahmbi has sent 100 criminals back in time. The TXP pill aligns a person's molecules to the delta wave transmissions of TRAXX, thus enabling the transfer of molecules. At present, the body can only withstand two doses of TXP; thus the limit is one round trip in time.

On June 21, 2193, a thief named Seth Dietrich (Michael Warren) steals the gun that killed Abraham Lincoln from the Smithsonian. SELMA identifies the thief, but before Darien can apprehend him, he uses the gun to kill a political figure. Dietrich is then caught and imprisoned. He is not permitted visitors, but he is allowed to receive mail. A blue envelope arrives that, when opened, causes Dietrich to vanish.

When Elissa reads an account of the incident in the paper, she approaches the arresting officer (Darien) and tells him about her and Dr. Sahmbi's project. A confrontation between Darien and Dr. Sahmbi occurs. During the struggle, Dr. Sahmbi takes Elissa captive and activates the TRAXX machine. Dr. Sahmbi, who had previously taken a TXP pill, vanishes (he reappears in 1993 Washington, D.C., where he plans to seize power and become king). Elissa, not protected by TXP, dies. Darien is enraged and vows to return to the past and capture Dr. Sahmbi.

The nation's government, the NHA, takes over the TRAXX project. Its chief (Henry Darrow) assigns Darien the task of not only capturing Dr. Sahmbi, but to retrieve the 100 criminals Sahmbi sent back to 1993.

SELMA is programmed with 179 new databases from 1993 plus a profile on each of the escaped criminals. Darien is given a miniature pellet gun (made to look like a hand-held car alarm) with three buttons: blue (to fire a two minute immobilization pellet), green (a three hour knockout pellet) and red, the TXP pellet (after being fired, SELMA emits a special frequency that allows TRAXX to locate and retrieve the felon). SELMA is disguised as a credit card when not in her holographic state. Darien, given era money, clothes, a driver's license, and an ATM card, is to communicate with the future by placing ads in the *Washington Post*.

Darien takes the TXP pill, enters the TRAXX chamber and vanishes. He reappears in the basement of the Smithsonian on June 15, 1993, at 9:38 P.M. in what was then the women's restroom. Darien is arrested as an intruder but let go when he explains that he was accidentally locked in the building. Prior to Darien's arrival, the Smithsonian had been robbed — of the gun that killed Abraham Lincoln. Darien theorizes that it must be Dietrich. With SELMA's help, Darien learns that a man named Seth Dietrich has booked a flight to Hawaii — where the President of the United States is to give a speech.

Darien books a flight for Hawaii; he is unknowingly followed by Annie Knox (Elizabeth Alexander), a Secret Service agent who has been assigned to follow him (Annie, an ancestor of Elissa's, had been assigned to investigate the gun theft. When her superiors became suspicious of Darien but could not prove anything, Annie was told to keep an eye on him). In Hawaii, Darien is detained by the Secret Service and brought to Annie for questioning. When alone, Darien uses the blue pellet to stun Annie and escapes. With only seconds to spare, Darien finds Dietrich and prevents him from killing the president. Dietrich, shot with the red pellet, is retrieved by the TRAXX team. Darien hands Annie the stolen gun and is allowed to go. Annie doesn't understand but tells him, "I may need your help at a future date."

Darien's driver's license was issued in Illinois, where he is listed as living at 3249 Ledgewood. He is a fan of the Chicago Cubs; even though Annie says they're a losing team, he says "I'm sticking with them because in 155 years they're going to win the pennant." Darien accomplished part of his goal and "can pop myself with a red pellet and return home, but I won't because I pledged to rid this place of those who came to plunder." As the series progressed, Darien told Annie about his mission and about Elissa. Together they join forces to retrieve the criminals from the future who have made a new life of crime for themselves in 1993. Gary McDonald and Laurie Stone composed the theme.

140.   *Tom Corbett, Space Cadet* (CBS, 1950; ABC, 1951-1952; NBC, 1951, 1954-1955; DuMont 1953-1954)

It is the year 2350 and the planets Earth, Mars, Jupiter and Venus have been colonized. They are part of the Solar Alliance and protected by the Solar Guards, a celestial police force that is based at Space Academy, U.S.A., a training school for aspiring Solar Guards. In this futuristic time, war as we know it no longer exists and guns have been outlawed. Men no longer wear suits (their everyday clothes are made in one piece) and women wear short skirts. Navigators have been replaced by Astrogators and nucleonics officers have replaced engineers. Pilots use tele-tranceivers for visual communication with Space Academy and the Strato-Screen allows for visual exploration of space. The Paralo-Ray (which causes temporary paralysis) is the most common weapon for the Solar Guards (only used, however, when they set out to explore new areas of the universe).

Science has developed immensely. There are blood pills (to heal the deepest wounds), personal telephones (worn on the belt and capable of calling anyone on any planet), light sticks (tubes that contain a material that shines constantly), a ceiling paint that captures light during the day and illuminate rooms at night, and the Study Machine (allows one to learn while sleeping). Phone numbers, however, haven't changed; they reflect the 1950s (a 1950 episode gave the phone number Andover 3-7800 as a way for futuristic kids to order the Study Machine).

Space Academy itself enlists men of high school and college age to train as Solar Guards. While not readily explained, women are not permitted to be Solar Guards. They can, however, train as Auxiliary Cadets to assist the Solar Guards in times of emergency. The series focuses only on the male students: Tom Corbett (Frankie Thomas), Astro (Al Markim) and Roger Manning (Jan Merlin). The cadets live in a dormitory room and must adhere to curfews and intense study to pass difficult exams. Major Connell (Ben Stone), called "Blastoff" by the cadets, is the roughest, toughest and meanest officer in the Solar Guards, while Dr. Joan Dale (Margaret Garland, Patricia Ferris) is the kindest of the instructors at Space Academy. Space Week is a tradition at Space Academy that allows the various spaceship crews (each of which consists of three members) to vie for top honors by competing in space races. The Academy's Electro Scope (an electronic telescope) allows cadets to view the vast regions of space without leaving the academy. The Servo Unit has been developed to automatically steer academy spaceships (which include the *Polaris*, the *Falcon*, the *Orion*, the *Vega* and the *Ceres*). There is also the Rocket Graveyard, an eerie site on a distant, uncharted planet, where the remains of dozens of lost rocket ships have accumulated over the past 200 years.

Tom, Roger and Astro are assigned to training on the *Polaris*. While supposedly only a cadet, Tom appeared to be more of an academy official (he gave orders, charted flights and booked space maneuvers). He was strong and forceful and showed leadership qualities. He was also quick thinking, assertive and popular with all those he worked with. Early episodes find Tom as the storyteller. He is seated in an official-looking office and welcomes viewers to relate an adventure he shared with Roger and Astro. A flashback type sequence is used and Tom returns at the end of the story to relate the moral and bid farewell with his famous "So long for now and spaceman's luck to all of you."

Astro was the alien member of the team. He was born to Terron parents on the planet Venus (at a time when it was just being colonized) and was considered to be a Venusian by his colleagues. He was a natural born engineer and his job was to oversee the rocket motors on the power deck of the *Polaris*. Astro had a quick temper and frequently acted without thinking first.

Roger was a wiseguy, sarcastic and always causing trouble (especially with his habit of playing practical jokes). He often taunted Astro and caused endless rifts between them. While he did work on the radar bridge (near the nose of the *Polaris*) he also thought he was better than everyone else (boasted of his own accomplishments while downgrading those of his colleagues). Why Roger was not expelled is a mystery, but in time of dire need he became helpful (but in the end he would always give in to temptation to belittle others). When something went wrong Roger would say "Aw, shucks"; when he was annoyed at someone, he would utter "Blow it out your jets." He was replaced in the last season episodes by Cadet T.J. Thistle (Jackie Grimes), a non–practical joke playing student who had a chip on his shoulder (he felt his shorter height prevented him from achieving success).

Dr. Joan Dale was the only regular female presence at the academy. She was a professional and dedicated to teaching (Astro appeared to have a difficult time comprehending scientific-related courses). Joan was not a femme fatale (a girl always in need of rescuing). She was not only beautiful, but educated, intelligent and capable of defending herself (she is, in 1950, the first role model for girls in the viewing audience). Joan was also a researcher and inventor. She invented Tom's rocket-powered space suit as well as new rocket fuels and the Hyper Drive (which allowed the Solar Guards' rocket cruisers to reach nearby stars). Joan was not all work. She had a human side and would worry about her superior, Captain Steve Strong (Edward Bryce) and Tom's crew when they were off on dangerous missions. Joan wore a calf-length dress which was based on the military style dress uniform worn by the cadets.

Commander Arkwright (Carter Blake) was the stern principal of Space Academy; Cadet Eric Rattison (Frank Sutton) headed the crew of the *Vega*; Rex Marshall appeared as Lieutenant Saunders in commercials for the show's longtime sponsor, Kellogg's Cereals (it was also sponsored by Kraft foods and Red Goose shoes).

Announcer Jackson Beck opened early episodes with these words: "Space Academy, U.S.A, in the world beyond tomorrow. Here the space cadets train for duty on distant planets. In roaring rockets they blast through the millions of miles from Earth to far flung stars and brave the dangers of cosmic frontiers, protecting the liberties of the planets, safeguarding the cause of universal peace in the conquest of space."

Later, when the product became a part of the opening, it began with this example from 1954: "Kellogg's Pep, the build-up wheat cereal, invites you to rocket into the future with Tom Corbett, Space Cadet." Tom would then say: "Stand by to raise ship. Blastoff minus five, four, three, two, one, zero." (Announcer:) "As roaring rockets blast off to distant planets and far flung stars, we take you to the age of the conquest of space with Tom Corbett, Space Cadet."

141. *Tracker* (Syndicated, 2001)

Migar is a solar system of six planets. Sartop, its moon, has been colonized and serves as a prison for criminals from the various planets. Guardians oversee operations; Trackers capture felons and guard them. The Guardian Zin (Geraint Wyn Davies) is a scientist who has discovered a wormhole and believes it can lead to another world. Zin also seeks power and feels his scientific achievements are not appreciated. Not willing to risk his own life in the wormhole, Zin releases the prisoner Ree (Joanie Laurer) and sends her through the portal. Ree's safe arrival on Earth prompts Zin to send 218 additional prisoners to Earth before he, himself, enters the wormhole. Zin plans to use the prisoners as soldiers to do his bidding (which includes killing and committing crimes).

A young woman named Mel Porter (Amy Price-Francis) is stranded by an inoperable car near highway 88 in Illinois. A short distance away, the wormhole appears in the sky. A beam of energy is discharged and follows the path of a high tension wire tower that is part of the landscape. The beam discharges itself and hits the ground near a grove of trees. An unknown entity emerges and begins to wander. It stops near a highway billboard for Cole (men's briefs) and assumes the image of the model depicted in the ad. As the entity walks it spots Mel and approaches her. Mel is apprehensive at first — until the alien places his hand on her car and the engine starts. Mel offers to give the good Samaritan a lift to town. As Mel speaks, the alien begins to understand English. When she suggests "You look like the Cole guy," the alien assumes Cole as his name.

Cole's true name is Daggon. He lived on the planet Cirron and was a Tracker on Sartop. He has come to Earth to capture Ree, the being responsible for killing his wife and daughter (very limited information is given about Daggon's life. There are no filmed sequences to follow; all information is contained in brief exchanges of dialogue in various episodes). It appears that Daggon (Adrian Paul) had previously captured Ree and was assigned to guard her. It is not explained how Zin managed to release so many prisoners without arousing suspicions or how he was able to contact Ree to tell him the wormhole was safe. How Daggon found the wormhole is also not explained.

When Ree arrived on Earth, it is assumed she killed a young woman and consumed her life force (Cole explained that he assumed an Earth image as opposed to consuming one). Zin has apparently killed to appear human also (it is explained that Zin provided Earth life forces for those 218 prisoners by killing passengers on a train that, by coincidence, had exactly 218 people on board). Only the transfer of Daggon from Sartop to Earth is shown. There is a tremendous atmospheric disturbance, not to mention an equally powerful explosion when the wormhole appears and discharges someone. How this was not detected by anyone on Earth is also a mystery (considering the wormhole had to be used 221 times to account for the prisoners, Ree, Zin and Daggon).

Mel is the owner of a bar called the Watchfire in Chicago's Criminal Courts District (340 is the number on the building). She has inherited the bar — and her assistant, Jess Brown (Leanne Wilson) — from her late aunt. It is here that a very trusting Mel allows Cole to stay (in one of the rooms above the bar, where Mel also lives). Cole immediately takes matters into his own hands and converts a computer (with additional parts from various items, like a microwave oven) into a device to track Ree (Ree and others like her discharge an "excitement hormone" when they kill or commit a crime. The "tracking device" hones in on that hormone). Mel believes Cole is either an FBI or CIA agent. When Cole discovers Ree's whereabouts, he asks Mel for help. Cole is too late to save a girl Ree kills for pleasure, but it is when Cole places a sphere-like device near Ree's neck and captures her life force, that Mel learns he is an alien and must recapture Zin and those 218 prisoners (Cole stores all captured life forms in a special container in his room that he plans to send back to Sartop; he also faces the problem of finding a new wormhole to do so as it appears the one he used to get to Earth has closed).

Before Cole was a Tracker, he was an educator and studied many different fields in college. He believes human physiology is very primitive and is having trouble adjusting to his human life. He wears clothes that were left by one of Mel's former boyfriends and enjoys all types of Earth foods, especially corn on the cob. He can mentally stop time and alter it for a split second. Cole can manipulate electronic equipment with the power he emits from his fingers. He can also change his appearance by studying a picture of someone and assuming that image. He has incredible strength and can leap to fantastic heights. Cole can sense when a prisoner is near or where one has been; he can also sense one by touching an object it touched. Cole believes that the Roswell incident could have been a Cirron ship that contained treasure hunters and crashed in New Mexico. Extraordinary feats weaken Cole ("It takes one solar day for me to regenerate") and becomes numb if exposed to cold weather. Dean McDermott plays Victor Bruno, the police detective Cole and Mel help.

The Watchfire Bar was originally a cop bar and has its original Louis Sullivan 1940s wood finish. Mel not only inherited it and Jess "but debts, bills and no customers." She has tried to change it into an upscale bar, but it is too far from the business district to be successful. Mel has also inherited the white car she drives (plate LY 3W89) and has Cole working at the club to protect his true identity. Mel is fearful when Cole takes the car (he has no license and no identification and could be exposed if he is caught).

Jess is British and believes Cole "is a hunk but a little nuts" (she believes he is either CIA or FBI). She has numerous ideas for the bar, but they rarely work when Mel lets her try them. Donald Quon composed the theme.

142. *Ultraman* (Syndicated, 1967; 1979; 1992)

Over the course of 31 years (1967–1998) 11 series dealing with the adventures of Ultraman, a being from another galaxy who battles evil on Earth, have been produced. Only three of these series, *Ultraman* (1967), *The Ultraman* (1979) and *Ultraman: Towards the Future* (1992) have appeared on U.S. television. With the exception of the 1992 version (produced in English), the other versions were produced in Japan. The 1967 and 1979 versions were dubbed into English but presented without dubbing credits.

The 1967 version, titled *Ultraman*, begins as two unidentified flying objects approach Earth. During their flight the ships collide. One veers off course and crashes into a lake in Japan. The other strikes a Scientific Patrol Headquarters exploratory ship and kills its pilot, Iota. A mysterious being from Nebula M-78 in the fortieth galaxy, emerges from the grounded alien craft. Guilt ridden for having taken a human life, the alien restores Iota's life by giving him a special capsule that enables him and Iota to become one. In times of emergency, Iota can become Ultraman, a 400-foot-tall, indestructible crusader, to battle the dangerous and monstrous phenomena on Earth. Iota is a member of the Scientific Patrol, an organization that safeguards the Earth from alien invaders.

The 1979 Version: In a galaxy millions of light years away, the rulers of the star Ultra dispenses one of their men to help the Earth battle space monsters that are beginning to appear at frequent intervals. Because of his strange, robot-like appearance and height, it is decided to implant the vast energy resources of the Ultraman into the body of Matt Gordon, a young Earth-based Space Force trooper. In times of danger, Gordon can call on amazing Ultra Powers and transform himself into the 400-foot-tall Ultraman yet still be capable of keeping his identity a secret from his fellow troopers. Gordon is a member of the Earth Defense Force. By absorbing energy from the sun, Gordon transforms himself into Ultraman and acquires his powers (incredible strength, the ability to fly and the ability to discharge energy bolts as a weapon).

The 1992 Version: The Universal Multi Purpose Agency (UMA for short) is an Earth-based organization that investigates extraterrestrial matters. It has also begun the exploration of other planets. During an exploration of the planet Mars, two UMA astronauts encounter an alien creature that is threatening to kill them. Suddenly, a humanoid being called a Vigor comes to their rescue. In an ensuing battle, one of the astronauts is killed. The other astronaut, Jack Shindo (Dore Kraus) is injured. Vigor approaches Jack and uses the powers contained in a crystal he wears not only to heal him, but to become part of him. Vigor, a creature 400 feet tall, then takes Jack back to Earth. Jack learns that a Martian virus called Gudas Cells have entered the Earth's atmosphere and have the ability to infect small or microscopic life forms and transform them into hideous and gigantic monsters. To battle these creatures, Jack calls on his secret alias by activating the crystal (the Delta Plasma Pendant) he wears around his neck on a chain. Jack is his normal height when he is himself. When he becomes his other self — whom he calls Ultraman — he grows to a height of a 20-story building but can only maintain his new image for a period of three minutes each seven hours. The pollution in the Earth's atmosphere destroys the energy cells he derives from the sun. As Ultraman, the warning light on Ultraman's chest blinks when his three minutes are nearly up (giving Ultraman the needed time to disappear from sight so that he can revert back to Jack without arousing suspicions).

Ultraman, called "The Savior from the Stars," has the ability to fly, ultimate strength, and the ability to discharge energy bolts from his hands. Arthur Grant (Ralph Cotterill) is the head of UMA; Jean Echo (Gia Carides), Kim Shoamin (Grace Park) and Charles Morgan (Lloyd Morris) are members of UMA. Steve Apps and Robert Simper play Ultraman; Mike Read and Johnny Halliday are the various monsters. John Bonney narrates and Jay Hackett performs the theme vocal.

The Ultraman series (as of 12/31/01): Ultraman (1967), Ultra Seven (1967-1968), Return of Ultraman (1971), Ultra Ace (1972-1973), Ultraman Taro (1973-1974), Ultraman Leo (1974-1975), The Ultraman (1979-1980), Ultraman '80 (1980-1981), Ultraman: Towards the Future (1992), Ultraman: The Ultimate Hero (1993), Ultra Tiga (1997-1998).

143. *V.I.P.* (Syndicated, 1998–2002)

Vallery Irons (Pamela Anderson) is beautiful, young and single. She has no special skills, little business experience, no knowledge of computers, but is an expert on makeup and fashion. She is also the owner of V.I.P. (Vallery Irons Protection), a high profile Los Angeles–based protection service that charges $25,000 a day plus expenses plus a $100,000 retainer fee (the fee was also said to be $5,000 a day). "At V.I.P., the client's needs always come first. We don't work by the hour, you can't provide proper protection," says Vallery.

The Commerce Bank of Beverly Hills lists the following personal information on Vallery: Social Security Number: 904-38-2832. Birth: 7-1-73. Age: 26. Place of Birth: Columbia Hospital (Vancouver, B.C., Canada). Height: 5'6". Weight: 120 pounds. Eyes: Green. Race: Caucasian. Hair: Blonde. Distinguishing Marks: Mole, left shoulder. Address: 9600 Sunset Blvd., Beverly Hills, California, 90210-0176. Lessee: Vallery Irons. Landlord: V.I.P. Holdings, Inc. Telephone: 310-555-9276. Account Name: Vallery Irons. Account Balance: $1,182.42. Occupation: Chief Executive Officer. Employer: Vallery Irons Protection. Address: 9100 Sunset Blvd., Beverly Hills, California, 90210-0176. Federal I.D. Number: 904-38-2812.

Bank Account Information: Account Number: 390005641. Account Name: Vallery Irons. Account Balance: $8,610.14. Criminal Record: None.

Prior to this information, given in the third season, V.I.P. was said to be on the ninth floor at 3500 Hollywood Boulevard and its phone number 310-555-1847 (or 555-1-VIP; later phone number: 555-0199). Vallery was first said to live at 10867 Whittier Boulevard, then at 299 Ocean Avenue and finally at 209 Ocean. Her phone number was seen on the V.I.P computer personnel file as 310-555-1836. Tasha Dexter (Molly Culver), Nikki Franco (Natalie Raitano), Quick Williams (Shaun Baker), Kay Simmons (Leah Lail) and Johnny Loh (Dustin Nguyen) are Vallery's employees.

Prior to the job at V.I.P. Vallery was the owner of a Tail of the Pup fast food franchise. She is attending a Hollywood movie premiere when an assassin tries to kill the film's star, Brad Cliff. Brad, a coward, sees Vallery and uses her as a shield. When the assassin approaches, Vallery hits him over the head with her penny-filled purse and knocks him out. As the media approaches, Brad covers for his cowardice by saying that Vallery is his bodyguard. Vallery lies and agrees.

The following day, Tasha, Nikki, Kay and Quick find themselves as the owners of the debt-ridden Colt Arrow Security Services when its owner skips town and leaves them to pay IRS taxes and penalties. Later, while in a park, Tasha recognizes Vallery from her newspaper picture and asks her about the incident. Vallery confesses, "I lied about the whole female bodyguard thing." Because of all the publicity surrounding Vallery, Tasha asks her to join their company "as a figurehead; you won't be involved in cases." Vallery is reluctant until she hears about the company jet, car and luxury apartment. "It sure beats working at the hot dog stand," she says. The company name is changed to Vallery Irons Protection and while not supposed to be involved in cases, Vallery does what she pleases, bringing her inexperience to complicate matters (although always saving the day in the end).

Vallery is called "The Bodyguard to the Stars." She buys her lingerie at Sheer Elegance (and makes sure it can be seen by wearing see-through outerwear). She shows ample cleavage and was first said to wear at 38D bra; then 36DD and finally 34D. She has a wardrobe of 8,762 outfits and loves short skirts and high heels (which often cause more problems than making a fashion statement; she has difficulty running in them and the heels often get caught in things). The lingerie company, Cleo's Passion, introduced a line of sexy lingerie and active wear called "The Vallery Irons Undercover Collections—Undergarments to Cover You."

Vallery's knowledge of criminal activities came from watching reruns of *Law and Order*. She also enjoys the interview program *Donny and Marie* (the real series with Donny and Marie Osmond) and going to the 7-11 "to see what the latest slurpee flavor is." Vallery reads *Vogue* and *Open Toe Monthly* magazines and hyperventilates when she gets scared. She became a contestant on the reality TV show *Danger Island* (a fictional version of *Survivor* on the FTS network) in an attempt to win two million dollars. She also did a TV commercial (spokesgirl) for Oliver King's Rare Treasures.

Vallery attended Eastern Vancouver High School, Class of 1990. She was an *A* student, a gymnast and captain of the volleyball team. She is currently taking classes in hypnotism at U.C.L.A. in her spare time.

Vallery's purpose at V.I.P. "is to pull in the rich and famous." While called "the best in the business," Vallery "is better at fashion and makeup than she is at protecting." Her haphazard crime fighting skills (accomplishes everything by accident) have led criminals to believe that her incompetence is her secret weapon and meant to strike fear in their hearts.

Vallery has the ability to have a good time in any situation. She has several strong convictions ("I don't eat meat, I don't cheat at Yahtzee and I don't date men who kill other people") and frequents a bar called Foam. She has a robot dog named Bowser and a red Viper (then Jaguar) with the plate VIP VAL. Although she drives quite recklessly, Vallery hates car chases—"You gotta watch out for speed bumps and baby squirrels."

As a child Vallery had an invisible friend named Dirk. She was raised by her mother, Carol Irons (Loni Anderson) after her father, Jed Irons (Lee Majors) deserted the family. Vallery's last memory of her father is a *Star Wars* kite he bought for her. Jed was a CIA agent and abandoned his family to protect them when a mission went wrong and he was framed for killing agents. Vallery believed her father was a house painter. Carol now works for STX Consolidated, a computer company in Vancouver, Canada.

Vallery shares her apartment (all addresses given) with Maxene Della Cruz (Angelle Brooks), a fashion designer. Max, as Vallery calls her, calls Vallery "Val Gal." They have their hair and nails done at the Transcend Salon and became addicted to what Val calls "cyber shopping" (TV home shopping clubs). They also enjoy watching old movies on TV while eating popcorn and potato chips. Max is an amateur inventor and created "The Maxi Case," an attaché-like case "that holds a girl's makeup, curlers and fax machine." "The Evil Me," as Vallery calls Joan Archer, is Vallery's double (Pamela Anderson), an ex-undercover cop who was drummed out of the police department and uses Vallery's identity to commit crimes. Vallery makes her own "Shrinky Dink" bracelets and has the computer password "Val Gal."

Tasha is the most ruthless of the V.I.P. girls. She was a CIA double agent ("I was a spy for the Soviet Union before I switched sides") and can speak six languages. Tasha, well versed in the martial arts, will "sleep with the enemy" to get information but gets really angry "if I did it for nothing or it didn't pay off in results." Tasha, a licensed helicopter pilot, was also a former KGB operative, a member of the Israeli Army and an agent for MI-5. She has also been married four times and spent one year in a KGB prison. She also mentioned she was a fashion model before becoming a spy. Tasha has a short attention span and "I get an itchy finger if the baddies take too long to respond to my questions." She also says "I do all the dangerous work and Val gets the credit." Tasha is also uptight around Vallery because "no matter what case we are on, Vallery needs protection." VIP TSH is her blue Mustang license plate and 310-555-9816 is her phone number. She is famous for her veggie lasagna and *Born Free* is her favorite movie.

Nicollette Franco, called Nikki, is a member of the Franco crime family "but I have nothing to do with the crime end of it." Her grandfather, Don Franco (David Groh), is a mafia boss in Los Angeles. Nikki is the most violent of the V.I.P girls and feels bullets and guns are the only way to deal with the enemy. She carries two 357 magnums with her at all times and a grenade launcher is her favorite weapon (which she carries in the back of her yellow and white Mustang, plate VIP NIK; later it's a Dodge). Nikki, also an expert on bombs and explosives, has an electronic "sniffer" (bomb detector) shaped like a dog she calls Rex. "When I get depressed I like to blow something up," says Nikki (who is also seen discharging alarming amounts of ammo on a firing range when she is upset). Nikki's phone number is 323-KL5-2245; she attended the Catholic high school, St. Theresa's School for Girls. Nikki likes high speed racing and drove the XJ-219, an experimental electric-powered car. Val calls her "Queen of Explosives" and "Car Czar."

Quick is a former boxer who uses the skills he learned in the ring to defeat his enemies. In an early episode he said he was called "The Iron Bull" in the ring; later he was called "The Boxer with Mighty Quick Hands." He had to quit the ring when he refused to take a dive and was framed on drug charges. Quick can tap dance, served a hitch in the army (stationed at Fort Irving) but was sentenced to a psychiatric ward for running naked across the base. Quick (no other name given) is quick with his fists and skilled in the martial arts. He lives at 3430 Alto Cello Drive in Los Angeles and 323-555-7704 is his phone number. As a kid, astronaut Dex Dexter was his hero ("I even had a toy action figure of him"). Quick says "that if you retain us, the only down payment we require is full disclosure." He reads *Variety* and his subscription (number X0684A1334) expires March 5, 2000.

Kay is the agency's sexy and brilliant computer expert (Kay is the only other V.I.P girl who wears revealing tops and shows cleavage). Kay would like to become more active in the field and be like Tasha and Nikki ("I can be mean and vicious as long as I don't hurt anyone"). Her middle name is Eugenia and says "I rather it be Danger; anything is better than Eugenia." At the age of seven, Kay was enrolled in Neo Tech, "a school for brainy kids." She won the seventh grade science fair "with my Black Plague in a shoebox diorama" but was picked on by other kids and called "Cry Baby Kay." Kay was editor of her college yearbook for three years "including one year after I graduated." Kay is a fan of the *Star Trek* TV series and movies. Kay (and Val) are members of the Champions of Freedom (a conservation group) and like Val, her favorite TV show is *Donny and Marie*. Kay lives at 817 Oakdale and her phone number is 818-KL5-9415. She often helps the team on assignments but gets nervous after doing so and always asks Tasha, "Do you have any Mylanta?" VIP KAY is Kay's minivan license plate and her electronic wizardry and monitor skills lead Quick to say, "Who needs manpower when you've got Kay power?" Kay's computer name is "Muffin Girl" ("I like muffins") and curiosity is her Achilles heel.

Johnny, a skilled marital arts expert, worked previously as a Hollywood stunt man. He rides a motorcycle (plate J00158) and has the phone number 213-555-8202. He reads *RIDE* magazine.

Frankie Blue composed the theme. The program opens with these words: "The beautiful and lethal Vallery Irons. Plucked from obscurity to lead an elite protection agency. They know how to get things done ... eventually." See also *Dangerous Curves*.

144. *Viper* (NBC, 1994; Syndicated, 1997–2000)

Viper is a crime-fighting car of the future. "It prowls the streets in the pursuit of justice. It is the perfect weapon for an imperfect future." Viper's origins are secret ("it's 21st century technology"). The Viper, originally red (NBC), then blue (Syndicated) morphs into the indestructible silver Defender at the touch of a button (people who see the Defender report it as "a phantom vehicle"). The police disavow any knowledge of its existence, fearing to create a panic if it is known an attack vehicle prowls the streets. The car can reach a top speed of 180 miles per hour, is bulletproof and contains a miniature self-propelled Probe that flies and can be used for spying (Probe can get into places Defender cannot).

The original car, a 1992 red Dodge Viper RT/10 Roadster, was used for the NBC version and the first two seasons of the syndicated version. It had four wheel drive with raised suspension and tire enlargers, a grappling hook, static pulse, a holographic projector, and a tunneller missile. The first season of the syndicated run added a 50 caliber machine gun and an auxiliary turbine for speed. The third season added a grenade launcher and a flame thrower. The final season kept the abilities of the prior car but incorporated them into a stock 1990 Dodge blue Viper GTS Coupe. When morphed into the silver Defender, it had the added capabilities of a hovercraft and torpedo launcher; it also carries cluster and canister bombs. The car, made of "an armor skin," can withstand temperatures up to 1500 degrees.

The NBC Format: Viper was created by Julian Wilkes (Dorian Harewood) as a secret project for the Chicago Police Department. Delia Thorne (Lee Chamberlain), a commander with Metropole Police, funded the project as a weapon to fight a criminal organization called the Outfit. At this same time, master thief Michael Peyton (James McCaffrey) is seriously injured in a car crash while attempting to escape from a robbery. Peyton is taken to County General Hospital and unknowingly becomes part of the Viper Project. Delia believes Peyton's skills as a thief as well as a driver make him the perfect candidate to drive Viper.

Peyton's memory is surgically altered to create the identity of Joe Astor, a police officer who was a former auto racing champion. A chip is implanted in Michael's brain to suppress his memories and create his new identity (to cover their tracks, the police department releases a statement saying Michael Peyton died in a mysterious blast). However, before the Viper Project can be launched, it is scrapped due to corruption in the police department. In an attempt to save the project, Joe and Julian kidnap Viper and set up a secret headquarters in an abandoned power station they call "The Batcave." They are assisted by Franklin "Frankie" Xavier Waters (Joe Nipote), the police department motor pool mechanic who works as their inside man. Figuring she can accomplish more away from the department, Delia quits and joins the Consortium, a group of people who work with honest cops to stop the Outfit.

Syndicated Version: The setting has changed to Metro City and the FBI is now in possession of the Viper Project (which is housed in a secret headquarters called "The Viper Complex." The 30-year-old abandoned subway station has been outfitted with the latest in crime detection equipment and the complex gives Viper access to the entire city via a series of tunnels). When Joe objected to the way the government ran the project, he quit.

Thomas Cole (Jeff Kaake), a former maverick CIA operative turned FBI Special Investigator, is assigned as Viper's driver. Julian leaves for a post in Washington; the Outfit/Consortium/Delia aspect is dropped.

Cameron Westlake (Heather Medway), badge 881, is a patrol car officer with the Metro City Police Department. Her father, a captain, and her two brothers, law enforcement officers, have gold shields for outstanding work. Cameron demonstrates the same potential and is promoted to detective. She is assigned to the Viper Project as Cole's assistant and becomes the liaison between Viper and the police department. Frankie (Joe Nipote) is transferred from the police department to the Viper Complex as the chief mechanic. Dr. Allie Farrow (Dawn Stern) is the engineer responsible for Viper's computer and weapons systems as well as maintaining the complex's "nerve center," the computer base of operations (from which Allie can monitor all areas of the city, call up crime files and track any vehicle via the Crime Analysis Tracking System). Season three adds J. Downing to the cast as FBI agent Sherman Catlett.

Changes occur in the final season. Viper is destroyed in an explosion at the same time Cole decides to leave to pursue other career opportunities. Allie also leaves work for a government think tank in Portugal. Frankie becomes the new computer expert (and mechanic) as the FBI commissions Julian Wilkes (Dorian Harewood) to create a new Viper (the 1990 Dodge, plate 369 BPF4). Julian, wheelchair bound in the NBC version, is now able to walk due to a morphing device he invented that was implanted in his spine. He is also kidnapped and held for ransom: Julian for the Viper. When Joe Astor (James McCaffrey), assigned only to deliver Viper to the complex, learns that Julian has been abducted, he and Cameron use the Viper to rescue Julian. Although Joe defied the FBI by using Viper, he is asked to return as the car's driver and assist Cameron and Frankie. Julian rejects an offer to return as he has been offered "a job at NASA" that he can't refuse. Catlett becomes the liaison between the FBI and the Viper team.

All addresses "are classified." Cameron first drove a 1996 Dodge Avenger, then a 1998 Jeep Grand Cherokee Limited. Frankie first drove a 1971 Plymouth Barracuda (NBC), a Dodge Challenger (Season 2) and the Barracuda again. He has a dog named William, hates guns and is allergic to oat bran. Shirley Walker composed the original theme (NBC), Eddie Jobson the syndicated theme version.

145. *V.R. Troopers* (Syndicated, 1994–1995)

Ryan, Kaitlin and J.B. (Brad Hawkins, Sarah Brown, Michael Bacon) are friends who live in a place called Crossworld City. One day while working on his computer, J.B. receives a message for Ryan: "Greetings from Virtual Reality. I have gone to great lengths to contact a young man, Ryan Steele."

J.B. contacts Ryan and they learn the message came from Professor Horatio Hart (Julian Combs). By contacting Hart, Ryan learns Hart has a message from his father, Tyler (David Carr), who mysteriously disappeared ten years ago. Ryan is instructed to meet Hart at his lab. There, Ryan, Kaitlin and J.B. meet the professor and are given virtual reality glasses "to see our world from the virtual reality world." Ryan learns his father has stepped into virtual reality to stop Grimlord, an evil being trying to break out of that realm and release an army of mutant robots on the real world. Professor Hart and Tyler need Ryan and his most trusted friends to become their V.R. Troopers. J.B. and Kaitlin agree to help. They are given power jewels that transform them into soldiers when they touch the jewel and say "Trooper Transfer, We Are V.R."

Grimlord has the ability to cross over into both worlds. In the real world he is a powerful industrialist named Ziktor (head of Ziktor Industries); in the virtual reality world, he is Grimlord (both played by Gardner Baldwin). Ziktor calls on the forces of darkness to transport him to virtual reality. There, as Grimlord, he commands mutants, known as Skugs, to do his bidding. Once he has taken control of the world, Grimlord hopes to combine with Ziktor and become all powerful and rule the world. The program is strong on action and has little additional character information. Kaitlin works as a reporter for a newspaper called the *Daily Underground Voice*; Ryan and J.B. are instructors at the Tao Dojo Karate Studio (Richard Rabago plays the studio owner, Tao Dojo). Jed, Ryan's dog, also assists the troopers on assignments. Shuki Levy composed the theme.

146. *The Wild Wild West* (CBS, 1965–1969)

The *Nimrod* is a luxurious passenger train coach that serves as the mobile base of operations for Major James T. West (Robert Conrad) and his partner, Artemus Gordon (Ross Martin), Secret Service operatives for President Ulysses S. Grant in the west of the 1870s.

James, called Jim, had served in the U.S. Cavalry for ten years before being selected by President Grant (James Gregory, Roy Engel) for duty as an undercover intelligence officer. The *Nimrod* is pulled by an 1860 2-4-0 steam locomotive (engine number 3) and its attached coal car. Its is actually a government loan but as far as the outside world is concerned, the train is the sole property of James T. West, a big spender from the east who is known as "the dandiest dude who ever crossed the Mississippi in his own train."

Artemus, called Artie, is a brilliant actor turned agent who uses the wizardry of his craft (disguises) to help Jim apprehend criminals who pose a threat to the safety of the country. Artie, favorite color red, gets the less glamorous assignments — nondescript characters who are there to help Jim.

Artie can read and write English, Latin, Greek, German, Chinese and Braille. He can't read Russian but he can speak it. His everyday wardrobe accommodates smoke bombs, putty explosives and knockout powders. Jim, who uses advanced scientific weapons, has pop-out guns up his sleeves, a tiny derringer concealed in the heel of his boot, a skeleton key hidden behind his jacket lapel, a sword in his pool cue and small bombs concealed under his holster.

The *Nimrod* contains an assortment of weapons (rifles, guns, knives and explosives), a secret wardrobe for Jim's undercover assignments and a pool table for relaxation. The car also contains several cages that house Artie's homing pigeons (Anabella, Arabella, Henrietta and Henry). The marker lights at the tail end of the *Nimrod* (there is no observation car on the train) actually serve two purposes: an alert to other trains on the same track and a signal that something is wrong (for example, if Artie is out of the car and Jim is in trouble, he switches on the lights).

While Jim and Artie battle many notorious villains (in some cases using surveillance techniques and weapons that had not yet been invented), their most diabolical enemy was Dr. Miguelito Coyote Loveless (Michael Dunn), an evil scientist who owed his villainy "to the curse of my midget size." He also believed the U.S. government took the country away from his grandfather and getting back at the government was his way of seeking revenge.

Tennison (Charles Davis) was Jim's manservant on the train; Voltaire (Richard Kiel) and Antoinette (Phoebe Dorin) were two of Loveless's assistants. The series was originally titled *The Wild West* (same music and characters; title graphics are the only difference). Richard Markowitz composed the theme.

Note: Two pilots were made in an attempt to revive the series:

1. *The Wild Wild West Revisited* (CBS, 5/9/79). It is 1895. Robert T. Malone (Harry Morgan) is now head of the Secret Service. Jim West (Robert Conrad) has retired to Mexico; Artemus Gordon (Ross Martin) is an actor with the Deadwood Shakespearean Strolling Players Traveling Tent Show. When a new enemy, Michelito Loveless, Jr. (Paul Williams), the diabolical son of Jim and Artie's old adversary, threatens to take over the U.S. (by cloning heads of state), Malone recruits West and Gordon to stop him.

2. *More Wild Wild West* (CBS, 10/7, 10/8/80). Jim West (Robert Conrad) and Artemus Gordon (Ross Martin) are called upon by Robert T. Malone (Harry Morgan) to stop Professor Albert Paradine II (Jonathan Winters), a daft megalomaniac who seeks to rule the world with his diabolical weapons of doom.

147. *Witchblade* (TNT, 2001)

The Witchblade is a mysterious, ancient bracelet with a mind of its own that has attached itself to strong women throughout history (from Cleopatra to Joan of Arc to World War II spy Elizabeth Bronte). It is said to be "a branch ripped from the tree of knowledge to balance good and evil." When possessed by the Witchblade, its wearer gains extraordinary abilities to fight evil. The bracelet becomes a chameleon-like powerhouse: a bullet-deflecting bracelet, a bayonet-like knife, a Samurai sword, a suit of armor — whatever its preordained champion needs to protect herself as she battles "to cleanse the world and make it pure." A gift of the Witchblade is the power to slip back and forth in time. A refusal to wear the bracelet or fight its power could result in death.

Sara Pezzini (Yancy Butler) is a young woman who lives in a Greenwich Village loft (number 416) and works as a homicide detective with the 11th Precinct of the N.Y.P.D. She wears badge 322, drives a car with the license plate RFD 960 and is called "Pez" by her partner, Jake McCartey (David Chokachi).

Kenneth Irons (Anthony Cistaro) is a mysterious billionaire who heads Vorschlag Industries. He is also the owner of the Witchblade (he killed Elizabeth Bronte 30 years ago when he could not use her to acquire its power). He is also growing old and fears he will die before he can harness the power of the Witchblade (in order to control the Witchblade, Irons must control the woman who wears it). He lives on an estate at 1111 Faust Street.

On November 11, 2000, Sara's life changes forever. It is the day the Witchblade chooses her as its wielder. A robbery suspect, being pursued by Sara, takes refuge in the Mid-Town Museum. During an exchange of gunfire, a bullet shatters a display case exhibiting the Witchblade. As Sara seeks cover, the Witchblade attaches itself to her. A bullet hits the bracelet, is deflected and ruptures a gas pipe. An explosion results and kills the suspect. Sara emerges unharmed. She has little memory of what happened and conceals the gold band, red ruby bracelet while being questioned. Later, while investigating a mob plan to take over a nightclub, Sara meets Kenneth Irons, a man who displayed the Witchblade as part of his Joan of Arc collection. Sara also learns of her destiny.

Irons has a mysterious link to the Witchblade; he can feel its power when in use but cannot control it. Irons begins by showing Sara two marks (circles) on his hand — the same circles Sara has on her chest (the circles represent the light and dark powers of the Witchblade. Sara claims "the marks" are "from shrapnel I got during a SWAT raid 11 months ago"). Sara was destined to wear the Witchblade (only women can wear it because women are more elemental; they are closer to nature than men and the Witchblade finds them superior). Sara was meant to find the Witchblade and Irons was meant to find Sara (although Sara is unaware of Ken's real intentions. The Witchblade chose Sara for her courage and her concealed vulnerability).

The Witchblade will not allow Sara to remove it from her wrist. She must accept it and earn its power; if she does not, it will abandon her (it is written that Joan of Arc's sword came to life during her battles. After her capture, her weapon disappeared from her hand — "the Witchblade has a way of slipping from its wielder's grasp just when you need it most"). In order for Sara to receive the full power of the Witchblade she must first spill some of her own blood (which happens when she is wounded by a suspect in a subway shooting. It was then that she could command the Witchblade to protect her). The Witchblade is a mystery wrapped in a riddle. Irons would like to solve the mystery. "The Witchblade has many powers," Ken tells Sara, "and only the person who wields it can truly know it all." Sara, Irons and the Witchblade become a trio formed by destiny.

Sara can now see things other people cannot (for example, what happened at a crime scene by looking at a photo or visiting the scene). She acquires strength and can pierce the veil of the senses to extract more from the universe than the normal person. She cannot fight the power of the Witchblade. If she fails to use its power she will die. Once chosen, a wielder cannot rid herself of the Witchblade (it will return to her. If she tries to abandon it, the bracelet will punish her by inflicting pain).

Cleopatra, Joan of Arc and Elizabeth Bronte (Yancy Butler in flashbacks) are Sara — not a reincarnation, but a continuation of their lives in different centuries to serve the Witchblade. Sara once lived by the law; she must now become the law. When something upsets Sara, she goes into a deep depression until she overcomes it. She relaxes by shooting pool and carries a spare gun in her boot.

Jake, a former world-famous surfing champion, had a bad spill that forced him to retire. He became a cop "because I'm a neat freak. I want to make my corner of this insane world a little more orderly." Jake, badge 405, amazes Sara with his ability to come up with pertinent information without apparent federal connections (it is later revealed that Jake is an FBI agent assigned to expose the White Bulls, an organization of ruthless, renegade cops who act like crusaders for justice but dispense their own brand of justice to anyone they feel is harmful. Sara's father, James Pezzini, was one of their victims. Sara has vowed to find her father's killer and Jake feels working with Sara will give him the best opportunity to bust the White Bulls).

Ian Nottingham (Eric Etebari), called "The Man in Black" (for his black trench coat) by people who see him, is Irons' mysterious assistant. He is Sara's "Guardian Angel" and has been assigned by Irons to watch over Sara. He can catch bullets in his hands and be wherever Sara is in the blink of an eye. Also helping Sara is Danny Woo (Will Yun Lee), the ghost of her original partner (killed during an assignment at a movie theater). While Danny cannot physically assist Sara, he tries to help her understand the powers of the Witchblade.

In the last episode (8/21/01) it is learned that Elizabeth Bronte had a daughter who did not wield the Witchblade. This daughter had a child and from that child Sara was born. Sara, however, was kidnapped by a man named Lazar and given to James Pezzini to raise and to eventually wield the Witchblade. When Sara acquired the Witchblade it bonded with her and gave her a unique genetic makeup — something no other person has. When Irons came in contact with the Witchblade, it gave him a longer life, but he needs blood from the wielder to survive; without it, he will age and wither away.

The final scene leaves the viewer with the impression that everything that happened to Sara was a dream. With Jake's help, Sara brings down the White Bulls. She is enraged when she discovers its leader is Kenneth Irons. In a confrontation with Irons, Jake is killed by Ian. Sara wields her blade and destroys Ian (Ian's first duty is to protect Irons). Kenneth is beginning to age and in a desperate measure, stabs Sara in the back (for unexplained reasons, the Witchblade armor Sara was wearing while fighting Irons did not protect her). Sara pulls out the knife, dripping with blood, from her back. As Sara moves away from Irons (knowing the blood will save him), the ghostly image of Elizabeth Bronte appears to tell Sara that she has the power to reverse time; it is, however, a one time only gift of the Witchblade, and Sara will have little memory of what happened to her as a wielder. She uses the power. And, as a montage of scenes from past episodes flash across the screen, Sara is returned to her car seated next to Danny moments before they entered the ill-fated theater. When Danny sees the suspects enter the theater, he tells Sara, "Let's go." Sara pauses—"Something doesn't feel right" and saves Danny's life by preventing him from getting out of the car. The scene fades to black as Sara and Danny drive off. Joel Goldsmith composed the theme, "Witchblade."

148. *Wonder Woman* (ABC, 1976-1977; CBS, 1977–1979)

Paradise Island is an uncharted land mass in the Bermuda Triangle (refraction of light prevents the island from being seen). The unknown metal, Feminum, can be found there and its inhabitants are a race of super women called Amazons. Paradise Island was established in the year 200 B.C. At this time, the rival gods Aphrodite and Mars battled for control of the Earth. When Aphrodite suffered a defeat, she retreated to the island and created her race of women ("There are no men here. It is free from their wars and barbaric ways. We live in peace and sisterhood"). Aphrodite chose Hippolyta as their queen. As the war continued, Mars resorted to skullduggery and used Hippolyta's own weapon of love to defeat her. Hoping to achieve forgiveness, Hippolyta fashioned a small statue out of clay and offered it to Aphrodite. Aphrodite brought the statue to life as the baby Diana. As the centuries passed, Diana, groomed by Hippolyta to become a ruler, grows into a beautiful young woman.

In 1942 the idyllic life of Paradise Island is shattered when man once again threatens its serenity. U.S. fighter pilot Steve Leonard Trevor (Lyle Waggoner) is on a mission to intercept a Nazi plane (en route to bomb the Brooklyn shipyards) when his plane is hit by gunfire. Although wounded, Steve manages to eject himself from the plane and his parachute lands on a beach near a cave on Paradise Island. There he is found by the Princess Diana (Lynda Carter) and nursed back to health. When Diana learns from Steve that the world is engaged in a war and the Allies are battling a fierce enemy called Nazis, she asks her Queen Mother for permission to use her abilities to help America. Hippolyta (Cloris Leachman, Carolyn Jones) is reluctant, until Diana proves herself superior in an Olympic contest (number XXXIII) to determine which Amazon should take Steve back to America.

Hippolyta presents Diana with a gold belt (to retain her cunning, strength and immortality away from Paradise Island) and a magic lariat (which compels people to tell the truth). To signify her alliance to freedom and democracy, Diana receives a red, white and blue costume. She is also given a gold tiara (with a red ruby star in the middle) and a set of gold bracelets, made from Feminum, to deflect bullets ("The Amazon mind is conditioned for athletic ability and academic learning. Only we have the speed and coordination to attempts bullets and bracelets").

"Go in peace my daughter," Hippolyta tells Diana. "And remember, in a world of ordinary mortals, you are a Wonder Woman." "I will make you proud of me and of Wonder Woman," promises Diana. Steve is given a drug from the Hybernia tree to erase his memory of Diana and the island. The invisible plane enables Diana to fly Steve back to Washington, D.C. (where she brings him to the Armed Services Hospital to regain his strength). Diana adopts the alias of Diana Prince, becomes a Navy yeoman and is assigned to the War Department as Steve's secretary.

Diana lives at 2890 West 20th Street; Capitol 7-362 is her phone number. Steve, based in the Military Building (Air Corps Intelligence Division) on D Street has the phone extension 0277; 24-36-33 is his office safe combination number. To become Wonder Woman, the plain looking Diana places her arms in the air and performs a twirling striptease. In addition to her super strength, Wonder Woman possesses the ability to impersonate any voice and run and jump at an accelerated speed.

Wonder Woman's sexy costume is a strapless one piece bathing suit ("her satin tights" as the theme says) which has a blue bottom with white stars and a red with gold (around the bustline) top. For modesty, Hippolyta also fashioned a removable blue and white skirt that Diana rarely wears.

While it is not known how to kill Wonder Woman, her enemies have discovered that she can be subdued with chloroform.

After several months, Hippolyta feels Diana has spent enough time in America and must return home to assume her duties as heiress to the throne. She discharges her younger daughter, Drusilla (Debra Winger), to find Diana and bring her home. Drusilla, however, becomes fascinated by the American way of life and talks Diana into letting her stay with her (through dialogue it is learned that Diana has spoken to her mother and has been allowed to continue her fight for freedom).

Drusilla, as Wonder Girl, possesses the same powers as Diana, but her costume is not as revealing. She wears a red top with white stars, a silver belt, silver tiara and blue bottom. Dru, as Diana calls her, poses as a typical 15-year-old high school girl to hide her true identity. Dru finds ice cream the most fascinating part of American culture. She does a twirling striptease to become Wonder Girl, but acts on impulse and changes without thinking of the consequences. There is no explanation given as to how Drusilla came to be.

The first commandment of Paradise Island is never to tell anyone about it. Diana and Drusilla can find Paradise Island "because we know where it is." The Nazis believe Wonder Woman is a top secret U.S. weapon. The ABC version ended with Steve and Diana battling Nazism in 1945. It is assumed that Diana returned to Paradise Island when the war ended. General Philip Blankenship (Richard Eastham) is Steve's superior; Yeoman Etta Candy (Beatrice Colen) is Philip's secretary. The Charles Fox Singers perform the *Wonder Woman* theme vocal. The program is also known as *The New, Original Wonder Woman*. The pilot aired on 11/7/75.

CBS Version: *The New Adventures of Wonder Woman.* In 1977, a sabotaged plane lands on Paradise Island. By coincidence, Steve Trevor, Jr. (Lyle Waggoner), the son of the major Diana helped 35 years ago, is aboard. When Diana learns the modern world is threatened by evil, she receives permission from her Queen Mother, Hippolyta (Beatrice Straight) to save the free world from its enemies. Diana (Lynda Carter) uses her invisible plane to guide the jet back to Washington, D.C. There, Diana adopts the alias of Diana Prince and acquires a job as Steve's assistant at the I.A.D.C. (Inter-Agency Defense Command). Diana's Wonder Woman costume is the same as before and Lynda is depicted as a much lovelier and sexier Diana (her hair is not pulled back, as in the ABC version; her daily wardrobe is casual, not a restrictive uniform; and her eyeglasses are flattering, not matronly looking). There is little factual information in this version as addresses, phone numbers, and personal information is simply not given. Diana does reside in a flattering apartment in Washington, D.C., and is prone to the same weakness as in the prior version: chloroform. Diana revealed her true identity to only one person: Tina (Julie Ann Haddock), a pretty girl from the undersea kingdom of

Ilandia (she rescued her from kidnappers but could not find a way to return her home). When Diana is Wonder Woman, she can be seen in high-heeled boots. During a running sequence, the boots have flat heels; they switch back to high heels when the running sequence is over.

Joe Atkinson (Normann Burton) is Diana and Steve's superior. The agency's main source of information is the I.A.D.C. computer, IRAC (voice of Tom Kratichzil), whom Diana and Steve call "Ira." Artie Kane composed the revised theme.

First Pilot: In 1968, 20th Century–Fox produced the first known *Wonder Woman* pilot with Ellie Wood Walker as Diana Prince/Wonder Woman. In this unaired six minute test film, Diana is 27 million years old and lives in a modern-day apartment with her domineering mother (Maudie Prickett). Diana appears to be misadventure prone (for example, she falls off a chair while reading the newspaper) and is very vain. She is not as busty or gorgeous as Lynda Carter's Wonder Woman, but wears a similar outfit (a bosom-revealing red and gold top and a blue bottom with white stars). Diana loves to look at herself in a mirror and admire her figure. "She knows she has the strength of Hercules, the wisdom of Athena, the speed of Mercury— and she thinks she has the beauty of Aphrodite," says the narrator (William Dozier).

Mother is worried that she has "an unmarried daughter Diana's age" and fears what the neighbors are saying about the situation. Mother refuses to let Diana go out of the house in bad weather or become Wonder Woman on an empty stomach ("Where do you think all that strength comes from? Those gods? From my cooking! Eat first, save the world later"). When Diana decides to fight crime and become Wonder Woman, she takes her blue bracelets out of a dresser drawer, approaches a wall in the living room and pushes it. The wall revolves to reveal Diana's secret dressing room. When she emerges as Wonder Woman, she admires herself in the mirror, climbs out the window and says, "Away, away you vision of enchantment, you've got a job to do." She is then able to fly under her own power (something Lynda Carter's Wonder Woman couldn't do). When Diana admires herself, the song "Oh, You Beautiful Doll" is played in the background. "Ellie Wood Walker as Wonder Woman" is the only screen credit.

Second Pilot: *Wonder Woman* (ABC, 3/12/74). On Paradise Island, which is inhabited by a race of women called Amazons, the beautiful Princess Diana (Cathy Lee Crosby) is approached by her Queen Mother (Charlene Holt) and instructed to assist the world in its battle against evil. Diana adopts the alias of Diana Prince and travels to Washington, D.C. There, she acquires a job as secretary to U.S. government agent Steve Trevor (Kaz Garas). Diana's adventures, as she battles the enemies of the modern world, were to be the focal point of the series. The pilot finds Diana battling Ahnjayla (Anitra Ford), a renegade Amazon who is now Diana's enemy, and Abner Smith

(Ricardo Montalban), a thief who has stolen books that contain the names of America's top agents. Artie Butler composed the theme.

149. *Wonderbug* (ABC, 1976-1977)

Susan, Barry and C.C. (Carol Anne Seflinger, David Levy, John Anthony Bailey) are teenagers seeking an affordable used car. In a junkyard they find Schlep Car, a conglomeration of several junked cars. As they admire the car, Susan finds an old horn and places it on the car. Suddenly, Schlep Car is magically transformed into Wonderbug, an amazing dune buggy that can talk (voice of Frank Welker), think, fly and travel on water. A squeeze of the magic horn transforms Schlep Car into Wonderbug and vice versa. The four join forces the battle crime.

There is no background information given on the teens (not even if they attend school). Susan is the real brains of the group (comes up with all the plans) but it is Barry who takes the credit (he says, "I've got a better idea," then repeats Susan's idea; C.C. agrees with what Barry says, not realizing it was actually Susan's idea). Schlep Car (also voiced by Frank Welker) is not your typical run-down car. It needs a paint job, can barely carry the weight of its passengers (huffs and puffs), loses parts as it rolls along, hesitates, eats gasoline, and expels too much exhaust. Its windshield has two bandages in the shape of the Red Cross that is apparently holding it together. As Wonderbug, all the problems disappear. Not only is the car spotless, but it can drive by itself and thus come to the aid of Susan, Barry and C.C. when they need help. The headlights act as Wonderbug's eyes while its two-part front bumper (upper and lower) act as its mouth. Broadcast as a segment of *The Krofft Supershow*. Jimmie Haskell composed the theme.

150. *Xena: Warrior Princess* (Syndicated, 1995-2001)

Amphipolis is a small village in ancient Greece that is home to Xena (Lucy Lawless), a young woman who works in a tavern run by her mother, Cyrene (Darien Takle). Xena's father is unknown. He deserted his family when Xena and her brothers, Lyceus and Toris (Aaron Devitt, Joseph Kell) were young. When the warlord Cortese threatens Amphipolis, Xena organizes reluctant-to-fight villagers into a small army that manages to defeat Cortese. Xena, however, is blamed for a needless war and the deaths of many villagers, including Lyceus. Now, guilt ridden, Xena leaves Amphipolis to build an army to defend her homeland against future attacks. Xena's abilities and bravery earn her the name Warrior Princess, but she is soon corrupted by power and fights for the thrill of battle.

Xena will not kill women and children. When she stops her lieutenant from killing an infant, she is believed to be weak and loses control of her army. She seeks the help of Hercules (Kevin Sorbo) and together they defeat Xena's rogue army. Xena sees the evil person she has become and vows to Hercules to use her skills to help people.

A short time later, when Xena saves the village of Poteidain from the warlord Draco, she meets Gabrielle (Renee O'Connor), a young woman who becomes fascinated with Xena and attaches herself to her. Although Xena is reluctant to have a traveling companion, she finds Gabrielle's proficient gift of speech a valuable asset when she returns to Amphipolis and is saved by Gabrielle when she talks angry villagers out of attacking her. Gabrielle feels she is meant to be more "than just a village girl" and is welcomed by Xena, although Xena refuses to teach Gabrielle how to fight.

Gabrielle's true skill is that of a bard. She keeps records (called "The Xena Scrolls") of her and Xena's adventures. She had one produced in the style of a Broadway play called "Gabrielle and Xena: A Message of Peace." Gabrielle later attended the Academy for Performing Bards in Athens and daisies are her favorite flower. She is also a cook and treasures her frying pan.

People think of Gabrielle as "that irritating little blonde" that travels with Xena. She was one of the Followers of Eli (a religious prophet who professed love) and was called "The Visionary Voice of Athens" after she wrote the play *Fallen Angel*. Gabrielle and Xena traveled great distances—from Greece to Rome to India. In India-based episodes, Gabrielle becomes a peacemaker. She wears tattoo-like symbols called Mandie, which gives her the power to trap and destroy evil. Life changes for Gabrielle when she risks her life to save a wounded Amazon (a warrior daughter of Ares, the God of War). Ephiny (Danielle Comack), the Amazon queen, bestows the title of Amazon Princess on Gabrielle and teaches her how to fight. Gabrielle becomes proficient with her wooden staff, but is also an expert with a sword and a knife.

Xena, proficient in the art of swordsplay, has a deadly and powerful weapon called the Chakram (a flat, round piece of iron with razor sharp blades). She is also feared for "the pinch" (a technique that stops the flow of blood to the brain when a nerve on the neck is pinched). Xena's horse, Argo, loves apples and will only allow Xena to ride her. In addition to Xena, Lucy Lawless played three other roles (all resembling Xena): Meg, a harlot; Diana, a princess who could speak ancient Hestian language; and Annie Dey, a present-day girl who publishes a paper called *Joxer the Mighty* and is a member of the Xena society, C.H.A.K.R.A.M. (the Center for Historical Accuracy and Key Research in Ancient Mythology).

Gabrielle and Xena had children. Gabrielle, impregnated by the evil god Dayhawk, became the mother of Hope. Hope, however, was evil, and Gabrielle "destroyed" her by placing her in a basket and setting her adrift on a river in a raft. Xena had two children, Solon (David Taylor) and Eve (Adrienne Wilkinson). Solon was born shortly after his father, Borias, died under mysterious circumstances. To protect Solon from her enemies, Xena gave the infant to the half-man, half-horse Centaur leader, Kalcipus, to raise.

Eve's history is rather complex and evolves from a number of complicated, if not confusing episodes. Eve was called "The Bringer of Twilight" and as such, could end the reign of the gods on Mount Olympus. Ares, the God of War (Kevin Smith), was the most upset and set out to destroy the infant before she could grow to fulfill her destiny. To protect Eve, Xena gives her to a trusted friend (Octavius) to raise. In a fierce battle against Ares, Xena is able to stage an accident that makes it appear Eve is killed. Her plan backfires when she and Gabrielle are seriously wounded and thought to be dead. Ares, who had tried to return Xena to her wicked ways, takes Xena and Gabrielle to a cave in Mount Etna and places their bodies in ice coffins. Twenty-five years later, an avalanche cracks open the cave and sunlight melts the ice. Xena and Gabrielle, perfectly preserved over time, return to life.

During this time, Eve, given the name Livia by Octavius to protect her, had been seduced by Ares and has become the evil "Champion of Rome." Xena realizes Livia is Eve and confronts her. Livia refuses to believe her. When Livia is captured by the Amazons and put on trial for murder, Xena intercedes on her behalf. Livia realizes Xena is her mother and she is really Eve. Livia is spared the death sentence when she is cleansed by a prophet called the Baptist and becomes a messenger of peace.

The last episode reveals that before Xena met Gabrielle, she ravaged China and caused the deaths of 40,000 people, the souls of whom were claimed by the Lord of the Darkland. Xena's "sidekick" at this time was Akim (Michelle Ang), a Chinese woman who taught her "the pinch."

In an out of the blue storyline change, Xena decides to return to China to release those souls. She initially fails (killed) but with Gabrielle's help, her spirit defeats the Darkland Lord and the spirits are released. Gabrielle returns home alone. Xena's spirit appears to tell Gabrielle that she must continue fighting for right and that she will always be with her in her heart. It had been suggested that Xena and Gabrielle were lesbians. Although Gabrielle told Xena she loved her and vice versa, they never kissed.

Joxer (Ted Raimi) is a well-meaning but bumbling warrior trying to make a name for himself as Joxer the Mighty. He carries a lucky rabbit's foot, is more talk than action and accomplishes things by accident. Joxer is unable to kill. He wears armor, a helmet and carries a sword and shield. He and Xena met for the first time on the road to Corinth (when he offered to help her). Joxer receives an unkind fate. When Xena and Gabrielle emerge from the ice cave, they find Joxer running a tavern. He is now the father of Virgil (William Gregory Lee), a man who writes epic poems. Joxer joins Xena in her quest to find Eve but is killed in a battle. Virgil, a brave warrior, becomes Xena and Gabrielle's new aide.

Callistro (Hudson Leick) is a beautiful but lethal warrior who is out to kill Xena because "you barbecued my family." Years ago, during Xena's raid on the village of Sera, a fire was accidentally started that killed Callistro's family. Callistro, a young girl at the time, vowed to destroy everything Xena loved. Xena encounters Callistro for the first time when she learns someone is raiding villages and killing people in the name of Xena. Even though Xena appears to defeat Callistro— even doing nothing as Callistro drowns in quick-sand — Callistro always returns to fulfill her vow. "I smell burning" is the phrase Xena uses to indicate to Gabrielle that Callistro is near.

Aphrodite (Alexandra Tydings) is the Goddess of Love. She often speaks with a 1980s style Valley Girl accent and believes there is no one as beautiful as she. Aphrodite treasures the shrines mortals have built for her and is very protective of them. She is friendly, fun-loving and playful ("I'm a material girl," she says). "Love at first sight is my specialty" and "Just doin' the god thing" is what she says when she casts her love spells—whether they work or not. She calls Xena and Gabrielle "my favorite girl group." Aphrodite's enemy is Discord (Meighan Desmond), a goddess who delights in undoing Aphrodite's good deeds. Discord dresses in black (Aphrodite in either white or pink) and uses fireballs as her weapon. See also *Hercules: The Legendary Journeys.*

Joseph LoDuca composed the theme. The program opens with these words: "In a time of ancient gods, warriors and kings, a land in turmoil cried out for a hero. She was Xena, a mighty warrior princess forged in the heat of battle. The power ... the passion ... the danger. Her courage will change the world."

151. *Zorro* (ABC, 1957–1959; 1960-1961; CBS, 1983; Family Channel, 1990–1993; Syndicated, 1997-1998)

ABC Version: Don Diego de la Vega (Guy Williams) is a Spanish nobleman who is returning to his home in Monterey, California (1820), after three years of study at the University of Spain. Don Diego has been summoned by his father, Don Alejandro (George J. Lewis) to help fight a tyrant, the new Commandante, Enrique Monasterio (Britt Lomond), who has imposed harsh laws and taxes on the people in his quest to become the richest man in California.

Aboard ship Don Diego tells his mute servant, Bernardo (Gene Sheldon) he must find a way to deal with Monasterio without arousing suspicion that his father has summoned him home. Bernardo uses sign language to suggest force—"No, Bernardo. I'm dealing with a powerful enemy. We must play another game." Just then Don Diego recalls a proverb: "When you cannot clothe yourself in the skin of a lion, put on that of a fox." He devises a plan: "I must convince the new Commandante that I am perfectly harmless ... instead of a man of action, I shall be a man of letters, an innocent scholar interested only in the arts and sciences." Fearing that he will be searched in Los Angeles, Don Diego has Bernardo burn his father's letters and discard his fencing trophies from the university.

As Don Diego adopts his new character (he wears a maroon-front jacket with gold braid and carries a walking stick), Bernardo motions that he wants to help. "Very well, you shall play the fool. You shall be the eyes and ears behind my back. You cannot only not speak, you hear nothing."

As Don Diego suspected, he is searched when he arrives in Old Los Angeles. He has fooled Monasterio's soldiers; now he must fool his father.

That night, Don Alejandro tells his son about the intolerable conditions that exist. Don Diego responds by saying "I'm going to sit down and write a detailed letter of complaint to the governor." This angers Don Alejandro, who believes his son is a coward. Don Diego next tells Bernardo that he has chosen a disguise: "From now on I shall be el Zorro—the Fox" (he draws his sword and carves his first *Z* on a sheet of music on the piano). He then chooses a black mask and outfit to disguise his true identity.

The following morning, Don Diego and Bernardo are seen in a hilly area of the de la Vega ranch. Don Diego whistles and a black horse comes into view. "I've brought you here to meet a third member ... Tornado. An old shepherd has been keeping him for me. He was a colt when I left... Even my father would not recognize this horse." (Don Diego, as himself, is seen riding a tan and white horse named Phantom.)

The de la Vegas are the most important family in southern California. Zorro's base is a secret cave below his hacienda in Monterey. (The entrance is through the fireplace. Don Diego found it as a boy and believes it was built by his grandfather as a means of escaping Indian raids.) Zorro's trademarks are the carved sign of the *Z*, his black hat, mask and cape. He carries both a sword and a whip, and in the opening theme Zorro leaves a warning for Monasterio—"Beware, Commandante. My sword is a flame, to right every wrong. So hold well my name—Zorro." Monasterio has posted the following: REWARD. 1000 PESOS WILL BE PAID FOR THE CAPTURE—DEAD OR ALIVE—OF THE BANDIT WHO CALLS HIMSELF ZORRO.

While Zorro is an expert swordsman, Don Diego pretends to be inexperienced at fencing (at the university, Diego was the fencing champion). To further cover his tracks when he is Zorro, Don Diego teaches Bernardo to play the guitar (to make it appear Diego is in his room practicing when in reality he is out as Zorro). Although Zorro helps the people, he is considered a criminal by the authorities. Zorro, "a friend of the people," is "the defender of the oppressed" and "the champion of justice."

Captain Enrique Monasterio is the real threat to Zorro (he is based in the Pueblo de Los Angeles, which was founded in 1781). When the viceroy (John Dehner) arrives to inspect the Pueblo and discovers that Enrique is corrupt, he arrests him. Enrique's second in command, the bumbling and dimwitted Sergeant Garcia, is appointed the temporary commandante. In the episode of 3/20/58, Captain Arturo Pollidano (Peter Adams) becomes the new magistrato—and enemy of Zorro's.

Sergeant Demetrio Lopez Garcia (Henry Calvin) is a soldier of the king of Spain (the king's lancers); in second season episodes, the overweight Garcia becomes the acting commandante when Arturo is dropped. "How did one so stupid become a sergeant?" "It was easy. I was a private for a long time. Then one day I saw the commandante kissing the magistrato's wife, and the next thing you know, I am a sergeant ... because I possess the natural qualities of leadership." The Pasada de Los Angeles is his favorite watering hole; Garcia and other lancers are paid every six months.

Cresencia (Penny Stanton) is the de la Vega maid; Anna Maria Verdugo (Jolene Brand) is Diego's romantic interest; Ricardo Delano (Richard Anderson) is Don Diego's rival for Anna Maria's hand. In episode 52 ("Amnesty for Zorro," 1/1/59), Don Alejandro learns that his son is Zorro (he prevents Don Diego from dueling with Delano for the hand of Anna Maria so he can fight on for the liberation of the peasants).

Annette Funicello appeared in both ABC versions of the series, but in different roles. In 1959, in half-hour episodes, Annette played Anita Cecilia Isabella Cabrillo, a beautiful girl from Spain who journeys to Los Angeles to find her father, Don Miguel Cabrillo (Arthur Space); with Zorro's help she discovers that he is Gonzales, the stable master. In the third hour-long episode, "The Postponed Wedding" (1/1/61), Annette is Constansia da la Torres, a girl Don Diego and Sergeant Garcia have known since she was a child. Constansia lives in Santa Clara and comes to Los Angeles to marry Miguel Serano (Mark Oamo), a scoundrel Zorro exposes as a fortune hunter seeking Constansia's money.

CBS Version: *Zorro and Son.* Old California in 1845 is the setting. Twenty-five years have passed and Don Diego (Henry Darrow) is still defending people as Zorro, but "The old gray fox isn't what he used to be." Realizing that Don Diego is aging and unable to perform as Zorro, Bernardo (Bill Dana), Don Diego's faithful servant, sends to Spain for Diego's son, Don Carlos de la Vega (Paul Regina) in the hope that the young man will help his father. When Don Carlos arrives in California and discovers that the new commandante, Paco Pico (Gregory Sierra), is unfairly imposing his law on the citizens, he is inspired to help them. Seeing this, Don Diego reveals to his son that he is Zorro and begins training Don Carlos as the new Zorro. Zorro rides a horse named Tornado; Bernardo, who can talk in this version, has a donkey named Rosita. Sergeant Sepulveda (Richard Beauchamp) is Pico's bumbling assistant; Corporal Cassette (John Moschitta, Jr.) is Pico's informer, a fast talker who can repeat overheard conversations word for word.

Family Channel Version: *Zorro.* The format of the original ABC version is recreated. Here Don Diego/Zorro (Duncan Regehr) battles the evils of Alcalde Luis Ramon (Michael Tylo) then Alcalde Ignacio DeSoto (John Hetzler). Felipe (Juan Diego Botto) is Don Diego's mute but not deaf servant; Don Alejandro (Efrem Zimbalist, Jr., Henry Darrow) is Don Diego's father; Victoria Escalante (Patrice Cahmi Martinez) is Don Diego's love interest and owner of the Pueblo's tavern; Sergeant Mendoza (James Victor) is the Alcalde's assistant.

Syndicated Version: *Zorro* (also known as *The New Adventures of Zorro*). The story is set in Old California but deviates greatly from the ABC version in that Don Diego/Zorro (Michael Gough II) uses not only his whip and sword to defeat the evil Captain Montecero (Earl Boen), head of the Los Angeles Garrison, but futuristic devices unheard of in the 19th century (for example, submarines, robots, steam powered wheelchairs, automatic guns). Zorro is aided by Isabella Torres (Jeannie Elias), the daughter of his neighbor. Ursula (Mary Kay Bergman) is an Indian sorceress who conjures up ghosts and ghouls. Sergeant Garcia (Tony Pope) assists the captain; Don Alejandro (Pat Fraley II) is Don Diego's father. See also *The Queen of Swords.*

Zorro and Son see *Zorro*

Appendix A:
Superheroes by Name

Batgirl *see* Batgirl, Batman
Batman *see* Batman
Batmanuel *see* The Tick
Black Scorpion *see* Black Scorpion
Buckethead *see* Honey I Shrunk the Kids
Captain America *see* Captain America
Captain Astounding *see* Honey, I Shrunk the Kids
Captain Justice *see* Once a Hero
Captain Liberty *see* The Tick
Captain Marvel *see* Shazam!
Captain Midnight *see* Captain Midnight
Captain Nice *see* Captain Nice
Captain Scarlet *see* Captain Scarlet and the Mysterons
Captain Video *see* Captain Video and His Video Rangers
Crimson Crusader *see* Once a Hero
Dare Devil *see* Dare Devil
Daring Dragoon *see* Jack of All Trades
Dyna Girl *see* Electra Woman and Dyna Girl
Electra Woman *see* Electra Woman and Dyna Girl
The Flash *see* The Flash
Greatest American Hero *see* The Greatest American Hero
Greatest American Heroine *see* The Greatest American Hero

The Green Hornet *see* The Green Hornet
Hercules *see* Hercules: The Legendary Journeys
Isis *see* Isis
Mantis *see* M.A.N.T.I.S.
Mr. Terrific *see* Mr. Terrific
Night Shade *see* The Flash
NightMan *see* NightMan
NightWoman *see* NightMan
Queen of Swords *see* Queen of Swords
Robin the Boy Wonder *see* Batman
Spider-Man *see* The Amazing Spider-Man
Spider-Woman *see* The Amazing Spider-Man
Superboy *see* The Adventures of Superboy, Smallville and Superboy
Superman *see* The Adventures of Superman, Lois and Clark: The New Adventures of Superman
Superpup *see* The Adventures of Superpup
The Tick *see* The Tick
Ultraman *see* My Secret Identity, Ultraman
Ultra Woman *see* Lois and Clark: The New Adventures of Superman
Wonder Girl *see* Wonder Woman
Wonder Woman *see* Wonder Woman
Xena *see* Xena: Warrior Princess
Zorro *see* Zorro

Appendix B:
Superheroes
by Mortal Name

Andrea Thomas (Isis) *see* Isis

Andrew Clemens (Ultraman) *see*
My Secret Identity

Barbara Gordon (Batgirl) *see*
Batgirl, Batman

Barry Allen (The Flash) *see* The Flash

Billy Batson (Captain Marvel) *see*
Shazam!

Brad Steele (Captain Justice) *see*
Once a Hero

Britt Reid (The Green Hornet) *see*
The Green Hornet

Bruce Wayne (Batman) *see* Batgirl,
Batman

Carter Nash (Captain Nice) *see* Captain Nice

Clark Kent (Superboy) *see* The
Adventures of Superboy, Smallville,
Superboy

Clark Kent (Superman) *see* The
Adventures of Superman, Lois and
Clark: The New Adventures of
Superman

Darcy Walker (Black Scorpion) *see*
Black Scorpion

Desmond Powell (Night Shade) *see*
NightMan

Diana Prince (Wonder Woman) *see*
Wonder Woman

Dick Grayson (Robin, the Boy
Wonder) *see* Batgirl, Batman

Don Diego (Zorro) *see* Zorro

Drusilla (Wonder Girl) *see* Wonder
Woman

Holly Hathaway (Greatest American
Heroine) *see* The Greatest
American Hero

Jack Stiles (Daring Dragoon) *see* Jack
of All Trades

Jessica Drew (Spider-Woman) *see*
The Amazing Spider-Man

Johnny Domino (NightMan) *see*
NightMan

Judy (Dyna Girl) *see* Electra Woman
and Dyna Girl

Laurie (Electra Woman) *see* Electra
Woman and Dyna Girl

Laurie Jarvis (NightWoman) *see*
NightMan

Lobo Fuerte (Masked Wrestler) *see*
Los Lochadores

Matt Murdock (Dare Devil) *see* Dare
Devil

Miles Hawkins (Mantis) *see*
M.A.N.T.I.S.

Peter Parker (Spider-Man) *see* The
Amazing Spider-Man

Phil (Street Sweeper) *see* Dark
Angel

Ralph Hinkley (Greatest American
Hero) *see* The Greatest American
Hero

Stanley Beemish (Mr. Terrific) *see* Mr. Terrific
Steve Rogers (Captain America) *see* Captain America
Tessa Alvarado (Queen of Swords) *see* The Queen of Swords

Wayne Szlinski (Captain Astounding) *see* Honey, I Shrunk the Kids

Appendix C:
Crime Fighting
Machines by Show

Airwolf (helicopter) *see* Airwolf
AutoCar (car) *see* Automan
AutoCopter (helicopter) *see* Automan
Batcar (car) *see* The Tick
Batcopter (helicopter) *see* Batman
Batgirl Cycle (motorcycle) *see* Batgirl, Batman
Batmobile (car) *see* Batman
Battle Cruiser 100 (rocket ship) *see* Space Patrol
Beast (car) *see* Team Knight Rider
Beta (rocket ship) *see* Rod Brown of the Rocket Rangers
Black Beauty (car) *see* The Green Hornet
Chrysalid (ship) *see* M.A.N.T.I.S.
Dante (car) *see* Team Knight Rider
Defender (car) *see* Viper
Domino (car) *see* Team Knight Rider
Electra Car (car) *see* Electra Woman and Dyna Girl
Electra Plane (plane) *see* Electra Woman and Dyna Girl
Galaxy, Galaxy II (rocket ships) *see* Captain Video and His Video Rangers
Kenworth Project (truck) *see* 18 Wheels of Justice
Kat (motorcycle) *see* Team Knight Rider

KITT (car) *see* Knight Rider
Lobo Ride (car) *see* Los Luchadores
The Mantis (car) *see* M.A.N.T.I.S.
Orbit Jet (rocket ship) *see* Rocky Jones, Space Ranger
Plato (motorcycle) *see* Team Knight Rider
Plymouth Prowler (car) *see* NightMan
Polaris (rocket ship) *see* Tom Corbett, Space Cadett
ScorpionMobile (car) *see* Black Scorpion
SID (satellite drone) *see* Knight Rider
Silver Dart (plane) *see* Captain Midnight
Silver Moon (rocket ship) *see* Rocky Jones, Space Ranger
Sky Flash (rocket ship) *see* Flash Gordon
Street Hawk (motorcycle) *see* Street Hawk
Terra IV, Terra V (rocket ships) *see* Space Patrol
Viper (car) *see* Viper
Wing (plane) *see* Human Target
Wonderbug (car) *see* Wonderbug
X-9 (rocket ship) *see* Captain Video and His Video Rangers

Performer Index